*Jewish Bankers and the Holy See*

# THE LITTMAN LIBRARY OF
# JEWISH CIVILIZATION

EDITORS

*David Goldstein*
*Louis Jacobs*
*Lionel Kochan*

*This Library is dedicated to*
*the memory of*

## JOSEPH AARON LITTMAN

# Jewish Bankers and the Holy See
## From the Thirteenth to the Seventeenth Century

LÉON POLIAKOV

*translated from the French by*
MIRIAM KOCHAN

ROUTLEDGE & KEGAN PAUL
LONDON, HENLEY AND BOSTON
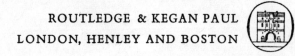

*First published in France as*
Les Banquiers juifs et le Saint-Siège
du XIIIe au XVIIe siècle
© *École Pratique des Hautes Études, Paris*, 1965
© *Calmann-Lévy*, 1967
*First published in Great Britain and the United States of America in* 1977
*by Routledge & Kegan Paul Ltd*
39 *Store Street*
*London WC1E 7DD,*
*Broadway House*
*Newtown Road*
*Henley-on-Thames*
*Oxon RG9 1EN and*
9 *Park Street*
*Boston, Mass.* 02108, *USA*
*Set in Monotype Bembo*
*and printed in Great Britain by*
*Willmer Brothers Limited, Birkenhead*
English translation © Routledge & Kegan Paul Ltd 1977
*No part of this book may be reproduced in*
*any form without permission from the*
*publisher, except for the quotation of brief*
*passages in criticism*

ISBN 0 7100 8256 8

# Contents

Judaeum esse est delictum,
non tamen punibile per Christianum

[To be a Jew is an offence,
not, however, one punishable by a Christian]

(Angelus de Clavasio, 'Judaeus', *Summa angelica*,
Lyons, 1519)

# Preface and Acknowledgments

A set of legal records from the Roman ghetto which Professor Fernand Braudel kindly mentioned to me in 1956 was the starting-point for this book. When I examined them at the Archivio di Stato in Rome, my attention was drawn to two folders containing the minutes of the Congregatio de Usuris, a committee created by Clement IX in 1668 to study the Jewish money trade from both the theological and the economic points of view. The protection accorded by the Holy See to the Jewish *banchieri* (pawnbrokers), as well as their taxation by the Apostolic Chamber have been known since the works by Ermanno Loevinson and Vittorio Colorni were published,[1] and I was interested in the origins of an institution of this type. It seemed to me that it served merely to give its blessing to the general custom of 'engaging' (*conducere*) these bankers, a custom which had grown up spontaneously in Italy in the fourteenth and fifteenth centuries, and which was sanctioned by the most reputable Italian canonists. Although the way it was practised has been studied by various authors (in particular by Gino Luzzatto and Attilio Milano), the canonical doctrine regarding it has not.[2] I have endeavoured to reconstruct its main features and its gradual development, while, at the same time, being careful to discuss it in terms of the economic situation at each stage. Without this additional information, a doctrine, far from throwing light on the attitude of men of the past and thus providing a more complete view of the facts, remains an intellectual exercise, an academic structure.

I hope, by thus swinging the spotlight back and forth, to be following the advice of the unforgettable Lucien Febvre:[3]

> . . . to incorporate or re-incorporate theology in history and, by an inverse process, history in theology; to cease regarding the latter only as a collection of concepts and arguments clustering together like crystals in a vacuum chamber; on the contrary, to compare them with the hundreds of other contemporary manifestations of thought and feeling and find out the essential connections linking them with each other; in short to try to perceive the psychological realities concealed behind the academic formulae . . .

and in the present case, the 'terrible question of interest', one is justified in including also the economic realities. The economic history of the Jews has been studied either by historians of Judaism or by economic historians; but while the first have steadily advanced the knowledge of the subject in the last decades, the second, over some thirty years, have embarked on nothing but isolated incursions into this field. The very honourable reasons for such reserve can be guessed. My greatest efforts were directed towards scouring the most recent research works in economic and social history, insofar as these touched on (as they very often do) the financial activities of the Jews of Italy, in order to link them to the erudite chronicles of the historians of Judaism. For this purpose, I found the works by Fernand Braudel, Gino Luzzatto, Raymond de Roover, Armando Sapori and numerous other contemporary scholars enormously valuable. My major concern at each stage in my work was therefore to isolate and analyse the relationship between the actual life of the Italian cities, such as I can envisage it in the present state of knowledge, and the 'bell-shaped curve' which the business dealings of Jewish financiers in Italy from the thirteenth to the eighteenth century seem to form.

I hope that the results I have obtained will stimulate further research. I have not resisted the temptation to use these results myself for a general conclusion on the Jews and economic life which might perhaps contribute, forty years later, to the revival of a discussion 'around Sombart', interrupted in 1932–3, following on the articles by Henri Sée and André Sayous.

In the course of my research, I received a great deal of understanding and help from many French and foreign scholars. My work would not have been possible without the kind support of M. Braudel and the generous co-operation of the Centre national de la recherche scientifique and of the VIth section of the École pratique des hautes études (EPHE). I shall never forget the welcome I was given at the Archivio di Stato of Rome, in 1956–8, by Adriano Carelli and his colleagues. I was also able to maintain contact with the Eternal City over the years thanks to the kindness of M. E. Toaff, chief rabbi of Rome, and the knowledgeable assistance of Mme Lia Calderoni, who did a good deal of indispensable checking with the best grace in the world.

A stimulating correspondence with Professor Siegfried Stein of London University in 1960–1 gave my work a final impetus. Dr E. Dichter, the founder of 'Motivation Research', gave me the benefit of his work on the psychology of the money trade. Rabbi G. S. Rosenthal of Fair Haven (New Jersey) generously put his collection of Responsa of Italian rabbis at my disposal. My friend Joseph Gottfarstein helped me to translate talmudic texts; Rabbis André Chekroun, Ernest Guggenheim and Charles Touati checked my translations and interpretations. As far as canonical doctrine was concerned, similar help came from Abbé Louis Grégoire, vice-chancellor of the archbishopric of Paris, whom I cannot thank enough for his great goodness, and from Professor Bogdan Kieszkowski, Dozent of the University of Warsaw, Gavin Langmuir of Stanford University, Pierre Nora, agrégé of the University of Paris, and Émile Touati, Doctor of Law, who all undertook the thankless task of reading the manuscript to give me the benefits of their friendly criticism. I received varied and valuable co-operation at the VIth section of the EPHE: Professor R. Kherumian brought me up to date on the present state of knowledge of the anthropological origin of the Jews. Penetrating comments by Maurice de Gandillac influenced the final revision of the work before it went to press. And the whole work owes infinitely more to its director, Ruggiero Romano: in a field which is not only unexplored but also obscured by controversy, where, on several occasions, I had to embark on hazardous paths, he was the director of my scientific conscience.

This edition of the book is basically the same as that which appeared in 1965 in the series 'Affaires et gens d'affaires' (EPHE, VIth section, published by SEVPEN), except that the plates and the voluminous bibliography have been omitted, as well as some of the appendices and notes; quotations given in the original language have been translated, and other cuts made. My warmest thanks go to Mlle Renée Drouelle for her kindness in participating in this task as well as to M. Braudel, President of the VIth section of the École, who gave me permission to publish the present abbreviated edition.

# PART ONE

# The Rise of the Jewish Money Trade

# The Significance and Basis of the Protection Granted to the Jews by the Holy See

Generally in those days, the world over, the Jews were taken and burned, and their possessions were confiscated by the lords on whose land they were living, except at Avignon and in Church lands under the wing of the pope, as the Church did not think it necessary that they should be put to death since they would be saved if they would return to our faith—Jean Froissart, *Chroniques*, ed. Luce, Paris, 1873, vol. 4, pp. 101, 332

Nothing can give a better idea of the closeness and complexity, even the ambivalence, of the secular links between the Jews and the Holy See than the cycle of legends (Judeo-Italian and Judeo-German) about a 'Jewish pope' which was woven from the early middle ages on.[1] According to the oldest version (fifth century), the first pope, Simon Kefa or Simon Caiaphas, was fundamentally a loyal Jew. Disturbed by the rapid progress of Christianity and afraid that this heresy might seduce the Chosen People (or again in another version: because the Christians were threatening to massacre the Jews if they did not rally to their ranks), he pretended to be a Christian. His purpose was to make his way into the bosom of the rival sect and divert the dangers that threatened. He was also concerned to reserve the blessings of the Hereafter solely for the Jews, and to that end to widen the gulf between the two religions. Consequently, so it was said, Simon diverted Christianity on to paths which made it unacceptable to Jews. On the other hand, he forbade Christians to convert Jews by violence. He may have adopted the name of Petrus, but this was because he had exempted or 'absolved' (*Pator* in Hebrew) the Christians from their loyalty to Mosaic practices. Once his task was completed, he is said to have retired to a tower where he lived as a hermit and composed the *Nishmat* prayer which forms part of the Sabbath liturgy.

He is an astonishingly composite personality, this 'Simon Caiaphas': he is assigned the historic role of the apostle Paul, while he also bears the surname of the high priest said to have committed Jesus for trial!

According to a later version (twelfth to thirteenth centuries), it was the father of the 'Jewish pope' who was called Simon. Under this name he is identified with a historic character, the liturgical poet Simon the Great, who lived at Mainz round about the year 1000. His son Elchanan, who had been stolen by a Christian servant and baptised, made a brilliant career for himself as a theologian, and was raised to the throne of St Peter. In order to see his father again (in one version, he remembered him; in another, he was suspicious and forced his servants to reveal the truth to him), he decreed that the Jews of Mainz be persecuted. They sent a deputation led by Simon the Great to Rome and immediately got in touch with the Jews there who expressed great surprise, because the pope was known to be friendly towards the Jews. In fact, the pope received the delegates kindly and embarked on a theological discussion with Simon, astonishing the Jews by the depth of his rabbinic knowledge. A game of chess ensued in which the son beat his father, using a manoeuvre which the father thought was known to him alone. The son then revealed his identity, nullified the decree of persecution, and after publicly announcing that he was a Jew, killed himself (according to one version) or (according to another) fled to Mainz.

These legends and their multiple variants reflect not only the diverse aspects of the relations between the Jews and the Holy See, and, of prime importance, the outstanding significance of papal protection in theory, but also the special role that pertained in these circumstances to the Jewish community of Rome.

To begin with papal protection: Catholic historians, like Jewish authors, have not failed to emphasise the importance of this protection for the very survival of Judaism. In the seventeenth century, a period of decadence and of persecution of the Jews in Italy, the Venetian rabbi Simone Luzzatto gave the following evidence on the subject:[2]

> The Zealots state that to tolerate those who do not follow the commonly approved religion is a sign of contempt for that religion; the simple answer to them is that they should moderate their pious zeal and note that the supreme head of the Christian religion tolerates Jews in the city where he himself resides: they have been settled there for over eight hundred years, have a stable domicile there and are governed there with justice and charity; so that no one should claim to know more about religious matters than he.

I will do my utmost throughout this book to study at their varied levels alternately the bases and methods of this protection. From the point of view of traditional attitudes, it is interesting to note the specific Hebrew term of uncertain etymology which designated and still designates the pope: *Afifior, avi* or *abi pior,* most probably a corruption of Father Peter or Abbot Peter.

It is well known that the protection of the Jews by the Holy See was justified by the theological idea, going back to the Fathers of the Church, of the necessity or utility of preserving the 'witness people'. It was this motive, as well as Christian charity, that the sovereign pontiffs invoked when they intervened with Christian princes on the Jews' behalf. It goes without saying that this argument only meant anything insofar as the popes themselves set an actual example of this preservation by granting the Children of Israel the absolute freedom of the city of Rome. At most periods, this freedom imposed quite substantial reciprocities on the Jews; in particular, it will be seen how, under the Renaissance popes, the Holy See drew not inconsiderable sums from the guild of Jewish moneylenders, by means of appropriate pressure. It would be rash to claim that protection rested on this alone. However, the specific training of the economic historian makes him approach the practical bearing of the theologians' concepts with caution. He will therefore tend to look for another interpretation of the exceptional fact of the peaceful continuance of a Jewry in a town which happened to be the capital of Christianity. The exceptional situation itself contributes to obscuring the terms of the problem thus posed. If it is not easy to identify, even when documents are plentiful, the sorts of reasons (religious hatred? economic competition? demographic increase?) why Jews were, as a general rule, expelled, it seems even more difficult to say why, when the sources are necessarily silent, they were not. The scanty references available exist only for a late period, namely the great pontificate of the Counter-Reformation under which expulsion was decreed. At that time, Pius V is seen stating almost in one breath that if he is sparing the Jews at Rome and Ancona while expelling them from other towns of the States, it is because certain members of the former communities are useful to trade, and that a limited number of the Children of Israel seem to him sufficient to bear witness (the utility of which he does not deny) in favour of Christianity. We are therefore hardly any further forward, except to note that the conjunction of patristic tradition and the financial interests of the Holy See were perhaps necessary to save the Roman Jews from the fate of their co-religionists in the great Catholic states (a fate the pope did not fail to mention). What can, on the contrary, be suggested with a degree of certainty is that the liquidation of the Rome ghetto would, in the short or long run, have sealed the fate of the other ghettos which still existed in Italy and throughout the German Empire. It can therefore be maintained that in 1569 the future of western Judaism was balanced between Pius V and the Jewish businessmen of Ancona and Rome.

This brings us back to the ambiguity of the relationship between the Jews and the Holy See. The collective unconscious of the ghetto in its own way spun a myth around the fragile margin of security left it by papal toleration–protection in the form of belief in a secret ally, the 'Jewish pope'. But such a dream of power, with its precise details, is legitimately open to additional interpretations. It will be noticed, *inter alia*, that the Jew Simon is a secret Jew in the first version of the legend and becomes a declared Jew, father of the Christians' pope Elchanan (which means 'favoured by God'), in the second. Perhaps we may be allowed to discern here both an allusion to the dialectic relationship between the mother and the daughter religion and a gleam of secret pride in the temporal success of the Jewish child who becomes the sovereign pontiff of the Christians. In any case, the theological contest between father and son, Jew and pope, reflects a concrete and living form of this relationship. It evokes the favour which so many scholars, particularly so many Jewish medical men, enjoyed at the papal court, to the great benefit of the Children of Israel as a whole. The fact that a number of medieval popes, in defiance of warnings, entrusted the health of their bodies to Jews perhaps contains a message of its own that we will on no account attempt to decipher. It was mainly a question of affinities between men whose education, reading, intellectual level and even certain preoccupations were not so different, thus facilitating a dialogue of which many examples will be quoted later. In short, the impression emerges that it was this sort of cultural affinity, rather than a point of doctrine, which was the determining factor in the protection granted to the Jews. In trying to fathom the secret of their continued existence at Rome, it must also be remembered that in the capital of the Church, it is the clergy who set the tone.

The abduction of the Jewish child by a Christian servant is a strange story which recurs throughout history. It is a permanent nightmare of Judaism and a symbol of those forced conversions which decimated the populous Jewries or, in certain regions, even put an end to their existence.

As for the Jewish delegation which hastened from Germany to Rome to report a decree of oppression, this detail also corresponds to a constant practice. Jewish chronicles abound in mentions of such missions coming to solicit favours and bearing presents, some of which are crowned with success, some fruitless. But another incident testifies even more eloquently to the prestige and renown of the papacy throughout the four corners of the Diaspora. From the distant island of Negropont (Euboea), a Venetian possession at that time, a Jew victimised by a co-religionist came to Rome in about 1400 to ask the pope for justice. The letter of recommendation he bore (which is our source of information on this episode) asked the leaders of the Jewish community in Rome to intercede with the Curia on his behalf.[3] We can thus see that this community enjoyed particular importance as a natural intermediary between the papacy and the Diaspora in Christian lands. The Jews of Rome probably obtained various advantages from these comings and goings and might even have been able to cash in on the support they granted the supplicants.

A good time to begin our study of them is the second half of the twelfth century, a period when moneylending became widespread throughout Europe and of major concern to the Holy See. There was then a community of about a thousand souls, whose situation, on the evidence of Benjamin of Tudela (*c.* 1165) left nothing to be desired. If, as this traveller says, the Jew Yehiel, grandson of a famous rabbi, was entrusted with the administration of papal finances at this period, the majority of Jews pursued crafts—just as they did further south in the kingdom of the Two Sicilies, which at that time sheltered several thousand Jews at least; while in northern Italy, in the territories of the nascent communes, the Jewish population was very scattered or still non-existent.

This was still true in the following century. While Sienese and Florentine merchants who swarmed throughout Christendom were becoming the financial agents of the Curia and developing techniques for transferring funds, there is only a single known case of a diploma issued to Jewish merchants—this was by Alexander IV. 'Curiam nostrae sequentes', says the text, and not 'mercatores camere' as for the official Christian bankers—Yves Renouard has shown the importance of this subtlety.[4] Further search, in the chronological registers of Pressutti, reveals a Jewish banker in Rome connected with a Florentine consortium; but he was a converted Jew.[5] It is Renouard again who seems to provide the key to this relative omission of early Jewish finance to take advantage of the situation. On the subject of the Venetian or Genoese traders, he notes that their organisation was not the same as the Tuscans' and that they lacked 'both capital and stability in their affairs'. 'It is only in the Tuscan companies', he continues, 'that [the popes] found stable, powerful, universal bodies . . . with which regular collaboration was possible and could even be accompanied by foresight.'[6] From the point of view of the frequency of unforeseeable risks, the Jews were probably in the same boat as the Venetians or Genoese.

Even if there are no documents actually to prove it before 1360, it is very probable that some Jews, better off than the rest, were carrying out loan transactions at Rome to pilgrims and prelates, or to citizens. They would thus have laid the foundations of a Jewish bank which began to expand beyond the Eternal City at the end of the thirteenth century, as will be shown later. But the greatest number remained tied to crafts and would remain so in the following centuries, just as in southern Italy.

In short, as early as the thirteenth century, the Jewish community of Rome demonstrated the same socio-economic features that were to characterise it in later days. It was headed by an aristocracy of lenders at interest, whose existence is vouched for both by the Roman origin of men who went and settled in the provinces from the end of the thirteenth century and by a statute of 1360 which regulated the practice of the profession. Then came the merchants, particularly pedlars of cloth, trading in silk and other goods. Finally there were the masses, pursuing every sort of craft. Observers were struck by the fact that the majority of them worked with their hands. A memorandum which a Bavarian Dominican friar attached to the court of Nicholas V sent to his duke on the subject of Jewish 'usury' concluded: 'that they live amongst the Christians as they do in Rome, where they wear the *rouelle* [the circular badge], buying and selling, and working with their hands'.[7]

The predominance of craftsmanship was even more pronounced among the Jews in the kingdom of the Two Sicilies. Thomas Aquinas was certainly thinking of the latter when he held up the Italian Jews as an example to the duchess of Brabant: 'It is preferable that the Jews be forced to work with their own hands to earn their living, as they do in the Italian countries'. But such professions and means of existence do not always seem to have been propitious to the preservation of Judaism in Christian lands.

There is no lack of interest in the problem thus stated, especially

9

as it seems as if every type of attitude has contributed to preventing it from being stated in these precise terms. That is why we are going to take a brief look at the Jews in the south of the peninsula.

According to a paraphrase attributed to Rabbenu Tam, a twelfth-century French Talmudist, 'the Law will go out from Bari, and the word of the Lord from Otranto' (a paraphrase of the lines from Isaiah 2:3: 'Out of Zion shall go forth the law, and the word of the Lord from Jerusalem'). He was referring to the brilliance and prestige of the Jews of southern Italy under the Normans and the Hohenstaufen. Their number is said to have risen to 3 per cent of the population (according to Raphael Straus), or to at least 30,000 souls (Milano's figure).[8] From the socio-economic point of view, the structure of this Jewish community, particularly in Sicily, continued on the eastern pattern of a 'vertical nation', within which several peoples coexisted and a variety of activities was carried on. Crafts predominated and trade played a relatively secondary role, with the Jews specialising particularly, as in the East, in cloth-dyeing and silk manufacture. Under Frederick II (1194–1250) these two occupations became a monopoly which the Jews operated on the state's behalf. The craftsmen engaged in them were tied to their workshops in such a way that it has been possible to describe the system as 'state slavery' (Straus). Others belonged to the Church, to which Roger I, who conquered Sicily, or his successors, had transmitted his claims over them. In his *Itinerary*, Benjamin of Tudela described at length the peaceful, hard-working life of these communities, and provided useful statistical data on them.

Under the Angevin dynasty which was allied to the Church, the Dominican order embarked on an energetic missionary campaign in the kingdom of Naples, which reached a culminating point in 1290–4. The Talmud was burned and pious persuasion was probably accompanied by threats. According to Fra Giordano da Rivalto, 8,000 Jews at Trani converted at one go. But details of these persecutions remain obscure, and the results are hardly better known. Joshua Starr states that Judaism had practically disappeared from southern Italy at this period.[9] According to Milano, the number of Jews was halved. The resulting situation can be gathered from the instructions sent by John XXII to the Inquisitors of Apulia twenty-five years later at the request of the bishop of Trani.

The bishop had complained to the pope that the Jews of his diocese, who had been a substantial source of Church revenue when they were numerous in the past, were so over-taxed by the Inquisitors that the small number left provided only a slender profit for it. The Inquisitors, added the bishop, oppressed the converts in the same fashion, 'paying more attention to their profits than to the edification of these neophytes'. The pope decided that the plaintiff was right, and suspended all actions in progress against both Jews and converts for two years.[10]

This state of affairs brings out the vulnerability of these southern Jewries and the fact that their structures were ill adapted to the specific conditions of Christian Europe. They apparently did not have sufficient means either to emigrate or to buy royal or papal protection. (Jacob ben Elijah, a Judeo-Provençal polemicist of the period, whose work is quoted in the appendix to this book, thanked God 'for having multiplied our wealth, because this enables us to protect our lives and those of our children, and to halt the schemes of our persecutors.')

Jews who converted in these circumstances lived for generations as crypto-Jews in what would later be described as a 'marrano situation'.[11] They married only among themselves, and their specialisation in commercial activities became even more marked, with the result that *neofito* became synonymous with 'merchant' in Apulia. In 1453 Pope Nicholas V described the latter thus: 'Descendants of Jews who, 150 years ago, became Christian by force rather than by desire.'

At the end of the fourteenth century numerous Jews who had been driven out of Spain settled in the kingdom of Naples, whence they were expelled in 1540. Others once more led a marrano existence for a few generations. It is not known whether some subterranean thread links this to the strange spontaneous emergence of a Jewish community at San Nicandro in Apulia in the 1930s and 40s.[12]

Does the case of the Jews in the kingdom of the Two Sicilies not make it possible to approach the old, attractive, and many-sided question of the relationship between economy and religion in a new way—when the religion is that of a minority group? But perhaps it is going too far to talk of a 'new way' in the context of an old theme in Jewish literature. One of the characters in *Solal*, by the novelist Albert Cohen, says: 'moreover, the money-lenders among us concern themselves with this metal in pursuit of a holy motive: to live, to withstand, to endure . . . Money is our fortress, we poor banished ones, poor wanderers'. Reading a remarkable book on the subject of French Protestants, one has the impression of a similar situation: emigration requires a minimum of means as well as freedom of movement. For poorer classes, there could be no choice between apostasy or martyrdom.[13] But a figure quoted by R. Mandrou in his *Introduction à la France moderne* is a reminder of the caution necessary when making this sort of comparison. Between 1549 and 1560, out of the 6,000 Protestants who passed through Geneva, only 200 were women. Now, a similar disproportion is unthinkable in the case of the Jews, for whom the cohesion of family ties within the framework of a whole way of life minutely arranged by the Torah (to the point where it becomes a sort of second nature) served as a break-water against the assaults of the Church.

I still think the question is worth posing, however, particularly as the great Jewish historians of the past were more disposed to play down the Jews' role in the money trade than to stress it in the preservation of Judaism.

# CHAPTER II

# The Doctrine of Usury
# and the Jews

I hereby warn the reader that this word [Jews] is generally used here in its popular sense: Jews, bankers, dealers in specie—Alphonse Toussenel, *Les Juifs, rois de l'époque*, Paris, 1845, p. 4

We now pass on to the doctrinal framework, that is to say the ideas held by both Christian and Jewish theologians on the Jewish money trade. An examination of these ideas, which mainly reflect the social conditions, will supply a few preliminary glimpses of this situation. But one comment must be made at the outset, or rather one warning formulated, about the way the texts should be read in order to avoid the errors made by generations of historians.

The warning is semantic in nature. In medieval texts, *judaeus*, *judaei*, and words derived from them, can have meanings other than *Jew* or *Jews*, in the strict sense of the terms, both literally and figuratively.

In the literal sense, the designation *judaeus* coupled with a name does not necessarily mean that its bearer was Jewish. It could be an ordinary surname with no particular implications—not even that the Christian so designated must be a converted Jew (there are grounds for presuming this only in certain special cases). There seem to have been very many examples of such wholly Christian *judaei* in Italy: Vittorio Colorni has pointed out half a dozen in the town of Cremona alone; Benjamin Nelson has studied an interesting case of this type at Genoa, the great merchant

13

'Blancardo the Jew'.[1] Was it to avoid such confusion that the Avignon Curia took care to specify in its accounts that Jewish *judaei* were involved when on occasions it was dealing with actual Jews, as Yves Renouard states?[2]

The same applies in the figurative sense. In the middle ages the designation 'Jew' exceeded its strict meaning of a follower of the law of Moses much more widely than now. According to a linguistic practice going back to the first Fathers of the Church, it could mean anyone (or everyone) who diverged from orthodoxy, and in this way it acquired a very general pejorative sense.[3] This comment has a significance of its own from the point of view of economic history, since 'Jewish usury', for example, does not necessarily mean that it is or was carried on by Jews. But it is not solely a question of usury—far from it. A good example of medieval terminology and even medieval attitudes, from this point of view, comes from two letters by Bernard de Clairvaux.

In one, he describes how the sumptuous decoration of churches 'prevents devotion, and almost makes me think of Jewish ritual'. The metaphor, because it is one, obviously has no connection with the bare and humble synagogues of his day, but is inspired by the prophets' fulminations against the ungodly ostentation of the Temple of Jerusalem. For St Bernard, and he is not alone in this, the Jews' depravity begins with their settlement in the promised land, and inevitably culminated in deicide.[4] In another epistle (no. 343, intended to prevent the massacres of the Jews at the time of the preaching of the second Crusade) he said, *inter alia*: 'Where there are no Jews, Christian usurers judaise in a much worse way—that is, if they can be described as Christians, for the designation of baptised Jews suits them far better.' It would be wrong to infer any definite conclusions from such a passage about the importance of the Jews' participation in the money trade in the second quarter of the twelfth century.

To be more precise, one would have to say that caution is all the more necessary in this matter, because while the terminology does actually correspond to the social situation, on the other (and more important) hand it is still dependent on traditional imagery, closely linked, throughout the centuries, to the scale of values of

Christian society. 'Christ was born and died to teach us to love, and not to judaise,' wrote Erasmus.[5] The remarkable fact is that at the end of the nineteenth century a man such as Jean Jaurès, also pleading the Jews' cause, expressed himself no differently from Bernard de Clairvaux and his like in the twelfth. 'True Jews', he exclaimed from the height of the tribune in the Chamber of Deputies, 'are those who know how to circumcise the saving of others, and in this sense there exist thousands of Christians who are Jews or ready to become Jews.'[6]

These precautions are obviously valid for other words in any way connected with Judaism. When the 1213 Council of Paris denounced the *synagoguas malignantium* erected by the *foeneratores et maligni ecclesie persecutores*, it was thinking only of Christian merchants and bourgeois, as the context shows.

Having cleared up the semantics, let us move on to the doctrinal ideas of the middle ages on the Jews' money trade.


Let us begin with the rabbinic views. The question can be described as both very complex and quite simple. It is complex, because the commentaries by the 'Sages of the Talmud' on the written Law of the Old Testament (in particular, Deuteronomy 23:20: 'Unto a foreigner thou mayest lend upon usury; but unto thy brother thou shalt not lend upon usury') express the most varied and contradictory views. It is quite simple, because in Christian Europe these views tended to be standardised quite early on. To put it briefly, it can be said that Talmudic tradition, though still praising crafts at the expense of trade, did not judge trade in money as absolutely good or absolutely bad. It judged it according to the influence that such an occupation (or any other practised by the Children of Israel) could have on strengthening Judaism and on its purity. Let us develop these two points.

1  Various passages of the Talmud, expanded by Near Eastern post-Talmudic commentators, forbid and condemn lending at interest in general. The principal propounder of this view was Rav Huna; in his words, 'profit from usury, even when it is taken from an idolater, is doomed to perdition'.[7] In his commentary on

15

this passage, the great Rashi (1040–1105) points out that 'unto an alien thou mayest lend upon usury' can also be read as 'thou mayest pay interest to an alien'. This not only illustrates the often enigmatic conciseness of archaic Hebrew, but is also a reminder that, at the time of their financial transactions, the Jews were just as often borrowers as lenders. It must be noted that charity towards the non-Jew might have been only a subsidiary motive in the minds of these scholars. They were mainly concerned with preventing Jews from 'following in the ways of the Goyim', with preserving the purity of their faith and, in addition, with avoiding the transition, once the habit was acquired, from usury in general to usury between brethren. An opinion reflecting this point of view is that Jews in general can lend at interest to non-Jews only in extreme cases, that is to say when compelled to do so, while scholars of the Law can do so without restrictions. (It is presumed that their knowledge will prevent them from tripping up[8]— which explains the ironic comment of a thirteenth-century rabbi that all his generation of Jews regarded themselves as scholars of the Law.[9])

Maimonides, on the other hand, is the principal defender of the opinion whereby it is a 'commandment' to charge interest to non-Jews. The contradiction with the preceding view is, in my opinion, only superficial. The fundamental motive always remains the purity of the faith, which runs less risk of being adulterated by lending at interest when relationships between man and man are restricted to business than by free loans which generate friendly relations (a position to which the Roman Church was to return, according to its own account, as far as the dangers of friendly relations were concerned, particularly from the thirteenth century). It was therefore a question, at this juncture, of strengthening the 'hedge of the Law' designed to protect Jewish particularism. But proponents of this view also invoked proselytising or charitable institutions in support: an unbeliever, they said, under pressure from and exhausted by usury, would more easily renounce the paths of idolatry[10] (a thesis which is found again among Christian theologians in justification of the 'Exception of St Ambrose', which will be mentioned later). However, behind all this we can see the effects of the social and economic changes—urbanisation, transition from agriculture to trade, dispersal and peregrinations—which affected the Jews' existence in the eighth to the twelfth centuries.

Finally, the Talmud recognised a middle way, which permitted (but did not recommend) both borrowing from and lending to non-Jews at interest. For example, Rav Simlay teaches that one of the means of attaining perfection is to lend to a foreigner, even an idolater, without interest; which in practice comes back to granting a wide degree of toleration to substantial loans.

2    This is the view which prevailed early on in Christian Europe: the justification for it also tended to become standardised, particularly among Franco-German and Italian rabbis. They noted a dual need: social (the scattered condition of the Jews frustrated all attempts to limit their contacts with non-Jews), and economic (trade, especially the money trade, had become their sole means of earning a living). Here, for example, is Rashi (on the subject of a Talmudic prohibition on trade with non-Jews): 'When this prohibition was pronounced, the Jews all lived together and could trade with each other; but now that we are a minority, we cannot subsist without trading with non-Jews, since we live among them, and also because we are afraid of them'.[11] Two generations later, Rabbenu Tam (first half of the twelfth century) put the emphasis more specifically on the money trade, which had obviously increased in importance in the interim:

> Today, people are accustomed to lend at interest to non-Jews . . . because we have to pay taxes to the king and nobles, and all these things are necessary to sustain us; we live among non-Jews, and we cannot earn our living without trading with them. Therefore it is henceforth no longer forbidden to lend at interest.

Rabbenu Tam's view, which merely sanctioned an established state of affairs, acquired the validity of *halakhah* or unwritten law. The rabbis of the following centuries scarcely felt the need to justify the practice at length,[12] and certainly not in the case of the Jews of Italy, among whom specialisation in pawnbroking was more advanced than elsewhere, as will be seen. A suspicion of a sigh of regret can sometimes be felt. For example, R. Jacob

Landau of Pavia (*c.* 1480), after noting that R. Tam and most of the authorities had permitted this practice, added: 'I have no power to forbid the practice, but anyone who shows strictness in the matter [i.e. anyone who will not lend at interest] will be blessed.'[13]

Two special cases nevertheless remained about which the rabbis maintained their reservations throughout the middle ages.

(a) They had to consider money lent at the time of Christian festivals or even on account of these festivals. The Pentateuch already warned Israelites against any action which implied participation, even indirect, in the festivals of idolaters, and the Talmudists, afraid that the services rendered on these occasions might involve serving the idol itself, formulated an extremely detailed doctrine on the subject. In Europe, the first relaxations date from the tenth century.[14] In Christian lands the most important question was whether Christians were 'idolaters'. In practice, although Rashi still regarded them as such, the twelfth-century Tosafists (glossarists) noting that they did not offer sacrifices in pagan fashion, paved the way for the contrary interpretation.[15] However, it would be regarded as reprehensible to lend them money interest-free at the time of their festivals.

(b) The rabbis demonstrated the same desire to preserve the purity of the Jewish faith (at the same time as a very understandable prudence) by objecting to the acceptance as pledges of objects of Christian worship.[16] It is known from many conciliar decisions that the Church for its part had the same anxiety. It is also known that such injunctions had no great effect.[17] Far vaster violations of the spirit and letter of both the Scriptures and the Talmud must have been introduced by European rabbis on the question of making loans at interest 'between brothers', that is to say between Jew and Jew. The most they could do was to try their utmost to safeguard the forms of these henceforth inevitable practices by prescribing participation by an unbeliever in the transaction, to purify or disinfect it in some way, in accordance with the obscure requirements of the medieval mind.

On this point, too, the basic texts come from the French rabbis, Rashi and Rabbenu Tam. That R. Tam should have sanctioned proceedings that Rashi, following all his predecessors, condemned is an additional sign of the great changes which had taken place in the socio-economic condition of the Jews in the first half of the twelfth century. R. Tam referred to the Jerusalem Talmud when he wrote:

> A Jewish borrower has absolute permission to send his pledge through the intermediary of a non-Jew or his serf [non-Jewish], and the lender can accept the pledge from the hand of the non-Jew, and give him the money, or even give it to the Jew [direct], provided that he says: 'I lend it to you for the non-Jew'; the lender must not in any circumstance rely on the borrower but solely on the pledge...

This roundabout method is based on a Talmudic ruling relating to personal possessions whereby 'in questions of movable goods, possession equals entitlement to the goods' (just as in French law, for example), which makes it possible to maintain the fiction that the loan has been made to the non-Jew.[18] This decision by R. Tam served as a precedent for numerous and very varied practices, all involving the real or fictitious intervention of a Christian. It will be enough to describe just one formal method of lending which also involved resort to the principle of *damnum emergens* and which, in its complexity, suggests the stratagems the Christian merchants of Italy formulated with the help of the canonists:

> A lent a sum of money to his co-religionist B, the contract stipulating that the loan was free; but B authorised A, in case of non-repayment when it fell due, to borrow an equal sum at interest from a Christian and undertook to bear the cost of the transaction. At the [fictional] date of maturity, new contracts appeared; another Jew who served as a figurehead for B advanced this sum, at interest, to a Christian, who in his turn lent it to A on the same conditions, and A thus found himself repaid. For lender A, the advantage of the transaction seems to have been twofold: not only had the prohibition been circumvented but it became possible for him in this way, under cover of compensation, to charge interest at above the legal rate.

Our knowledge of this sort of transaction comes from thirteenth-century English contracts.[19] As for Italy, where documents are less plentiful, it seems that the most commonly employed dodge consisted of concealing interest by means of various types of commercial associations, which resembled the *commenda*.[20] In the sixteenth century one also finds that the Jewish *banchieri* (pawnbrokers) of Italy did not always bother about such precautions, and charged interest direct between Jew and Jew. It was against such abuses that R. Yehiel Nissim da Pisa was protesting in his treatise *The Eternal Life*. As far as pawnbroking was concerned, this rabbi prescribed adherence to the principles set out by Rabbenu Tam and other Tosafists. On this point the *Shulhan Arukh* displays a certain amount of caution (168:7):

> When an Israelite says to a pagan: 'Go and borrow money from an Israelite at interest in your name in order to give it to me', he is going against the Law; as for the lender, he is innocent, since he did not know about the ruse. *Gloss:* 'Some people show great moderation and say that the pagan cannot be regarded as absolutely replacing the first Israelite. However, it is permissible to show moderation only in places where one is accustomed to do so.'

This moderation or this laxity, which the codifier accepts when it is consecrated by custom or practice, does not seem to me to be very far removed, as far as the prevailing spirit is concerned, from the canonical idea of *toleratio* which will be mentioned a little later.

Apart from *doctrine*, there is the question of the development of medieval Jewish *attitudes* in the matter. What 'value-judgment' could the Jews themselves have made about an occupation which the Church's educational endeavours increasingly brought into disrepute?

The answer is not easy, despite the existence of various Judeo-Christian polemics on the subject, which the polemicists later transcribed for the use of their audiences. Thus in the thirteenth century Jacob ben Elijah gave the following reply to the apostate Pablo Christiani on the subject of usury:

> among the Jews of the East, every man lives by the work of his hands, for the kings of Ishmael, however sinful and evil they are, have enough judgment to levy a fixed annual tax on them; from

the rich according to his fortune, and from the poor according to his. It is different in our countries; for as far as our kings and princes are concerned, they have no thought but to harass us and strip us entirely of our gold and silver. And now, look at and consider this court at Rome to which all Christians are subject . . . everyone is greedy for profit . . .

A colourful description follows of the customs of the Curia and the 'people of Tuscany' (see the Appendix): 'As for us, what sort of a life have we, what is our strength and our power? We must thank our God for having multiplied our wealth, because this enables us to protect our lives and those of our children, and to halt the schemes of our persecutors.'

This then was a regular counter-attack, and we recognise the same tones or the same tactics in similar writings, side by side with rational arguments which put forward the needs of economic life. But not until quite a late period do we come across any frankly disapproving attitudes or even the expressions of a psychological split created by the debasing trade to which the Jews were subjected. In Italy, such criticism or grievances are not encountered until the second half of the sixteenth century, and I will deal with them later. They can be attributed to the shock caused by the establishment of ghettos and by local expulsions as well as to the reflections arising out of the catastrophe of Spanish Judaism. A good example of this point of view is a scholarly 'Purim satire' from the beginning of the seventeenth century, *The Book of the Lender and the Borrower*, imbued with a sort of gallows humour. It uses hyperbole to make its point. The anonymous author threatens anyone who does not lend at interest, or who lends without having made sure of a pledge, with the worst maledictions. He must be whipped even if the debtor repays him, 'not because this is the law, but because the times require it.' This Jewish humour has been compared with the ironically spellbinding formula which, according to the apostate Morosini, was current in twelfth-century ghettos to justify usury between Jews. It consisted, it is said, of reciting Deuteronomy 23:20 in interrogative tones to make it mean the opposite of its obvious

21

B

sense: 'Unto a foreigner thou mayest lend upon usury; but unto thy brother thou shalt not lend upon usury?'[21]

In Germany, on the other hand, a text from the end of the fifteenth century very seriously praises lending at interest: it is a trade which not only leaves leisure for study of the Law but makes it possible to provide for the needs of pious Talmudists who devote themselves full time to the interpretation of the divine will:[22]

> If the Torah and its understanding are better disseminated in Germany than elsewhere, this is because the Jews here make their living from their money trade with Christians, and therefore have no need to work. Consequently, they have the necessary time available to study the Torah, and anyone who does not himself study provides, by his profits, for the needs of those who do.

There is not a trace of humour here. In the following century it is interesting to see a man like John Calvin himself—who is so severe on the subject of usurers—also putting forward the pious leisure it makes available to religious ministers as a point in favour of lending at interest:[23]

> Because it is more tolerable than trading or following some occupation which would distract him [the pastor] from his duty, I do not see why the act should be condemned in general. But none the less, I would like such moderation to be preserved that a fixed profit should not be drawn from it; but that one should be content, when lending money to some merchant—an upright man—to rely on his faith and honesty to make a fair profit from it, depending on how God makes his labour prosper.

We now come on to the dominant concepts of Christian theology.

It is interesting to note that the first ecclesiastical provisions relating to Jewish usurers do not appear until late in the twelfth century. At first (Council of Paris, 1188), they concerned solely the protection of the Crusaders' patrimony. Then, at the beginning of the thirteenth century, Innocent III issued general warning edicts. It must be remembered that, from the earliest Christian times, the Church had condemned lending at interest, that even in Charlemagne's era conciliar provisions as well as royal capitularies forbade it to Christians, and that the anti-usury battle became an early major concern of the Church, in the twelfth century, when 'usurers are legion everywhere' (as Jean Lestocquoy puts it), during a period of general economic upsurge. One can therefore wonder why both ecclesiastical and secular legislation remained silent for so long on the subject of the 'Jewish usurer'.

It must be assumed that while he played only a relatively secondary role in the money trade (itself still undeveloped), theologians found nothing to say against his activities from their point of view. In fact, they appeared to be authorised by the Law of Moses (Deut. 23:20). In addition, patristic doctrine supplied a supplementary justification in the shape of the 'Exception of St Ambrose' (which authorised usury 'between enemies' and was included in this form in 1140 in the *Decretus* of Franciscus Gratianus). But in the long run such a state of affairs could not fail to compromise the Church's anti-usury battle in its entirety. It can be assumed that the example thus set was hardly edifying; above all, the Jews' actual privilege multiplied possibilities for all manner of loopholes. A very good instance of this is a passage in the *Verbum abbreviatum* by Petrus Cantor of Paris (end of twelfth century) criticising both Christian usurers for 'becoming followers of the Jewish name' in order to be able to practise their trade with impunity, and also the nobles who protected them for covering them by claiming: 'Isti nostri judaei sunt.' If this particular type of subterfuge appears to be isolated (at least I have not come across any other references to it), it was a widespread and persistent practice for Christian financiers to turn to Jews *sensu stricto* to serve as figureheads for them.[24] Such practices suggest that there is a grain of truth in the simplistic idea that the Jews' medieval specialisation in lending at interest was a direct and immediate consequence of its canonical prohibition to Christians.

These were the circumstances under which restrictive legislation, rather vague and probably impromptu, on the Jews' money trade emerged under the pontificate of Innocent III, and one would have good grounds for supposing that it bore the marks of his personal opinion of the Jews. The two basic texts are his letter to the archbishops on remission of interest on Crusaders' debts

(August 1198, *Post miserabilem*) and canon 67 (*Quanto amplius*) of the Fourth Lateran Council (November 1215).[25] The first therefore applies to the special case of debtors who had taken the cross. The second, decreeing redress of the 'serious and excessive usury' extorted by Jews, appeared to mean that they were only forbidden to make loans at interest above a certain rate (but without specifying that rate). This could have been the primary intention of the legislator, still tied down by the old views. In any case, that was the way that the text was interpreted in the beginning. This emerges from the gloss itself, which later (when the two texts in question were incorporated into the *Corpus juris canonici*) pointed out the contrary interpretation in connection with *Quanto amplius*: 'Ergo moderatas [usuras] videretur permittere a contrario sensu: quod non est verum, *et ita cessat argumentum a contrario sensu.*' [Therefore, in the contrary sense, it would seem to permit moderate interest rates: this is not true, *and thus the argument in the contrary sense falls.*] As for the *Post miserabilem* decretal, the first part mentioning the Crusaders was omitted when it was included in the *Corpus*, and as a result, the obligation placed on princes to see that interest levied by Jews was refunded was transformed into a general and permanent obligation.

Nevertheless, in the eyes of medieval public opinion, the dishonourable but indispensable practice of usury remained a sort of moral prerogative of the Jews, justified by certain lines of argument. The principal one (which is not without a distant analogy to the role of Judas Iscariot in the economics of salvation) was that the Jews, who were in any case already condemned, were not placing their souls in danger by charging interest, and were at the same time contributing to the salvation of the Christians they replaced. A prince of dubious faith like Emperor Frederick II referred to this when he excluded Jews from the general prohibition on usury. A prince as irreproachably Christian as St Louis came up against the same opinion among his counsellors, who assured him that the people could not live without lending at interest. One can say that medieval opinion was almost solid on this score—to the extent that the wording of the texts advocating the replacement of Christian usurers by Jews has led some excellent modern authors into the error of writing that the Jews' money trade was not considered reprehensible, even from the doctrinal point of view[26]—which, as has been seen, cannot really be validated except for the period before 1200. But the inflexibility of the thirteenth-century canonists rapidly relaxed in practice.

In the course of the following centuries, scholastic authors most frequently agreed that it was simply a question of toleration in the case of the Jews, 'to avoid a greater evil'.

Reading certain views leaves the impression that the reasons why the Jewish money trade was tolerated were related to those prescribing toleration of Judaism: because the natural malice of men must be taken into consideration. 'The Church and Christians are not committing a sin when they allow Jews to observe their rites, since they do not sanction them but only tolerate and permit them, and since it is impossible completely to uproot the ill-will of men', Francesco Sforza was told by a theologian he consulted on the subject of Jewish usury. The Jews, according to unchanging tradition, are worse than other men, being *ipso facto* in a state of sin, and their souls are probably lost in any case; therefore usury can be left to them.

This seems to have been the basic belief of St Thomas Aquinas, among others, but it has been so inadequately elucidated that modern authors have interpreted it in a great variety of ways.[27] Most comments on St Thomas's views refer to his short work *De regimine Judaeorum*. This, however, was written for a specific occasion, in reply to an embarrassing question when the duchess of Brabant asked him for official authorisation *not* to expel the usurers, Jewish or otherwise, contrary to her husband's testamentary stipulations, and *not* to compel them to refund the proceeds of their usury. In these circumstances, St Thomas could reply only in the negative, the stumbling-block in the event being the profit that the *Christian prince* drew from Jewish usury; in other words, his active participation in the sin of usury. This was truly an insurmountable difficulty for the middle ages, and one which Italian Thomists later made two attempts to solve. One of these, as logical as it was impracticable, was to recommend that the Jews

25

be allowed to practise their profession without the Christian authorities concluding an agreement with them to this express end, levying taxes on them or drawing any other profit from it (this was Savonarola's opinion). The other was to create the fiction whereby the Christian prince did not in any way participate in the sin of usury when he dealt with Jews, since, as the representative of his subjects, he was, for the same reasons as they, only a *patiens*, a victim like them. This was the opinion of the Dominicans of Brescia in 1547, who compared the duke of Mantua to the faithful Christians who assisted and consoled the martyrs. The magistrates of Florence summed up the impasse with remarkable clarity in 1469: from the moment that a tax was levied on the Jewish *banchieri*, how could it be maintained that they were tolerated in the name of the needs of the people and not out of cupidity or greed?

St Thomas himself expressed his views ambiguously on these points. His reply to the duchess of Brabant has even been capable of interpretation (wrongly, I think) as a prohibition on 'Jewish usury'.[28] But when he examines the question of lending at interest in a general way in question 78 of the *Summa theologica*, right from the first article he notes the freedom enjoyed by the Jews to lend at interest to foreigners 'to avoid a greater evil'. Moses had permitted this (Deut. 23:20) so that their covetous natures should respect the prohibition on usury between brothers. It is true, and St Thomas does not fail to mention in the same article, that the New Law replacing the Old has made all men brothers. But in the case of the Jews, permission to do forbidden things does still seem to exist. For example, despite the indissolubility of the marriage bond, in view of their irascibility and in order to forestall the danger of homicide, they are still allowed to divorce or repudiate their wives. Discussing the problem of repudiation, he raises the question of knowing the reasons why this was permitted to Jews by their Law, and concludes that it was 'to avoid a major evil, that of uxoricide [assassination of the spouse], to which Jews were driven by their vice of irascibility. In the same way, they were permitted to practise usury in respect of

26

foreigners, because of their vice of covetousness and so that they do not practise it between themselves.'

In question 78, however, St Thomas, after examining the case of the Jews, states more generally in the response *ad tertium* that, 'because of the imperfection of men ... human law tolerates lending at interest, not that it considers it in any way consistent with justice, but so as not to injure the greatest number'—a juxtaposition which is certainly significant.

The prevailing ideas of medieval theologians on the position of the Jews shows implicitly through all this. They may, because of their transgression or inveterate malice, be condemned to perpetual servitude, as St Thomas mentioned in his reply to the duchess of Brabant. But they do at least benefit from the moral depravity they have demonstrated since the time of Moses by virtue of the prerogative he conferred to transgress certain prohibitions in order to avoid greater evils. This permission does seem to be working in the interests 'of the greatest number', that is to say of the Christian community. None the less, a watch is needed so that the Jews' exorbitant impunity is tempered by financial punishments or fines (which must not serve to enrich the princes), 'in order that their iniquity does not allow them to make large profits', as St Antoninus of Florence later put it.

Granted, St Thomas does not take the argument which emerges from this to its logical conclusion; perhaps because in his day and notably in his native Italy, pawnbroking was still practised mainly by Christian usurers. In the fifteenth century, on the other hand, when it was primarily practised by Jews, discussions by theologians on the subject were numerous and ideas became explicit. Three major currents of thought then seem to be discernible. Some people thought that the Jews should be fully authorised to lend at interest. According to others, on the contrary, the general prohibition should also be applied to them. Others again took the middle way of toleration or the 'negative act of permission' (as Cardinal da Luca later expressed it). It is this view which prevailed in practice until the dawn of modern times.[29]

The famous canonist, Pietro d'Ancarano (1333–1416), can be cited as a proponent of the first idea. The *Consilium* he wrote at the request of an Italian prince (probably the duke of Mantua[30]) seems to express very well the views of Italian jurists who, brought up on Roman law and, in addition, inspired by the prevailing economic upsurge, had a tendency to question the prohibition on lending at interest in general. The prince had asked Ancarano if it was legal to force Christian debtors to discharge debts they had contracted to Jews. Ancarano replied in the affirmative and supplied five reasons in support: 1. The Christians had not sinned by borrowing, nor the Jews (who were outside the Church) by lending; 2. The Justinian code authorised lending at interest; 3. If evil there were, it should be tolerated because otherwise the greater evil of Christians lending at interest would ensue; 4. The public good required it insofar as there was no other means of supplying the needs of the nation; in such cases, human law permitted what divine law forbade (homicide, for example, in certain cases); 5. People's acquiescence, the public 'consensus', legalised the use of force in respect of debtors and the purging of all vice.

However, notwithstanding all these excellent reasons, Ancarano did not venture to come to a conclusion, since *Post miserabilem* expressly stated the contrary. There was, he said, an irrational contradiction there—all the more as the most elementary honesty ordained payment of debts—but this problem was not within the province of the prince, so he referred it to the Holy See. The practice of papal dispensations and the establishment of Jewish *banchieri* operating with the authority of the Holy See (to be dealt with later) were heralded in this way.

The thought behind the *Consilium* Paolo de Castro (?–1445) gave to the Venetian authorities at the time of the conquest of the territory of the *terra ferma* was quite different.[31] He stated at the outset that usury was strictly forbidden, equally by divine as by human laws and that, to cut short the expressions of opinion by laymen 'who prefer to believe their heads rather than divine and human writings', the decretals of Pope Clement V ranked the contrary opinion as a heresy. However, the custom of entering into agreements with Jewish usurers was spreading throughout Italy because of the vast needs of the people. It must never be forgotten that this was nothing but a form of last resort; the idea that Christians could carry on usury between themselves must not be believed—a warning which suggests how the Jews' privilege was helping to challenge the canonic prohibition. It was therefore important to leave usury solely to the Jews, and de Castro described the practice of dealing with them as 'necessarius et salutifer'. Moreover, he stated, the custom was hardly new, and the Church was the first to tolerate it in the lands immediately subject to the pope. It was therefore not possible to attribute it to sin, while still treating it with grave misgivings and knowing that the Jews were carrying it on—thus jeopardising their souls.

The famous canonist Tartagni (Alessandro da Imola, 1424–77) developed and later rounded off the argument of Pietro d'Ancarano and Paolo de Castro.[32] To establish the power of the pope (and of him alone) to grant dispensations in the matter, he reasoned along the following lines, among others: by so doing, the pope was not causing a mortal sin to be committed for, as far as the Jews were concerned, it was pointless to ask if they were committing such a sin by carrying on usury, since they were already damned by their unbelief. He then returned to the comparison with homicide, forbidden by divine law but which did not constitute a mortal sin. He also compared Jewish usury to prostitution, which the Church tolerated as a lesser evil. Finally, he referred to the position St Thomas adopted in the *Summa theologica* and cited the 'Exception of St Ambrose' *en passant*. It is interesting to see that the Venetian patrician Marino Sanuto refers at the beginning of the sixteenth century to these scholars to justify recourse to the Jews who, he says, were at least as necessary to a country as its bakers.[33]

On the other hand, the canonist Alessandro de Nevo (?–1486), among other arguments in favour of prohibiting Jewish usury, refers to the responsibility of the Church in the salvation of the Jews in his four *Consilia* against the *Iudaeos foenerantes* written between 1440 and 1455 at Padua.[34] His major argument could be summed up as follows: as usury was a mortal sin, and a sin in itself, no one had the power to grant dispensations in respect of it, since God had not given either Peter or his successors permission to sin. Moreover, he concurred with the laxist view whereby only

29

the heavy *mutuum*, the 'consumption loan', constituted usury properly speaking. His argument on the subject of toleration is also interesting. He compares toleration of Judaism with toleration of Jewish usury, and embarks on a discussion of the difference between the two.

Let us now try and follow de Nevo's reasoning in detail, for it enables us to supplement our knowledge on several points. The most systematic account is found in his first *Consilium* in the form of five 'doubts' on the following points:

1  *Are the Jews sinning by lending at interest?* (In fact if they are not, it would seem that the Church has no authority to concern itself with the question.) He stated that several scholars of his day, heedless of the opinion of all the authorities, affirmed that Jews could lend at interest to Christians without committing a sin. To prove this, these scholars cited three texts. First, *Quanto amplius*, which only forbade 'excessive and serious usury' to Jews; de Nevo answers this with the restrictive interpretation of the gloss. Then the 'Exception of St Ambrose'; but this, he notes, was applicable only between enemies, so that Jews, toleiated by Christian piety and enjoying the status of Roman citizens, could in no way plead it. Finally, and most important, the Jews or their advocates invoked Deuteronomy 23:20. To reject this argument—the most impressive of all—to establish, in other words, that their Law itself forbade the Children of Israel to lend at usury to 'foreigners', de Nevo tried to show that the permission had been revoked by the old Law itself. He found his proof in Deut. 28:12 and above all in Psalm 15:5, which decreed a general prohibition on lending at interest and was, in his opinion, even more authoritative than Deuteronomy, since David was a king (*rex*), while Moses was only a leader (*dux*). De Nevo also uses another argument: if Moses allowed Jews to lend to foreigners, he did so as the lesser evil and because he was not sufficiently powerful to decree and enforce a total prohibition. The Christian princes now possess this power. They must therefore utilise it.

2  *Ought the Church to oppose this sin of the Jews?* To reply in the affirmative, de Nevo referred to *Post miserabilem*, and more generally to the Church's mandate to make the unbelievers who

happened to be under its sovereignty respect natural law; the ban on bigamy, for example. De Nevo produced a series of arguments in answer to the claim that, as the Jews were already damned in any case, the Church had no need to concern itself with their souls. He cited the centurion Cornelius, the Gentile whose prayers and alms were pleasing to God, who made no distinction between people (Acts 10:4, 34). Then, to show the Church's anxiety for the souls of the Jews, he recalled that every year, during Holy Week, it caused prayers to be said for their conversion. He also reminded his readers that it was necessary to love the unbelievers (who included the Jews), even in their evil, and that the commandment: 'Love thy neighbour as thyself' involved these neighbours, too. One last argument, however, took the line that as the passion of Christ made Christians free and Jews slaves, it would be a disgrace to allow the Jews to lend at interest and thereby dominate the Christians, 'since he who contracts a loan becomes the slave of the usurer.'

3 *Ought the Church to tolerate this sin or to condone it in order to avoid a greater evil, or in the name of a greater good which can probably ensue?* On this subject, de Nevo examined the three types of toleration or permission recognised by theological tradition. First, simple permission, when, to avoid a greater evil, punishment was abolished although guilt was not diminished. Next, permission of the second grade when the Church not only tolerated but, if need be, also removed obstacles to toleration, as it did in the case of the Jews when the Christians wanted to prevent them from practising their rites. Finally, permission of the third grade, consisting of giving direct help to a reprehensible practice such as Jewish usury. Why must Jewish rites be tolerated? Because, St Augustine said, they bore witness to the truth of the Christian faith. As St Thomas Aquinas had written (quoted from the text at this point), Jews 'observe rites which in the past represented those we observe; the resulting advantage is that we have in our enemies themselves a witness to our faith and that what we believe is in some way represented before us figuratively'.[35] (The practices of other unbelievers were quite different kettles of fish. They 'offer neither truth nor usefulness; they must

31

therefore not be tolerated in any way', with exceptions.) This being so, the Jews might therefore be tolerated; but not their usury, for that would be equivalent to abetting the evil—as inadmissible for the Church as directly supporting or co-operating in the celebration of Jewish rites. (It will be remembered that a similar type of anxiety, i.e. not to support 'idol-worship', was a major preoccupation of the Talmudists.)

None the less, in certain cases, usury seemed to be permitted by canon law. But this was only on the surface; in reality, these were not cases of usury at all.[36]

4 *Can princes or town communes and councils grant usurers' licences to Jews?* It was obvious that they could not, de Nevo replied, since they were less powerful than the Church, and he who can do less cannot do more. At this point, he embarked on a systematic criticism of the *Consilia* by Pietro d'Ancarano and Paolo de Castro cited above, and pointed out in passing that almost all the nobles and all the communes in Italy had been excommunicated for entering into agreements with Jews (here we do perhaps catch a glimpse of one of the anxieties of the opponents of the Jewish money trade which it was essential not to withdraw from the scope of ecclesiastical jurisdiction). Referring to the Epistle to the Romans (1:32), de Nevo added that the sin of the communal councils was greater than that of the Jews: 'Not only do they do it, but they approve of those who do.' He also challenged the argument of the public good, since people generally borrowed in order to gamble or to commit other reprehensible acts; sons stole their fathers' possessions to pawn them, and many other evils resulted. More generally (this is one of Bernardino da Siena's arguments), the man who did not firmly believe that the human race could dispense with overt usury was doubting the solicitude of God by so doing, and was therefore uttering a blasphemy.

5 *Can the Pope grant dispensations to princes or towns to take Jewish lenders into their service and conclude agreements with them, according to custom?* The reply was obviously a categorical 'no': usury was an evil that no reason could transform into a good; a *peccatum in se* and not a *peccatum secundum quid*, like fishing[37] (which

32

is not an evil in itself) on the Lord's day, for example. 'If the pope does not have permission to sin, he cannot grant it to others'. Finally, and if possible even more categorically, God could not act so as to disgrace the Christian faith.

In the following century a Dominican from Venice, Sisto da Siena, turned de Nevo's argument round in the following fashion: the major crimes of the Jews consisted in their unbelief and perfidy, which were an offence against God. Since our mother the Church none the less tolerated them, why not tolerate their usury when this was not contrary to the public good?[38]

For greater clarity in the above account of Alessandro de Nevo's argument, in some places I have interpolated in the analysis of the first *Consilium* quotations or examples from the three following *Consilia* in which the canonist developed his ideas or engaged in polemics with his adversaries. In the fourth and last *Consilium*, the dominant thesis seems to have weakened slightly. De Nevo introduces us, as it were, into the intimacy of these discussions. One evening, he tells us, Master Galvanus of the Servite order came to see him at Padua, brandishing a new argument in favour of Jewish usury built on the basis of an examination of the state of necessity according to St Thomas. De Nevo rejects the argument, but in the course of the discussion comes to agree that fear of scandal necessitates toleration of many things. Again it is important to know how to distinguish between one scandal and another. 'Now, in our case, it cannot be said that the fact of not engaging Jews constitutes a serious scandal.' Despite this, he agrees that because of scandal it is permissible to 'conceal'—in other words, to feign ignorance—and not to punish delinquents. This seems to mean that it might be possible to tolerate the Jews, if not as recognised usurers, at least as clandestine usurers; a position which is already resembling the line Savonarola later adopted. But it could also mean that Christian usurers might be tolerated for the same reason, the main point still being not to make an active pact with evil.

In the second half of the fifteenth century, de Nevo's *Consilia*

33

became the principal arsenal from which the Italian Franciscans drew their theoretical anti-Jewish arguments. What we will be attempting to examine in the rest of this book is how the order of St Francis became the champion of the Monti di Pietà, and to what extent it was thus serving the interests of the Christian bourgeoisie. As far as the Jewish usurers were concerned, it was, as we have said, the intermediate position defended by de Castro that prevailed and, in practice, the *banchieri* system, licensed by the sovereign pontiffs, functioned without being seriously challenged. It was so much accepted that there was no mention of either Jewish usury or papal permission, tacitly sanctioned in this way, at the Fifth Lateran Council of 1516 or at the Council of Trent, both of which spent time deliberating on Monti di Pietà, and, by legitimising them, sanctioned the legitimacy of the interest levied on 'consumption loans'. We still have to see the comments on this system by the great Roman canonist da Luca in the second half of the seventeenth century, on the very eve of its abolition in quite different economic and social circumstances.

In his *Theatrum veritatis et iustitiae* . . . , Cardinal da Luca begins by describing how it functioned under the popes of past centuries, particularly those such as Paul IV and Pius V who displayed strong feelings against the Jews. He then states that the popes could not give dispensations contrary to divine law, 'canonise generally and indefinitely', or legalise practices forbidden by this law. They did, however, possess the power to interpret it, and this they could and must do, '*non per viam dispositionis, sed per viam tolerationis*' [not through dispensation, but through toleration]. By granting licences to Jews, they were doing no more than utilising this power. To state the reverse was to state that many sovereign pontiffs, and the whole Church, had been in error for a very long time. *Il Dottor volgare*[39] (the edition of the *Theatrum veritatis* . . . which had been 'given a moral tone in Italian') takes up this argument again in a more succinct form. It mentions

a negative act of permission, or toleration . . . the Jews' usury is tolerated by a connivance based on reason, since they have no hope of salvation because of their essential lack of faith. The Church therefore has no motive for caring about the salvation of their souls, since the outcome will be the same, whether they pursue usury or not. Therefore the laws which prescribe a certain taxation on the usury of Jews are not canonising it by this action, neither are they declaring it legal and valid; they are merely placing certain limits on it which it cannot exceed, in order not to allow larger extortions.

In conclusion, it is interesting to note an example of the way in which the rabbis translated such concepts. According to Leon da Modena (1571-1648; the text given below dates from around 1625):[40]

Permission to practise lending at interest is given by the pope, on grounds of toleration (*savlanuth*), and the interpretation he gives of it is as follows:

According to strict doctrine, the Jews should not have been permitted to lend at interest to the 'nations'; nevertheless, I make an exception in favour of so and so in order that he can practise lending. I do not intend to make it a general rule but, when someone insists, I reserve to myself the right, after examination of each case, to grant permission or to refuse it.

# CHAPTER III

# *Preliminary Reflections on the Jewish Money Trade in Italy*

---

. . . let his approach be affable, let him answer anger with soft words, let him be rather of those who are insulted than of those who insult, let him welcome people with a friendly face and let them like to have dealings with him. If he lacks any one of these characteristics, he is unsuited to the practice of his profession—*The Book of the Lender and the Borrower*, I, 1

Let us now move on to the circumstances in which, relatively late, people in Italy increasingly began to have recourse to Jewish lenders, who were coming to compete with the 'Tuscans'.

The first agreements concluded by the small towns or *castelli* in central Italy with the Jews of Rome seem to date from the second half of the thirteenth century (only one or two documents may exist for an earlier period). By the terms of these agreements, called *condotte*, the Jews could settle in the city, lend at interest and on security there (at a statutory rate which varied according to the place, the amount of the loan, etc.), engage in all types of business and have complete freedom to practise their religion. In addition, they enjoyed extraordinary privileges such as exemption from wearing the *rouelle* and, sometimes, the right to carry weapons. In return, they were obliged to invest a certain sum of capital in the *banco*, to pay an annual fee proportional to this capital to the commune, and, when necessary, to advance funds to it at a reduced rate. 'The *condotta*', wrote Attilio Milano (who studied a large number of them), 'is a stereotyped contract: names vary, as do specific conditions such as some clause which may stamp it with a more or less liberal intent, but the wording follows a standard formula.'[1] He places great emphasis on the colonising role of the lenders as pioneers, from the point of view of Jewish history. The *banchiere*, strong in his licence to settle, became a focus around whom gathered other Jews, his servants or small craftsmen. Then, if the colony prospered, they were joined by scholars and even artists. It must not be forgotten that from the religious point of view, a quorum of ten male Jews (*minyan*) was theoretically indispensable. Thus, while in southern bureau-cratised Italy Judaism was in desperate straits, northern Italy, the Italy of the free towns, was opening up to it as a result of the money trade.

We refer the reader to Milano for the chronology of this 'upward march' (to use his expression) right through the four-teenth century of Jewish moneylenders from Rome, which in the Po valley come up against a similar stream of Jews coming from France and Germany. It is enough to add that as far as the begin-nings of Jewish 'banking' are concerned, there is no evidence of the existence of specific and definite links between Jewish lenders and the Holy See. The very most that can be noted is a clause in an agreement concluded between the Jews of Siena and the commune of San Gimignano in 1309 that in cases of non-observance of the *condotta* by the commune, it will pay half of the agreed fine to the Jews, and the other half to the Curia in Rome.[2] It can also be assumed that the economic depression in Rome during the 'captivity of Avignon' prompted some Jewish capitalists to seek their fortune elsewhere.

Gino Luzzatto is responsible for the most interesting comments on this expansion of the Jewish *banchieri*, who settled first in small or middle-sized towns and came to a lengthy halt before the walls of great commercial centres like Florence, Milan or Genoa.

On the one hand, Luzzatto states that in large towns, borrowers —individuals or municipalities—could find money on the spot, while the small communes were forced to call on outside finan-ciers.[3] On the other hand, he writes:[4]

It has been said and repeated by a large number of authors that the Jews were favoured in the practice of their art and almost pushed into it by the canonical laws which forbade the profitable money trade to the faithful. But we really cannot ascribe this power to canonical prohibition alone, when we see that the same trade was practised by so many merchants and business companies in the richest and most highly developed Italian cities at the same time as by the Jews, and with equal if not greater success. The principal cause is, on the contrary, purely economic and lies in the fact that Jewish leaders, like the so-called *Lombards*, *Tuscans* and *Cahorsins*, finding themselves at this time, by virtue of their particular circumstances, the sole possessors of a small amount of circulating capital, could find no lucrative way of using it except to lend it at interest. Still less can it be admitted that a specific ethnic attitude forced the Jews into this sort of trade . . .

This is perfectly correct as a starting-point. During the thirteenth century, in fact, and a good part of the fourteenth, short-term lending and pawnbroking were practised in Italy by both Christians and Jews (in a way which at the beginning might seem undifferentiated). Later, however, Jews supplanted 'Lombards' or 'Tuscans' in this field and ended up by ousting them completely. Despite Luzzatto's views, can this be regarded as a triumph for the moral ideas of the Church which, by making these activities odious, caused them to be left to the despised minority? Outside Italy, however, the evolution was not the same; the evolution, particularly in western Europe, might even be said to have been the reverse. The Jews were definitively expelled from England, France and some German towns; in many places, notably the prosperous Netherlands, it was the Lombard dynasties which ended up by monopolising consumption loans. Can conclusions be drawn from this diversity and, if so, what conclusions? Can the precise secret of the success of the Jewish lenders of Italy (to paraphrase Henri Pirenne) be sought outside Italy?

To clarify the picture, a few guidelines on the organisation of lending at interest throughout Europe are therefore essential at the start.

## THE LOW COUNTRIES

Following the work of Georges Bigwood, Raymond de Roover and Camille Tihon have thoroughly studied the money trade in these active countries, and especially that carried on by the Lombards, the professional pawnbrokers.[5] De Roover in particular, in his major work on Bruges, set out to provide information not only on the Lombards' techniques but also on their way of life and their social characteristics. He brought out the disapproval which surrounded them, and did not omit a comparison of their situation with that of the Jews. Even other Italians established in the same places, he writes, avoided the Lombards' trade and kept them at a distance.

The ostracism inflicted by their own compatriots on the Lombards would therefore denote the growing disrepute of usury. It might also have corresponded to the gradual assimilation of Italians settled abroad, which would have led them to judge the misdeeds of their compatriots, the pawnbrokers, even more severely and to stand aloof from them. Yet it is known that, while the Italian colonies abroad were preserving their own individuality, the merchant bankers, like the Lombards, were maintaining close links with their homelands and preferred to marry Italian women. Generation after generation, they remained foreigners in the eyes of the local population. Paul Aebischer made the same comments about Lombards settled in Switzerland. Only a few of them, he wrote, settled down in the place where they made their fortune.[6]

In these circumstances, it can be said that the Lombards' loyalty to their country of origin steeled or immunised them against the surrounding animosity, against the penalties of all types to which they were subjected, against their defamation from the pulpits of the churches. For the expatriate 'Lombard' or 'Tuscan', the public opinion which must have counted was that of his narrow circle, an extension for him of the homeland. His local reputation in the Low Countries, his opprobrium in the eyes of the 'natives', cannot have affected him unduly, precisely because of a 'social isolation' based on his dual status as a foreigner and a usurer.

A statement in an anti-usury sermon by Fra' Giordano da Rivalto, the Florentine preacher who lived at the beginning of the fourteenth century, supported this view. Certain pawnbrokers, he remarked, were ashamed to practise their profession in their native town of Florence, and they therefore fled to France,[7] where they then felt more at ease. Among the great merchant bankers, too, morals abroad were more easy-going. Jacques Heers points to the Genoese settled in London who, when they made commercial loans, turned up their noses at the precautions or camouflage in use in their head offices at Genoa, and openly entered in their accounts the interest due to them.[8]

Can we not conclude from this that a moneylender could practise his profession more comfortably in places where a national or cultural gulf separated him from the rest of the population?

Such subtle shades of attitude, we believe, have their importance in an examination of the circumstances in which dynasties of Lombard lenders survived in the Low Countries until the beginning of the seventeenth century. Jewish lenders made only timid inroads there and did not take root. The judeophobia characteristic of northern Europe must also have contributed to this state of affairs: in 1349–50 numerous Jews were massacred at the time of the Black Death; in 1370, following an accusation of profanation of the Host, almost all the Jews of Brabant were burned alive (they reappeared there only in the eighteenth century). Jean Stengers, who has made a very detailed study of these vicissitudes, thinks that Jewish lenders were not able to settle in the Low Countries first because the Lombards were already there, and second because the urban economy of these regions was relatively well developed. Central Europe, he says, offered their capital and their energy a freer and better field of activity.[9] But Italy, with an even more developed economic life, experienced considerable Jewish immigration from the fourteenth to the sixteenth centuries; and I think that this favourable reception accorded to the Children of Israel is explained precisely because Italy was, economically and culturally, the most developed country of Europe. The Jews' welcome was linked to the way in which the Italian popes, princes or communes at the period saw either their own or the general interest.

Stengers's first reason stands. What barred the Jews' road to the Low Countries was the traditional monopoly of the Lombards, who enjoyed the same advantages or 'aptitudes': strong internal cohesion, an inward-turning community, relative invulnerability to social disapproval. Finally, the canonical prohibition on interest must have played a more important role in these problems than Gino Luzzatto assumed. But its differentiating effect acted very unevenly, by slow and sometimes circuitous routes.


## OTHER EUROPEAN COUNTRIES

A rapid general survey will have to suffice for the rest of Europe, not only because the material is dangerously inexhaustible, but also because, with one or two exceptions, there is nothing resembling the research by Bigwood or de Roover on the Lombards of the Low Countries.

However, the impression emerges that the social distinction *sui generis* between merchant banker and pawnbroker which these authors describe was barely perceptible elsewhere, since no historian of the Lombards outside the Low Countries has noted anything of the sort or compared their social condition to that of the Jews. This is borne out by the very imprecision of the terminology whereby 'Cahorsin' or 'Lombard' indiscriminately designated the Italian merchant generally, in England or France.

In England—where the Jews, organised into a sort of nationalised corporation, the *'scaccarium Judaeorum'* or 'Jews' Exchequer', actually became the financial agents of the Crown in the course of the eleventh and twelfth centuries—their displacement by the 'Cahorsins' in the thirteenth century was rapid. In 1263 all English Jews were pledged by Edward, son of Henry III, to the Cahorsin firm of Beraldi. Impoverished and rendered useless, they were expelled in 1290.[10]

Information currently available does not make it possible to establish such a direct link between the appearance of the Lombards in France in the thirteenth century and the decline of the Jews, although these sorts of conjectures have often been put forward in a general way (particularly by Henri Pirenne). This field remains virtually unexplored.[11]

The expulsions of the Jews by St Louis appear to have been mainly theoretical; that by Philip the Fair in 1306 was, on the contrary, very effective and put an end to the existence of French Judaism in its traditional form. The readmissions in the fourteenth century applied only to specialised groups of lenders. In fact, expulsions alternately of Jews and Lombards are to be noted during the course of this century, with confiscation of money owing to them and remission of interest. What was involved was therefore an exercise of financial policy, coloured by the anti-usury struggle. In addition, business connections between Lombards and Jews are reported in certain documents which reveal very clearly the Lombards' financial superiority over the Jews. It is also interesting to note that the Jews were finally expelled from France in 1394, while the Lombards were expelled from the territories of the Two Burgundies at almost the same period. Elsewhere in France they also became fewer and disappeared earlier than in the Low Countries. It is tempting to relate this to the rise or reappearance of a bourgeoisie who felt that 'it is almost a conscientious duty to hire out money' (Lucien Febvre) and who, in order not to lose the profits from its clandestine usury, fought against the licensed and supervised lenders. In the end, only Italy and the Low Countries treated these with wise toleration.

For the German lands and eastern Europe, it is enough to recall that Lombard lenders in any number are reported only in the Rhine Valley and southern Germany (just as the Italian merchant bankers; perhaps in their wake?) and that Jews, as we know, were able to remain in all these economically less developed regions throughout the middle ages, and to play their role as 'sponges' in financial matters there. In the Iberian peninsula also, the hold of Italian finance on Spanish business dates only from the sixteenth century. In the middle ages, commerce and finance remained primarily the prerogative of Jews and Moors, solidly entrenched, thanks to the country's Moslem past.

The full multiplicity of the factors involved and the complexity of the picture can thus be seen. According to a classic theory, first suggested by Wilhelm Roscher almost a century ago, the Jews of Europe were the pioneers of trade, gradually ousted from all economic activities. In 1895 he wrote:[12]

> It can be said that the trend of medieval policy towards the Jews was almost the reverse of that of general economic development. As soon as nations became sufficiently mature to fulfil these functions themselves, they did their utmost to emancipate themselves from such tutelage over their trade, often through bitter conflicts. The persecutions of the Jews in the late middle ages are therefore, to a large extent, a product of commercial jealousy. They are connected with the rise of a national merchant class.

Almost all subsequent authors expressed similar views. Henri Pirenne, for example, produced the following concise formula: 'The more economically advanced a country was, the fewer Jewish moneylenders were to be found there.'[13]

Now it just happens that these types of theories and views are no longer applicable to the most advanced country of all. From the point of view of Jewish history, this is a remarkable exception. It is not uninstructive even to the historian of economic theories, concerned with the various solutions that medieval society found to the 'terrible question of interest'.

In these circumstances, the two-sided question might be asked: What in Italy was 1. the weakness of Christian usurers? 2. the strength of the Jews?

## THE ABANDONMENT OF PAWNBROKING BY CHRISTIANS?

In one of his short stories Franco Sacchetti tells of a priest who, tired of seeing the faithful reject his sermons, announced that he was going to demonstrate that usury was not a sin, and so succeeded in filling his church. Boccaccio could be quoted to make the same point. Or again, to illustrate the development of the money trade in medieval Italy, one might mention the banker Folco Portinari, the father of Dante's Beatrice, and Angiolotto Giotto, who was not above exploiting the weavers (as Davidsohn has maliciously recalled).[14] There were always swarms of occasional lenders in Italy: professional practitioners of the usurious money trade passed, roughly speaking, through the following three stages of development:

merchant bankers, non-specialist, undertaking consumption loans, *inter alia*;

the establishment of a class of professional pawnbrokers ('Lombards', 'Tuscans' and Jews);

the sole monopolisation of pawnbroking by Jews.

The transition from the first to the second stage is interesting in this context only to the extent to which, corresponding to progressive specialisation (bankers; money-changers; pawnbrokers), it also reflects the growing disrepute of pawnbroking. At the end of the thirteenth century the Gianfigliazzi of Florence, lenders to kings, were still also official agents of pawnbroking establishments in the Dauphiné and Provence.[15] In the fifteenth century, on the other hand, the Medici, as well as their principal colleagues, strained their ingenuity to camouflage in their books the interest due on funds deposited with them, since such investments were canonically reprehensible[16] (while profits arising from a partnership agreement were henceforth regarded as legal). The evolution which resulted not only from the anti-usury campaigns of the Church but also from the concessions it made to the requirements of economic life can be judged by the subtle distinctions of the theologians. According to Benjamin Nelson: 'the merchant-usurer of the early middle ages had broken down to yield two disparate figures who stood at opposite poles: the . . . manifest usurer-pawnbroker, as often as not a Jew; and the city father . . . a merchant prince.'[17]

Nelson has studied numerous wills in which Italian merchants at the point of death ordered restitution of their 'usuries', and points out that after 1330 none of the legatees, i.e. former customers, resided outside Italy. From this he deduces that the great international merchants ceased at about that time to bother with consumption loans, which were left, even in Italy, to relatively small traders.

Besides the effect of the anti-usury campaigns, and with some relevance to them, was the slow evolution of morals, a preliminary symptom perhaps of Italian commercial decadence in modern times, when 'the ennobled descendants of the great merchant dynasties preferred to enjoy themselves rather than take risks'.[18] On the subject of this fourteenth-century evolution, Amintore Fanfani in his study of the 'capitalist spirit' places the emphasis on the new 'instrumentality' of wealth, the principal function of which, according to him, was henceforth to increase reputation. He writes very expressively: 'Forward therefore, forward to accumulate possessions, the means of procuring honour.'[19] From the moment when 'overt and public usury' aroused general disapproval, the ardour put into making money in this way was of necessity somewhat chilled by the disrepute which was attached to it—to the greater advantage of the Jewish lenders.

Not that the Christian professionals withdrew rapidly—even after the Council of Vienne (1311) had excommunicated towns which entered into agreements with them, and declared to be heretics those who attempted to justify them. Nelson thinks that the thunderbolts of the Church were really effective only *in articulo mortis*, when the usurer, to be given a Christian burial, had to bequeath his patrimony wholly or partly to the customers he had robbed during his lifetime, or to the Church.[20] It was above all in this way that family continuity in the profession must have been interrupted from generation to generation, which makes it easier to understand the slowness of the process. In short, it seems that the Christian 'public usurers' did not finally disappear from the scene until the end of the fifteenth century, when the first Monti di Pietà appeared and multiplied in Italian cities. None the less, accounts of two miracles, one at Piacenza in 1478 and the other at Parma in 1481, mention overt usurers who, with the connivance of the clergy and without making restitution, were buried in consecrated ground, with ensuing diluvian torrents in

45

one case and bells ringing of their own accord in the other. Well-documented cases from Florence, Brescia and elsewhere, dating from a slightly earlier period (we will discuss these later), show how Christian lenders were able to forbid Jews access to these towns for many generations. The same interpretation can perhaps be given to the story of Tomaso Grassi, the millionaire usurer from Milan who pushed St Bernardino da Siena, 'little versed in the things of this world', into preaching against usury in order to embarrass his competitors and keep the field clear for himself.[21] Milan, in fact, had a tradition of keeping the Jews at a distance.

Finally, a few interesting facts are available about Nice, where the establishment of a *casana* for loans was laid down in the pact relating to the acquisition of the town by the princes of Savoy (1388). It was held from 1414, and perhaps earlier, by the Lombard family (from Chieri) of Busquetti or Busquette. In 1397 Mathieu Busquette bribed one Rostaing Blanqui to rob and kill a local Jewish merchant. When Blanqui was arrested, he justified himself by claiming that the assassination of a Jew was a venial sin. The last mention of two Busquette brothers in the role of 'casaniers' was in 1442. Then in 1448 the town was dealing with the *honestus et discretus vir* Bonnefoy de Châlons because, as the account of the reasons for the contract says, the 'casaniers' disappeared some time ago and the town was left without a *casana*. The impression emerges that the morality of the Busquette family left a great deal to be desired.[22] ('It seems', Sapori wrote of the Christian lenders, 'that the sin of usury infected their souls, to the point where they were transformed into veritable sinks of iniquity.')

In the end, the disrepute of usury is still not enough to account for the disappearance of professional Christian lenders. But there have been socially reviled professions, and volunteers to practise them, always and everywhere.

## THE JEWS' 'COMPETITIVE ADVANTAGES'?

Fear of eternal damnation and public disapproval were, as we have just seen, very slack curbs on the activities of Christian lenders, and essentially corresponded to a subjective state of mind. The question arises whether outside this, in the intersubjective lender–borrower relationship, other factors may not have intervened to give the Jews an advantage in their money trade.

The problem would then be to determine the professional qualities of the perfect lender, those which would ensure his success. Are they always the same everywhere? Fortunately, a document is available from Italy dating from a later period (early seventeenth century) which is a sort of 'handbook of the perfect Jewish lender' in a subtle and ambiguous form. This is the 'Purim satire' mentioned earlier, a scholarly entertainment stuffed with the puns, transliterations and biblical quotations proper to this type of work. They are not always easy to interpret, but certain passages could not be more informative. In the present context, it will be sufficient to quote the following recommendations:

I. The principal manager of the *banco*, whether the capital belongs to him personally *in toto*, whether he has a partner, or whether the capital belongs to a patron, must be a humble and modest man and his business must be conducted in a faithful manner, for it has been said: 'My servant *Moshe* (Moses) *is faithful in all mine house.*' (Num. 12:7) Now for *Moshe*, read *Macher* (lender). Therefore, let his approach be affable, let him answer anger with soft words, let him be rather of those who are insulted than of those who insult, let him welcome people with a friendly face and let them like to have dealings with him. If he lacks any one of these characteristics, he is unsuited to the practice of his profession.

II. Let him be a man who is whole in body and mind, well spoken, diligent, adroit, agile, prompt to receive and slow to return. Let him have a fine presence; let him be a good book-keeper, knowing how to write accurately and legibly, and endowed with a good memory; let him have a bushy beard and take care about his appearance, let him be dressed in the same way as the local people. Let him be of the male sex, for women are completely excluded from this profession by reason of their fickleness, and because it is to be feared that they may steal, following Rachel's example. (Gen. 31:19)

III. The *banco* must be built of hard stone, so that bandits cannot get in under cover of night. Doors and windows must be spaced out so that the building can be fortified against a possible break-in. The

47

windows should be protected by a metal grille and be closed at the bottom and at the top . . .

The *banco* must be situated in the best district of the town to give easy access, but not in the main street or the market-place, lest the rich be ashamed to go there.

The entrance to the *banco* must be low and narrow, protected by a curtain to shield it from the view of passers-by, so that the borrowers' faces cannot be recognised. This curtain must be blue in colour so that the bank is easily identifiable . . .

This last recommendation is, we believe, explained by the peculiarities of the money trade. In other types of business, the customer pays money to the trader and thus shows his affluence, so that it is in the trader's interest to have his own premises where he can welcome his customers sumptuously and before witnesses. Borrowing on security, on the contrary, is a sign of poverty and inferiority, it denotes weakness, it constitutes a humiliation; it is therefore to the trader's advantage to make the transaction discreet and himself humble. It would even seem that 'external signs of poverty' should form part of his conventional decor. In any case, Christian lenders in Florence and Lombards in Bruges in the fourteenth century had loan offices exactly the same as those just described,[23] so that the transaction could be shrouded in secrecy. You slipped in to the lender as furtively as you visited a prostitute. Later, in the sixteenth and seventeenth centuries, the embarrassment customers felt at the Monti di Pietà counters makes it easier to understand the persistent popularity of Jewish lenders, even though they demanded a much higher interest.

But on the other hand is there not a resemblance between the description of the qualities required for the practice of the profession of *banchiere* and Lucien Febvre's pompous portrait of the 'sixteenth-century merchant'? 'A man of prompt decision, exceptional physical and moral stamina, unrivalled boldness and resolution. He must be so, or else the profession crushes him. Moreover, aiming entirely for profit, he must pursue it by every means'.[24]

'An adventurer, in the etymological sense of the word', wrote Febvre again, and even 'a soldier'. Here, to be sure, the similarity ends. It even goes the other way: see the first recommendation: 'let him answer anger with soft words, let him be rather of those who are insulted than of those who insult'. This reminds us once again of the traditional humility of the medieval Jew, proclaimed as an essential virtue by contemporary rabbinic writings and corresponding to his lowly status within Christian society. If it is true that moneylending differs from other commercial acts of everyday life by the embarrassing situation in which it places the customer and by the secrecy with which the latter tries to surround it, may this not be a clue to one of the factors in the Jews' success in this field?

It is interesting and relevant to note that an Institute of 'Motivation Research' in the United States which embarked on an investigation on behalf of a loan company in about 1950 came to the same sorts of conclusions. The investigators[25] strongly emphasised the embarrassment felt by customers. They thought that they could note a more or less pronounced 'guilt complex' amongst the majority of borrowers, who felt they were committing a reprehensible act inconsistent with the conduct of a good citizen or *paterfamilias* (and even, in the extreme, 'very much like a crime, a theft of money'). Consequently, they advised loan companies to put their customers at ease, to do their utmost to neutralise their inhibitions by giving them a feeling of 'superiority' and to do this by avoiding, for example, receiving them in luxuriously furnished places. On the contrary, the firm should be satisfied with a rather bare establishment, while treating the visitor with discreet deference.

We thus come back to the literary archetype of the 'sordid usurer'; moreover, we think that well-conducted 'motivation research' can be no more than the orderly arrangement of old precepts and rules well known through the wisdom of nations. From this point of view, the study consulted contains other annotations which give food for thought on the intersubjective borrower–lender relationship in general. For example, it states that a number of borrowers, whatever they say or think about it, are very little concerned about the more or less exorbitant rate of interest that they will have to pay. Their real fears arise from another quarter: 'He fears his drives that made him give in to borrowing—so the Company becomes a devil who conjured him into it': a psychological process which must have played its part in the medieval 'diabolisation' of the Jew, even if factors of religious psychology are at the origin of the process. 'Any treatment which is not completely reassuring will be interpreted by the guilty borrower as harsh, much harsher than it is in reality': this is the light in which, I think, the frequent abuse of Christian usurers in the middle ages could be interpreted. The sources record that they were harsher than the Jews, 'skinning' the poor more. 'You have to sell the guilty borrower relief of conscience more than anything else': if this is so, would not relief come more easily from the outcast Jew?

That, according to correct procedure, such psychoanalytical conclusions are devoid of scientific precision, in addition that they are inapplicable as they stand to the socio-economic conditions of the past are obvious truths—yet they could provide a clue. And it seems to me no less true that contradictory and varied psychological factors—fear of losing face, ambivalent attitudes towards the abhorred Jewish usurer and the obliging lender, the Christian's contempt for the unbeliever—played their part during the competition between Jewish and Christian finance.

The American investigators strongly emphasised the fear the borrower felt in his relationship with the lender about the harshness which he attributed to him *a priori*. Remember the abuse directed at Christian usurers in the middle ages, accusing them of being harsher than Jews? As far as Italy is concerned, such assertions will recur throughout the remainder of this book; it is not rare to find them also on the other side of the Alps.[26]

In the light of the preceding consideration, it might be asked if it were all not just an illusion, since the hiring of money does not generally depend on the 'moral qualities' of the lenders. If the Jews seemed 'softer', was this not because of their manners? Did not the 'harshness' of the Christians just seem more shocking because it came from brothers in Christ?

None the less, numerous and conclusive proofs demonstrate, as will be shown, that in Italy the interest rate charged by the Jews was clearly below that charged by Christians when public and overt usury was involved. This phenomenon can be attributed to the following reasons:

1   Both were equally exposed to the taxes, fines, etc., levied by the civil authorities, but the situation was completely different where confiscation and condemnations pronounced by ecclesiastical justice were concerned. In Italy, I have found only a single instance (at Pisa in 1317) of a Jew condemned to make restitution by an ecclesiastical tribunal. This was therefore a 'debit charge' peculiar to Christian usurers.

2   Such material risks, run by Christians alone, were accompanied by risks of a spiritual nature, such as refusal of Christian burial and eternal damnation. One might therefore wonder, going back to the psychological subtleties from which these questions seem inseparable, whether the subjective state of sin in which they lived, their more dangerous state of existence, did not increase their hunger for profit, their 'inordinate covetousness', and may not, for example, have led them to take excessive financial risks, with corresponding repercussions for their customers.

3   It must also be recalled that, on the whole, the money trade remained the principal lucrative occupation open to Jews, and their primary means of earning their living. Because of this, and as a marginal group of the population, they had to know how to put up with smaller profits if necessary. This has been said many times; but perhaps the contrast has not been sufficiently emphasised between the Christian usurer living in a state of permanent sin, condemned by the Church, and the Jewish usurer whose activities were entirely justified in the eyes of the rabbis, as we have seen.

Did they have competitive advantages? Again, it is necessary to take into account that the Jews in Italy were more firmly rooted there than in France or Germany, so that their 'otherness' was much less obvious, and also to note the premature middle-class moral respectability: as early as 1221, a Florentine author could write: 'Today, respect goes primarily to His Majesty, King Money'.[27] If he was sufficiently rich, the Jewish *banchiere* could, as will be seen, be a respectable citizen of his town—and appeals were made to his loyalty to it; he could mix on a footing with officials and even have friendly relations with nobles. Such familiarity, which brought him closer in this connection to his Lombard or Tuscan competitor, probably reduced the possible advantages attached to his specific position as a Jew. On the other hand, psychological factors of this nature became decisive after the establishment of the Monti di Pietà, and it is in the light of these that one can understand the vitality of the Jewish money trade up to the eighteenth century, if not later. But insofar as private lenders, whether Jews or Christians, operating in similar conditions and with similar techniques, were involved, this type of preference could have been effective only within fairly narrow limits.

Having said this, it must primarily have affected customers with thinner skins, worried about their prestige; the 'rich' who, in *The Book of the Lender and the Borrower*, did not want to borrow in the sight and knowledge of the whole world, and for whom it was consequently important that the *banco* be suitably arranged. Now the administrators or officials who concluded an agreement with the *banchiere* and negotiated the terms of his concession obviously belonged to this category. While dealing with him *ex officio*, they were also able to resort to him in a private capacity, or even act as his sureties for municipal loans. In this way, the unconscious attraction towards the Jewish lender's humble and obliging manner must in their eyes have been masked by, and have blended with, their ideas on the way in which their office should be exercised and the interests of their city understood.

# CHAPTER IV

# The Rise of Jewish Banking in Italy

And if I, Marino Sanuto, had belonged to the 'Pregadi', as last year, I would have taken the floor . . . to prove that the Jews are at least as necessary to a country as its bakers, and above all to this one, for the general well-being—Marino Sanuto, *Diarii* . . . , 9 November 1519

The communal archives of the small towns of Todi, Ascoli and Matelica, north and east of Rome, contain the oldest agreements concluded with Jewish financiers from Rome at the end of the thirteenth century. They are not as yet the classic type of *condotte*, or specifically loans on security. Particularly curious is the contract concluded between the commune of Ascoli and a consortium of twenty or so lenders from Florence, Arezzo and Rome in 1297. On payment of 100 gold florins a year, they obtained the mono-poly of lending at interest in Ascoli and, if they wished, were allowed to bring other capitalists in. But what is interesting about the document is the association between Christian and Jewish lenders it seems to reflect, in that the eighteen Tuscans were Christians, while the four from Rome have Jewish names. The document, however, does not contain the clauses relating to the free practice of the Jewish religion that might have been expected. It does at least show that Jewish finance (at its beginnings) and Christian finance did occasionally combine.[1]

In contrast, the ten capitalists who lent 15,000 ducats to the commune of Orvieto in 1313 (to enable it to lift an excommunication Clement V had pronounced against this turbulent city in 1307, and after its officials had appealed to the Florentine banks of Mazzi and Sassetti in vain) were all Jews from Rome. By the agreement, they and their heirs were granted citizenship of the town and the right to practise any art or occupation there.[2] Like the Ascoli agreement, the Orvieto one makes no mention of the right to practise the Jewish religion: it can be assumed that this condition went without saying and there was still no need expressly to stipulate it.

The first information on the appearance of Jewish lenders in Tuscany dates from the same period. San Gimignano, in an attempt to attract *banchieri* within its walls, negotiated in turn with Jews at Rome, Siena and Pisa, but it is not known if any of them settled there permanently. From one of the documents relating to these transactions—which stretched over ten years (1309–19)—it emerges that, from this time on, Jewish lenders were doing their utmost to obtain protection from the Curia in Rome, and were trying to interest it in their affairs.[3] But generally, despite the presence of Jews in these regions since the eleventh and twelfth centuries, their role in the money trade remained insignificant. At most, they did perhaps succeed in getting a foothold before the middle of the fourteenth century in a few towns of secondary importance. At the same period, a tendency towards regulating the Christian money trade can be noted in the main centres of Tuscany. Local lenders came out of their semi-clandestinity; their activities were governed by communal statutes like those of other tradesmen, and not without protectionist provisions by the communes in their favour, at least in certain cases.[4]

In northern Italy at this time, no Jewish lenders are to be found in Genoa, Venice or the Po valley, only in fact at Trieste (and perhaps Treviso). In Friuli, where records show the arrival of Jews from Germany at the end of the thirteenth century, they must have been completely ousted by Tuscans.[5]

When the papacy under Clement V issued the *Ex gravi* in 1311 which protested against the custom of granting communal licences to overt usurers, it did not even mention Jews (which

enabled Giovanni da Imola, the Clementines' exegetist, to maintain in the following century that this provision did not apply to
them).[6]

A century later, the situation had changed completely. Before
studying it, it is worth considering whether the variety of crises in
the mid-fourteenth century could have acted in the Jewish
financiers' favour, and in what way.

From this point of view, the depopulation caused by epidemics
of plague, particularly in 1347–50, seems to have made the
marginal elements, the Jews, more favourably received in many
regions. As lenders they must have profited from the rise in prices
which followed the epidemic, from the dearth of money,[7] and
also from the frenzy of spending and the accumulation, in the
hands of countless heirs, of possessions which could if necessary
serve as securities. This observation may theoretically be true for
all the countries of Europe, but it is important to note that, in fact,
Jews were quite systematically burned in French and German
towns at the time of the Black Death, while in Italy, only as an
exception was this means employed to fight the scourge[8]—from
which a good number of the Children of Israel had suffered. It
was in these circumstances that the flood of Jewish capitalists
originating from Rome was joined by another coming from the
other side of the Alps in the wake of massacres and expulsions.
This immigration has left its mark to the present day on the
personal names and certain rituals peculiar to Italian Jews.[9]

In addition, the psychological and contingent consequences of
the catastrophe of 1348 in Italy must also have acted indirectly in
favour of the Jewish lenders, and contributed to the evolution in
Christian attitudes in the matter which has already been mentioned.

In one particular case, that of Lucca, the documents and their
dates make it possible to grasp vividly the relationship between
the fear of plague and the spontaneous or enforced abandonment
of usury. The epidemic which ravaged Sicily in the autumn of
1347 spread into Tuscany in January 1348. There its first step was
Pisa, whence it was brought on a Genoese galley. On 2 January
1348 the lessees of the *casane* of loans at Lucca, as well as of the inns
(also places of ill repute), were summoned to present themselves

before the judges of the town. On 8 January clandestine lenders were prohibited from lending at interest. These measures in the interests of public morality (which were probably fiscal measures as well) were followed on 14 January by an attempt to impose quarantine, entry to the town being forbidden to Genoese, Catalans and travellers from the east. On 28 January two lessees of *casane*, Vanni di Corso d'Arezzo and Fenzo da Prato, let it be known that they no longer wished to lend, and invited their customers to withdraw their securities within a fortnight; after that, they would be put up for sale. The proclamations (*bandi*)[10] from Lucca do not state how the retrieval of securities took place, but at least a partial remission of the interest due seems probable. Villani mentions the remission of interest by the Tuscan lenders in Friuli, '*convertiti a penitenza*', also in 1348—which he attributes to fear caused by an earth tremor.

Perhaps what occurred in this period was a genuine collective phenomenon. In any case, it can be seen how terror and the fear of divine punishment made Christians guilt-ridden (whether they were officials or pawnbrokers), as they had been told for a long time by their spiritual authorities that usury was a sin. Obviously nothing like this was to be found among the rabbis or their flocks.

But, whatever the varied consequences of the plague and their exact relationship to the gradual increase in Jewish moneylenders, the following situation can be observed in Italy in the second half of the fourteenth century.

At Venice—which in this, as in so many other points, sets the example—the monopoly of pawnbroking was granted to Jews (Germans in all probability) in 1366. Such were the origins of the 'Banchi dei Poveri', the famous Venetian pawnshops. In the Most Serene Republic, this form of social assistance remained the province of the Jews until the beginning of the nineteenth century. Genoa, by contrast, nearly always remained forbidden to Jewish *banchieri*. At Florence, which in the meantime had considerably extended its territory, the situation at the beginning of the fourteenth century is very typical: Jews could lend at interest in the majority of the towns thereafter under its control, but they were kept away from the capital itself. In 1406 the Florentines levied a global tax of 2,000 gold florins on Jewish finance in their territory; and we know how the total was divided, town by town.

Jewish *banchieri* settled in the duchy of Milan in the fourteenth or the early fifteenth century in the main provincial towns— Cremona, Como, Lodi, Alessandria, Pavia—but despite the Sforzas' protection, they did not succeed in gaining admittance to Milan itself, from which they were excluded until the eighteenth century. They had the right to go there for three days and there they handled multifarious business deals, but they never gained a foothold.

It was different at Siena. In the cradle of the Italian money trade, the practice of lending at interest was never forbidden to Jews. Yet documents for the end of the thirteenth century mention almost solely Christian lenders, though they do lead one to the conclusion that the Jews held a quasi-monopoly from the end of the fourteenth century. And moreover—although on two occasions (1393 and 1404) the General Council wanted to open pawnbroking to any citizen who asked—at a rate of 30 per cent and 'in the way in which the Jews lend'.[11]

At Lucca, where the maximum rate of interest had been fixed at 40 per cent in 1372 after the end of Pisan domination, Jewish lenders arrived and obtained a monopoly at the beginning of the fifteenth century under the easy-going tyranny of Paolo Guinigi. Documents mention the presence of Jews lending at interest at Pisa as early as 1317. The first known concession authorising them to lend on security on the same conditions as the Christian *foeneratores* is in 1400. About 1430 the activities of the wealthy Jewish da Pisa dynasty there became more specific. Isaac da Pisa settled with the creditors of the commune and seems to have exercised the functions of a communal treasurer-paymaster. The settlement in force of Jewish *banchieri* (the majority of French origin) in Piedmont, where they were protected by the dukes of Savoy, also dates from the first third of the fifteenth century. In 1424 they were admitted to Turin, 'probably out of hatred of Christian lenders, and because they charged a lower interest', wrote the historian Luigi Cibrario in *Storia di Torino* in 1848.

At the other end of the peninsula, too, the towns of the kingdom of Naples, where the economy was languishing, were asking for authorisation to keep the Jews, 'a great boon in these hard and iniquitous times, for otherwise the poor citizens would be forced to sell their possessions dirt cheap' (Brindisi, in 1409). These were not native-born or naturalised Jews, to be sure: some of these lenders came from Rome, others from Germany and Provence.[12]

It will be seen that when recourse to Jewish lenders finally became a custom, officials and princes took care to rationalise their decision by the need to preserve Christians from sin, as well as by the advantages the poor would reap thereby.

Except at Venice (see chapter XII), papal authorisation, based on the first of these two motives, became an indispensable condition for the conclusion of an agreement in the fifteenth century. The reasons why and the way in which the sovereign pontiffs participated in the agreement will emerge in the next chapter. But what were the real advantages involved, behind the good intentions thus expressed? Alfred Doren, the historian of the Italian economy, thought that the reasons thus put forward were only a pretext, and that Jews were preferred because they could be more heavily taxed.[13] This is a realistic but probably over-simplified view. Three centuries before him, the Venetian rabbi Simone Luzzatto, in his *Discorso* on the Jews, placed more emphasis on the political usefulness of recourse to Jewish lenders, neutral during struggles between factions, submissive and easier to control. What is known about Florence makes it possible to appreciate the significance of this distinction.

All that has been said so far goes to show that it was either small or middle-sized communes (which had to call on outside financiers anyway) or strong governments (concerned with public order) who turned first and from choice to the Jews. In the plutocratic towns, on the other hand, coalitions of local interests opposed to their admission were able to delay it. At Florence, throughout the fourteenth century, the Church fulminated and anti-usury prohibitions poured out in vain. Clandestine lenders, sometimes belonging to the highest strata of society, proliferated despite 'admonitions' and fines, while seven or eight public lenders, all Christians (one of whom bore the famous name of Bardi![14]) were lending on security at what seems to have been an unrestricted rate. At last, in 1396, the commune instructed the priors to invite the Jews and to authorise them to lend at 15 per cent. According to Davidsohn, this was merely a threat intended to impress local lenders. This unusually low rate lays the seriousness of the intention open to doubt; in any case it did not happen again, and the Christians retained their monopoly. In 1406, during a new anti-usury campaign, there is even mention of withdrawing the licences of Jewish lenders in the other towns of Florentine territory. In 1420 a maximum rate of 25 per cent was finally imposed on public lenders in Florence; in 1421 this was raised to 30 per cent, though in reality it seems to have been closer to 40 per cent.[15] In 1430 the commune once more decided to appeal to the Jews and to grant them the monopoly of pawnbroking, this time at the more realistic rate of 20 per cent. But again nothing happened, and Christians' licences were renewed for the last time in 1431. As for clandestine amateurs, Scipio Ammirato mentions a preacher who in the same year gave absolution even to usurers who did not make restitution. A probable assumption would seem to be that powerful coalitions of interests opposed the entry of the Jews and every time succeeded in preventing dealings with them on some religious pretext or other.

In contrast, when Cosimo de Medici returned from exile in 1434 and had a series of measures adopted which were intended to ruin his opponents, to humble oligarchic families and to benefit the poorer classes—by means of confiscations, substitution of direct and progressive taxation for indirect taxes—the matter was quickly settled once and for all. It seems that, to start with, pawnbrokers' licences for Christians were no longer renewed. Then at the end of 1437 the monopoly of lending was granted to a Jewish group.[16] The concession, established in the name of the banker Abramo di Dattilo da San Miniato, mentions papal authorisation, perhaps the first of the type to be found later in this book. Need it be recalled that Pope Eugenius IV lived in Florence at this time and must therefore have had to take Cosimo de Medici's wishes into consideration to a considerable extent? The Jews were obliged to invest at least 40,000 florins in four *banchi*. The rate of interest

was fixed at 20 per cent. It is worth noting that they set themselves
up in the same banks and under the same names ('Banco della
Vacca', 'Banco dei Quattro Pavoni', etc.) as their Christian
predecessors. The concession was decennial. It was renewed,
without too many difficulties, until the fall of the Medici; but
even under the Republic of 1494–1512—when it was not renewed
—the Jews were able to stay in Florence and go about their work
there. Beyond the floating capital of 40,000 florins, the amount
of the fines inflicted on *banchieri* on various pretexts (21,000 florins
on Salomone da Terracina in 1441, 22,000 florins on Vitale da
Montalcino in 1461) indicates the extent of the bargain made in
1437.

The settlement of Jews in the Italian financial capital seems to
mark their predominance in the money trade. It also corresponds
to the transition from the Italy of the communes to the Italy of the
seigniories. But, as has been seen, the two great commercial
centres of Genoa and Milan still remained forbidden to Jewish
*banchi*. Coalitions of local interests definitely opposed their settlement and there was no lack of supporters to plead the purity of
their convictions and the ardour of their Christian faith. The town
of Milan, for example, wrote to Philip II of Spain in 1595 that it
had never admitted Jews because it was 'more faithful than the
others to the spirit and will of Your Majesty . . . it has always
acted so as to have nothing to do with this breed and to keep it at
a distance.'[17]

It is probable that to achieve such a chorus, the Jews' competitors formed an alliance with the theologians, particularly with
the Franciscan popular preachers, and stimulated their fervour. In
chapter II the ideas of canonists such as Pietro d'Ancarano or
Alessandro de Nevo were analysed at some length, but without
mentioning who paid for their *Consilia*. Now it was obviously in
the Jewish usurers' interest to see their souls regarded as irrevoc-
ably lost, and in the interest of their competitors and adversaries
to propagate a more benevolent theology with regard to the
deicidal people. This conclusion, however humorous it may
appear to us, seems none the less reliable, and probably throws

some light on a generally unknown or neglected motive behind the thought of medieval scholars.

Where did commercial intrigue stop, and religious fanaticism and fear of God, in its specific form of medieval Judeophobia, begin? This is what is difficult to determine. Moreover, the sincerity of some medieval businessmen should not necessarily exclude the guile of others, and such demarcations run the risk of drawing the discussion towards the quicksands of individual psychology. I shall just incidentally mention a few confused rear-guard actions pursued by the opponents of Jewish finance, whether they had an axe to grind or not, on the basis of research by Italian scholars at the beginning of this century.

At Brescia, which has been studied by Agostino Zanelli,[18] the council's debates mention Christian *stochizatores* (extortionists) who were lending at 60 and even 80 per cent. The question of inviting the Jews who, it was said, were content with 15 per cent, also came up for the first time in 1431. But warnings, which Zanelli assumes were from interested parties, suggested that the idea was scandalous and that the scholars must first be consulted. Their advice must have been negative, because in 1441 and 1444 the subject was again debated, and the officials were of the opinion that Christian usury must be stopped at all costs and for this purpose the Jews should be called in. Taking advantage of an emissary's departure for Rome on other business, it was proposed that the requisite papal absolution be obtained through his offices. The results of the application are unknown, and it might well seem that Eugenius IV personally was hostile to this type of absolution. The fact is that once more nothing came of it. The council discussed the subject yet again in 1458; the proposal to call in the Jews was rejected by a majority of votes. Zanelli connects these fluctuations with the movements of the great Franciscan preachers who, every time they passed through Brescia, preached vehemently against vice, sin and Jews. Mean-while, clandestine Jewish lenders had appeared in the town, probably operating on the same terms as their Christian rivals and having, it can be assumed, the same interest at heart that the money trade at Brescia should not be regulated. Regulated it was

61

C*

in the end, however, since in 1463 a Jewish bank is found functioning officially there, with the approval of the cardinal legate.[19]

At Padua where, the historian Antonio Ciscato writes, 'the
council records at this time are entirely permeated with religious
terror', the documents he quotes do not mention obstruction
campaigns by Christian financiers. But we do learn from them
that, after their expulsion from the town in 1453, Jewish lenders
settled in neighbouring villages. Their customers in straitened
circumstances, particularly students, were coming along and
applying to them there, borrowing at 30 instead of 20 per cent,
since this was the legal rate in force for *forestieri* (foreigners).
Other Jews, who stayed in Padua illegally, were in these circumstances lending at 40 per cent. It can be assumed that local
interests were not unaware of such an absurd situation. Finally,
after thirty years of struggle (1452–82), the Jewish *banchieri* were
recalled to Padua.

The Pavia archives explored by Carlo Invernizzi[20] contain
information on complaints made by the Christian banker
Niccolino Colleoni in 1434 against the admission of the Jewish
banker Averlino da Vicenza, to whom he had eventually to give
way. Later, right through the sixteenth century, this town called
for the expulsion of the Jews with a relentlessness all its own.
What was involved in fact was a vow made following the death
at Pavia in 1494 of the blessed Bernardino da Feltre, champion of
Monti di Pietà and anti-Jewish crusades.

Two final glimpses of the money trade in the small town of
Castelgoffredo on the borders of the marquisate of Mantua and
the Venetian possessions will be enough to conclude this summary.
A Jewish *banco* had existed there since 1468. In 1477 the commune
asked the marquis of Mantua to abolish it, stating that it was
ruining the population 'by making pawning too easy'. The curate
of Castelgoffredo, on the contrary, was asking the marquis to
maintain the bank, as if it disappeared, this would force the poor
to turn to local *privati* (unlicensed lenders) on much more dis-
advantageous conditions.[21] It should be added that the bank at
Castelgoffredo could not have been doing bad business, because

at certain periods it profited from custom from the neighbouring towns and villages under Venetian domination.[22]

Thus, as at other times and elsewhere, the active opponents of the Jews of Italy consisted of some sections of the bourgeoisie and the mendicant orders, while their principal allies were the 'ruling classes' and the establishment, including, above all, the Rome Curia. The advantages of the alliances were definitely reciprocal, and one of these deserves particular attention, because it constitutes a basic position of strength of the Jewish lenders which has never been appropriately brought out—with one exception:[23] their financing by Christian capitalists, or even actual partnerships between the two. It is true that such affairs were as far as possible handled so that no traces remained. Scandalous for the financial backers, because of this they belonged to the realm 'of things which it is unnecessary to record in writing' for the Jews as well. Let us see what can be found out about them.

In the first place, there are references to them. At Mantua, according to the chronicler Ugo Calefini (about 1480), the Jewish *banchi* actually belonged to the Trotti, local financial potentates, who drew enormous profits from them, leaving the Jews only a modest share. At Florence, where the Republic could not make up its mind about expelling the Jews after the fall of the Medici, a 'reformer', Domenico Cecchi, demanded this expulsion because, he wrote: 'not content with sucking the blood of Christians, over the years, they have been behind what our Christian citizens make available for lending at interest under [their] cover, and many other evils which would take too long to mention.' But according to his biographer, Calefini was an enemy of the Trotti, and Domenico Cecchi, as a good popular reformer of his day, was hostile to the Jews. Their evidence may therefore seem suspect. The same criticism might be made of the evidence of Bernardino da Siena's preaching against Christians who deposited their money with Jews and who thus contributed to their financial hegemony. But more reliable sources are available to back up this opinion.

Naturally enough the Christian sleeping partners behind the Jewish banks should first be sought in the great old centres of the

63

money trade. At Siena, their existence is borne out by the following paragraph which was added to the Jews' *condotta* at the time
of its renewal in 1457:[24]

> Still declaring that, when the land survey or *lire* is made in the town
> of Siena, the aforesaid Jews can in no way be put to torture or be
> personally molested. But, on the demand of the estimators, the
> aforesaid Jews are bound to make known all the citizens and in-
> habitants of the town who have at present or have previously had
> money invested in their pawnshop. And to establish the truth, the
> Jews are bound to produce all their books and documents.

One reason which drove Christians to invest their capital in this
way thus emerges: tax evasion. The *Capitoli* of the Jews of
Florence, renewed in the same year (1457), contained a similar
clause, with the difference that the secret banker remained better
protected in the Italian banking capital. Jews were obliged neither
to produce their books nor to name Christian depositors; they
were compelled to declare only the total sum deposited with
them, and to pay a 10 per cent tax on this total. In 1475 this tax
was raised to 12 per cent. At the same time, the seigniory expressed concern at the increasing numbers of such investments,
'less helpful to the commune and to private persons, because
money is not utilised commercially but is invested in the pawnshops with dishonour to them [the depositors] and to the city,
and in addition to the perdition of their souls'.[25] It can be assumed
that St Antoninus of Florence (1389–1459) was aiming at this type
of usurious profit, more or less successfully camouflaged as
deposits, when he castigated the idle who did not want to work
and entrusted their money to merchants or usurers in order to
collect annuities from them.[26]

A transaction between Pius II and the duke of Milan in 1460,
without entirely satisfying our curiosity, provides supplementary
information on the great spread and notoriety of such practices—
to the point where they could be used as arguments in a question
affecting major politics.

To ensure the financing of the crusade against the Turks, Pius II
proposed to the princes he had assembled at the Diet of Mantua
the introduction of a new tithe on the clergy, one-thirtieth on the

laity and one-twentieth on the Jews.[27] The tithe and the thirtieth should affect incomes and production, as was customary, while the Jews' twentieth, as the pope saw it, had to be a tax on capital (special bull of 14 January 1460). The papal collectors got down to the task but soon came up against difficulties, as is learned from the situation in the duchy of Milan. What happened there was that on 22 March, Duke Francesco Sforza wrote to his ambassador at the Holy See instructing him to explain to the sovereign pontiff that at the Diet of Mantua, all that had been concerned was a tax on income, and that 5 per cent on the Jews' capital, three years later, would be 'too unbearable an affliction'. In a postscript to his letter, he developed these two arguments and spoke more plainly. He asked in fact that it be explained to Pius II that 'a great deal of Christian capital is in the hands of Jews, which must be taken into consideration, for a tax on Jews of one-twentieth of their capital would lead to the uncovering of a large and immeasurable number of men of ill will, and that it is important to consider that too much dissatisfaction must not be created'. He added that, according to his information, neither one-twentieth nor one-thirtieth was charged elsewhere in Italy, and that he would not wish to be 'the only one to make this move'.

The ambassador, having been granted an audience, replied that the pope had displayed a great deal of understanding, and that it would be sufficient to have the declarations written by the Jews themselves, thus avoiding bringing dishonour upon Christians who had invested money with them. On the other hand, it was also necessary to save the face of Pius II, and not allow it to be made known that he was waiving the tax on the Jews' capital. In order to camouflage the arrangement, they should therefore be dealt with on the basis of reasonable 'compromises'. Shortly afterwards, apostolic collectors of the duchy of Milan received appropriate instructions from the pope, which were, moreover, brought to them by the Jew, Simone da Piacenza—an expert, it must be assumed, on questions of taxation and other revenues to be drawn from the Jews by the Holy See.

A denunciation sent to the Sforza some fifteen years later by a man called Ganduzzi gives some facts about an individual case of deposits or trade in money between Christians and Jews. Two *banchieri* in Alessandria, Abraham and Micaël, were in prison for debt. Ganduzzi writes and tells the duke that numerous Christians have entrusted their money to them, and that a careful search would surely reveal all the Jews' pledges and goods lodged as security with one or other of their creditors. He insists on the severest penalties for these 'Christians, worse than Jews . . . who have committed the crimes of divine and human lèse-majesté; their punishment will enhance Your Majesty's reputation throughout the world.' The Franciscan preachers and their arguments had trodden this path before.

G. B. Piccotti, the editor of the documents just summarised, assumed on the basis of the close relationships that Francesco Sforza maintained with certain Jews that he himself deposited money with them. A. Lazzari, the historian of the court of Ferrara, had the same theory about the d'Este family in prosperous times; at other times they pawned their jewels at the Jewish bank of Norsa. As for the marquis of Mantua, a document cited by Piccotti establishes that he lent 130 ducats to a Jew in his entourage in 1491. All in all, the financial relationship between contemporary Italian princes and the Jews is reminiscent of that between the popes and their Florentine or Genoese bankers on the one hand, and between German princes and their 'court Jews' in the following centuries, on the other.

Let us go back to the examination of this sort of transaction. In the absence of written evidence, the exact nature of the relationship between the lenders and their financial backers is not known, but the forms they took were certainly very varied.

For financiers such as the Trotti, described by Calefini, the Jews could have been only firmly controlled figureheads. When the financial backer was a prince or a powerful political personality, the situation could not have varied appreciably. A quite different category of depositors could have been the 'monks, scholars, knights, ladies and other unknown characters' in quest of the lucrative and above all discreet investments which the merchants of Florence were talking about in 1605.[28] It should not be thought that the obloquy attached to such transactions constituted a strong deterrent, since any lucrative investment devoid of risks, in theory, remained reprehensible. To some people, investing with Jews must have seemed morally acceptable from the moment when interest was collected by them and not by Christians. But it can be supposed that the major part of the funds deposited with Jews belonged to important personalities—those implied in the correspondence between Francesco Sforza and Pius II—and that they were attracted by the realistic advantages of such investments: higher and, more important, regular interest. More complex schemes can also be imagined: the intervention of confidential agents, of the *familiari*, *segretari*, *agenti* of the prelates or other high personages who put the money of the Church or of their constituents to work, even unbeknown to them.

Raymond de Roover's research has shown how at the same period, in order to conform to the doctrine of the Church, or on the pretext of so doing, the Medici bank disguised the interest it paid to its depositors as *discrezione* or fictitious shares, which enabled it to pay none at all in certain years and, according to Raymond de Roover, put the client at the mercy of his banker.[29] In other words, in a situation where capital was seeking reliable investment outlets and return, one effect of the doctrine was to make the return uncertain. Here again, what was concerned were the effects of the canonical prohibition on lending at interest which, as can be seen, acted to the advantage of the Jewish *banchieri* in two different ways. To the moral monopoly of the overt charging of interest were in fact added better facilities for appealing to Christian capital or savings, whose owners thus benefited from the additional and sometimes not inconsiderable advantage of not exposing themselves to the criticism of lending at interest to their brothers in Christ.

What were the various implications of these phenomena for the Jews? The first question that might be asked is whether the privileged position of the Jewish lender in relation to the Christian borrower was not matched by the somewhat similar position of the Christian lender or financial backer, since Jewish tradition also forbade lucrative lending between brothers. In other words, did the Jews not seek out non-Jewish capital in preference, from scruples of conscience? On the whole, I do not think that they did. The many stratagems European Talmudists formulated to by-pass the prohibition in Deuteronomy (most frequently by the use of a Christian intermediary or dummy) have been seen above. Perhaps the special case of loans contracted by Jewish com-munities, as S. W. Baron thinks, was different.[30] But whether or not religious consideration did intervene, running into debt with Christians had an effect which makes one wonder how far it was unforeseen—the same effect moreover as debts on the part of influential Christians or Christian powers: namely, a strengthen-ing of the Jews' political position.

Here again, the Pius II–Sforza correspondence gives a glimpse of the reality: so as not to displease wealthy Christians who participated in Jewish business, the plan which would have inflicted 'too intolerable a hardship' on the Jews was abandoned. Similarly, the sight of the *banchieri* of Florence, officially expelled after the fall of the Medici and the establishment of a Monte di Pietà, continuing to go about their business as if nothing has happened, gives good grounds for thinking that the state of affairs people such as Cecchi were quoting to call for their departure— Christians lending at interest under their cloak—rightly con-tributed to their maintenance and their security. That indebted-ness could become a position of strength and a safeguard for the debtor, whom his creditors had an interest in protecting, is a conclusion that the Jews, always at the mercy of expulsion, must have come to early on. It will be seen later how in the seventeenth century, when the Jewish money trade was declining, the Jewish community in Rome played on the self-interest of its Christian creditors and brandished the threat of its own insolvency in the face of ecclesiastical sticklers who were calling for the closure of the lending *banchi*.

The political vulnerability of a group like this could thus in certain circumstances become an economic trump card. Moreover, the weakness could turn into a strength in various ways, for it is easy to understand that insolvency or the threat of insolvency were not the only factors that could serve as strong points; many other consequences of a dangerous existence could also fulfil this function. In a sense, medieval theology granted the Jews specific immunities to this end, and on this subject we refer the reader to the doctrinal discussions described in chapter II.

It is interesting to compare the theories formulated by Christian theologians on the Jews' particular position with rabbinic views on business relations with non-Jews, of which we get some idea from various passages in *The Book of the Lender and the Borrower*. Rabbinic knowledge, both out of concern for Jewish reputation and veneration for 'the Holy One, blessed be He', traditionally places strict limits on actions compromising to Judaism as a whole. A remarkable concordance between safeguarding the Law and the ethical principles, as well as the interests of the old oligarchies of the *banchieri*, can also be assumed. *The Book* storms against the 'scoundrels in Israel who think of nothing all day but depredation', because of whom 'the fortunes of the great heads of families [*balabatim*] totter and fall' (XI, 29)—in other words, the unscrupulous managers and other swindlers, quick to abscond, abusing the confidence both of their Jewish patrons and principals and of their Christian customers or financial backers. But seen in a sort of Sombartian perspective, they contributed on the same terms as the 'great heads of families' with well-established and prudently administered fortunes like the da Pisa, Volterra or Norsa to accelerate circulation and commercial exchanges, and to hasten the great economic changes.

The remaining question is: to what extent could phenomena similar to those just described have been reproduced in different circumstances of time and place, and have contributed, as a result of Christian participation or investment, to the Jews' supremacy in or monopoly of the money trade? Obviously all that can be done here is to point to a problem which is suggested by certain documents and has not passed unnoticed by several Jewish historians. Most frequently, when studying the method of building up the funds which served as the Jews' circulating capital, these historians have tended to emphasise the profits derived from big business before they had to abandon it, the proceeds from the sale of Jewish landed property, and even the direct import into Europe of precious metals, money or jewels. However, is it not plausible to assume that, from the early middle ages, numerous princes, prelates or monasteries were entrusting their capital to Jews in circumstances analogous to those in fifteenth-century Italy, and should not more attention be paid to this phenomenon than in the past?

# CHAPTER V

# The Banchieri *and the Holy See*

---

We have decided that at all events it is necessary to turn to our lord the pope, king of the Christians—may his life be long and his glory great—to intercede for our people and to ask him for new assurances and privileges and confirmation of the old ones, according to the tradition of the popes; and that this must be done without delay. For this, great expenditure is required, as all knowledgeable people will be well aware—Decisions of the rabbinic conference at Forli, 1418

The medieval papacy's benevolent interest in the Jews corresponded to a dual consideration, simultaneously theological and financial. In a nutshell, the Christian ideal decreed that Jews be protected, and also that Christians be turned away from the sin of active usury. The financial interests of the Holy See ordained that this protection be paid for as dearly as possible. Faced with two such discordant themes—or so they seem to modern ears—one needs to know where to draw the dividing line between protection of the Jews' lives and *religion*, and protection of their *business*, which is hardly easy, for the problem was all of a piece. After all, poor Jews (to adopt a witticism of Sixtus V) would have commanded even less respect than a poor pope. In any case, at the end of the middle ages, financial considerations persistently prevailed over theological considerations—which is not surprising.

The systematic and overt protection of Jewish banks in Italy through papal patents and corresponding taxation in fact seems to date from a very late period. Yves Renouard found nothing about it in his exploration of the archives and accounts of the Avignon papacy,[1] and the documents of the Rome Curia at the end of the fourteenth century maintain the silence. Even more interesting than this blank is the form taken by the first known 'absolution', which was granted by Boniface IX in 1401 to the duke of Mantua and sanctioned the *condotta* of the local Jewish lenders,[2] mentioning '*foeneratoribus aliigenis*', without specifying further. Everything suggests that Rome was still reluctant openly to protect the Jews' money trade. Under Martin V (1417–31) the system took more definite shape, and in my opinion its real genesis can be dated from this pontificate. Moreover, it was he whom the Jews of Rome and Avignon preferred to cite in the course of the following centuries for corroboration of their traditional privileges. This also tallies with the new departure the government of the Church took at this time when, after the Council of Constance, it was obliged to look for new resources, and to derive the greater part of them from its Italian revenues. But under Martin V, the Holy See's fiscal supervision and hold over the lending *banchi* in Italy was only sketched out, and protection of the Jewish money trade remained partially shrouded in the traditional protection of the Jewish religion. The relationship between Jewish banking and the papacy found its definitive form only some thirty years later. In a sense, the process as a whole is an interesting example of the way in which, historically, the Holy See has adapted itself to customs which it transforms into institutions. I am going to attempt to clarify the principal stages, particularly the early ones, as far as the documents allow.

Both Jewish and Christian tradition concur in saying that, as a pope, Martin V was 'a good thing for the Jews', perhaps even the best, according to some sources. From an account left by a Sicilian rabbi whom he received in audience, it emerges that there were occasions when he engaged in theological contests with Talmudists or put embarrassing questions to them. The names of two doctors, Elia di Angelo of Rome and Elia di Sabbato of Bologna or Fermo, can be picked out from among the Jews in his suite. Elia di Angelo, whose family had already been covered with honours under the preceding pontificates, was named 'governor' of the Jews of Rome in 1426. He lent small sums to the pope, made payments on his behalf and probably collected the Jewish taxes.[3] Elia di Sabbato, who was not only the pope's doctor but also that of Henry IV of England (he is the 'Elias Sabot' of English history), seems to have been a more prominent figure: Martin V used him for secret diplomatic missions, and it was in his house that the German translation of a papal bull in favour of the Jews was certified as a true copy in 1422.[4] A little later we shall meet a third doctor at the pope's court, Salomone di Ventura. The importance to the service of Judaism of the activities of practitioners such as these cannot be stressed too strongly. 'The practice of medicine depends too much on conversation; from conversation, friendship is born; from friendship, the protection of the Jews; and from protection, scandal, at the very least', proclaimed the Roman Inquisition in 1636.[5]

Coincidental with the ascension to the pontificate of Martin V was an attempt by the Jewish communities of Italy to federate into a 'super-community', the better to defend their interests and to achieve unity of action. The origins of this attempt are obscure: it could equally well have been dictated by the growing antisemitic agitation of the Franciscans in Italy itself as by the terrible blows which had fallen on Spanish Judaism since 1391. After a conference at Bologna in 1416—which was not perhaps the first of its kind—another meeting took place at Forli in 1418, and its conclusions (*takanoth*) are available.[6]

Represented at Bologna and Forli were the Jews of 'Rome, Padua, Ferrara, Bologna, Romagna, Tuscany', described collectively as Jews of the *romaneschi* communities. The *takanoth* decreed sumptuary laws 'to curb people's longings and not to arouse the jealousy of the Christians' and forbade gambling. Above all, they instituted a progressive tax on capital (from 0.5 to 1.5 per cent annually), 'given the fact that expenditure is necessary for the safety and security of the people' and 'in accordance with the taxation in force in Rome'. The proceeds of the tax were to be concentrated in the hands of the rich banker Jekutiel ben Emanuel

73

of Padua. Only 'those who lived on charity' were exempt from it.

As for the utilisation of this campaign fund, the *takanoth* gave the following explanation: 'We have decided that at all events it is necessary to turn to our lord the pope, king of the Christians—may his life be long and his glory great—to intercede for our people and ask him for new assurances and privileges and confirmation of the old ones, according to the tradition of the popes; and that this must be done without delay. For this, great expenditure is required, as all knowledgeable people will be well aware'.

In January 1419 at Mantua, the Jewish delegation formed as a result of these conclusions appeared before Martin V (who, from Constance, was gradually moving towards Florence) and obtained the promulgation of the traditional *Sicut Judaeis* bull expressed in the usual general terms.[7] As for the practical use of such bulls for the Jews, an indicative example can be found in the archives of Recanati, in the Marches of Ancona. In 1427 the blessed Giacomo of Monteprandone embarked on an anti-Jewish compaign, demanding in particular that Jews wear the *rouelle*—which was in accordance with canonic legislation, but contrary to their *condotta*. The Jews brandished the bull and threatened to leave the town, while the municipal council provisionally settled the case in their favour by 23 votes to 14.[8]

Meanwhile, from the fiscal point of view, it can be assumed that the papal treasury saw nothing but advantage in this 'confederation of Jews', which, as far as the Jews were concerned, seems primarily to have benefited those of Rome. In 1421 Martin V ordered the other communities to participate in the famous 'gaming' tax of 1,130 florins paid by the community of Rome.[9] There followed, as far as the documents have been preserved, in chronological order, a loan of 300 florins by Elia di Angelo to the Apostolic Chamber (10 January 1422), and a new bull in favour of the Jews (20 February 1422) which excommunicated *ipso jure* 'preachers of the word of God, mendicants or those of other orders' who stirred up the people against the Jews, as well as the inquisitors who acted in connivance with them. However, this bull was revoked as 'extortionate' on February 1 of the following year, without it being exactly known why; perhaps on the insistence of the Franciscan Inquisitor, Giovanni da Capistrano, as the latter let it be understood.[10]

In fact, the Franciscans' anti-Jewish agitation went on spreading. Inspired preachers such as Bernardino da Siena and particularly Giovanni da Capistrano were its main leaders. The impression emerges that their activity became a means of financial pressure in the hands of princes. This seems to have been the case in the Kingdom of Naples, where in May 1427 the fickle queen Joanna II gave Giovanni da Capistrano full powers to burn all the Jews' *condotti*. Representations ensued, as well as a mission to Rome by Salomone di Ventura. The pope intervened with the queen, and that August the Jews' rights were restored.[11] According to the registers of the Apostolic Chamber, this Salomone di Ventura lent 700 florins to the pope in November 1429.[12]

But at the court of Rome, the anti-Jewish party still remained active. The summons to a Jewish conference gathered in Florence in 1428 speaks, in veiled terms, of a dangerous 'prosecutor' of the Jews (Giovanni da Capistrano?) and 'filthy calumnies which are growing and penetrating the midst [of the Curia]', as well as of 'perils which are threatening the communities because they are exposed to the foul speeches of monks'. This summons criticised the Jewish communities for half-heartedness and urged them on to new sacrifices.[13] It must be assumed that, as a result, a fresh collective representation by the Jews took place, for a new and unusually long papal bull of 13 February 1429 repeated the terms of its predecessors. But it also spoke more clearly about 'concessions and pacts' concluded by Jews with 'magistrates and officials of cities and places', and demanded that they be observed, insofar as they were not contrary to the holy canons. Amongst other rights, this bull granted the Jews the right to frequent Christian 'studia e scholas' and to learn all branches of knowledge not contrary to the Catholic faith (this point certainly owed its appearance to the fact that the Jews had asked for it).

Notwithstanding, occasion did arise when the pope himself demanded the cancellation of a local *condotta*. This happened at Fano, where officials were excommunicated in October 1427 'because of the pact made with the Jews, contrary to the holy canons'. Likewise in June 1430, pacts concluded by the communes of Città di Castello and Borgo San Sepolcro with Jews (whose names are not known) were cancelled at the request of one Salomone Bonaventura on behalf of his family, 'because the interests of the Apostolic Chamber require it'.[14]

The documents for the pontificate of Martin V, despite their gaps, confirm what so much other contemporary evidence suggests—namely, that the pope's good intentions were bought at the price of money. This cannot be said of the pontificate of Eugenius IV (1431-47), although he seems to have been just as kindly disposed as his predecessor towards the Jews of Italy. Johannes Hofer, in *Johannes von Capistrano* which studies his anti-Jewish campaigns in detail, finds that they were discontinued throughout the pontificate of Eugenius IV. Could this be a clue? And would this pope, said to have been a determined adversary of simony, have found it repugnant to transform the traditional protection of the Jews into an instrument of financial extortion? This would seem to emerge from a declaration his nephew, the vice-camerlengo Francesco Condulmieri, made in 1441.[15] As has been seen, in 1437 Eugenius IV granted the commune of Florence the first known absolution to make explicit mention of Jewish lenders. But it can be assumed that the Curia did not derive a profit from it, since the Florentines themselves refrained from charging a tax on the *banchi* at that period—the tax would have implied participation in the sin of active usury from the doctrinal point of view, as has been seen in chapter II. On the other hand, according to de Nevo, writing in 1440-2, almost all the communes in Italy (as well as the authorities of Aragon) were excommunicated for having concluded substantial agreements with usurers; it is also known that in 1443 the duke of Milan cancelled all privileges granted to both Christian and Jewish usurers.[16] But this is all that is known about the ideas of Eugenius IV in the matter, and the question probably deserves to be studied in greater depth. It is also possible that the pope's attitude towards the Jews hardened in 1443, the year of his return to Rome.

The Holy See's hold on the Jewish money trade seems to have taken on its almost definitive form during the next pontificate, that of Nicholas V (1447–55), when a newly promoted generation of humanist prelates and secretaries filled the Curia. A few weeks after his elevation to the throne of St Peter, Nicholas placed the Jews of Italy under a fairly strict interdict, entrusting its enforcement to Giovanni da Capistrano, who was also instructed to deal severely with the heretic 'brotherhoods'. Christians were enjoined to break off all social and commercial relationships with Jews. The emotion which gripped the Jews is reflected in the correspondence between the rabbis of Ancona and Recanati at the end of 1447 or the beginning of 1448. These letters provide some evidence but are also even vaguer than usual. They refer to a recent persecution at Rome, to Giovanni da Capistrano (comparing him with the pitiless Haman), to rich and willing Jews who have left their businesses to go from community to community collecting, and to internal dissensions between these communities themselves. 'Unity of action' does not seem to have been easy to achieve, particularly given the traditional divergence of interest between the Jews of Rome, those of the Papal States and of the other regions of Italy.

Yet it can be noted that on 1 July 1448 Nicholas V authorised Jews in the marquisate of Este to trade with Christians and to practise pawnbroking, and he forbade preachers to incite the people against them. At the same time, the marquis of Mantua sent an emissary, Galeazzo Cattaneo, to Rome to obtain a similar privilege for his own Jews (more precisely to obtain the lifting of an interdict issued by the bishop of Mantua on account of the presence of Jewish *banchieri* in the town—following, I think, the pontifical bull of June 1447).[17] We have three letters Cattaneo sent to the marquis, describing his representations. It emerges from them that the Curia was instituting a fresh examination of these questions as a whole in the second half of 1448. Engaged in this examination, under the pope's own supervision, was his friend and confidant, Pietro da Noxeto, who fulfilled the eminently profitable duties of his first secretary.[18] The matter dragged on and the marquis grew impatient. The third message he received from Cattaneo told him that da Noxeto had again asked him to wait another fortnight, as it was necessary to avoid causing a great harm to His Holiness. And he added right at the end of the letter:

> Messer Pietro has explained to me in what way our lord's business would harm him. All the Jews generally are seeking to obtain a concession from our lord, and they must pay many thousands of florins; he would not want these individual concessions to impede the general concession. But [he tells me] that at the end of this fortnight I will certainly be given satisfaction. God willing! I have my doubts . . .

The marquis of Mantua finally obtained his concession, but only in 1452 it seems, since the privilege he granted to his bankers Aaron and Jacob di Gallis is dated 23 January 1453. As for the 'general concession', we do not know if it was arranged at that period. The fact that on 25 February 1450 Nicholas V renewed his June 1447 bull of indictment on the Jews would rather suggest that it was not. But a solution was found and as from 1451 the pope began to grant a profusion of 'individual concessions' (often signed or countersigned by Pietro da Noxeto). The following are known: Sicily, April 1451; Parma, 6 July 1451; Ferrara, the same date; Germany in the Holy Roman Empire, 20 September 1451; Lucca, 21 August 1452, renewed in April 1454; Pisa, 1453 or the beginning of 1454, and there were certainly others, in particular for the duchy of Milan. It is not known whether 'general concessions', that is to say collective payments made by Italian Jews to the pope, also existed during these years. In any case, the system of 'individual concessions' is easily explained by the multiplicity of the interests involved. Certain princes even forbade their Jews to pay anything whatever to the Apostolic Chamber.

After the death of Nicholas V there was some question whether the system thus worked out would be continued. Perhaps the temperament of the new pope Calixtus III laid it open to doubt. Contemporary Christian attitudes to the question are revealed in a debate in the municipal council of Padua. On the day it learned of the election of Calixtus III, and although it had already previously expelled the Jewish *banchieri*, the officials decided to make the first move and to send ambassadors to Rome to obtain absolution from the pope for having dealt with Jews in the past

78

and having rented houses to them. Because of this, it was said in the debate, 'their souls are caught in the net of eternal punishment.'[19] It can be seen from this what an effective instrument of financial pressure the fifteenth-century popes had at their disposal.

In quite a different style, Duke Francesco Sforza also took his own precautions under the new pontificate. It emerges from a letter he sent to his ambassador at the Holy See in January 1456 that the initiative for his representation had come from the Jews of the duchy of Milan who had, at the same time, promised him an annual tribute. Before writing to Rome, the duke had consulted local theologians and obtained their confirmation that the proposal was acceptable. He then instructed his ambassador to make the representation, providing him with a draft petition and giving him full powers to modify it if necessary before presenting it to the pope. In the draft petition it was said that the duke, 'for the greater peace of his conscience', asked His Holiness to ratify the agreement proposed by the Jews and to grant his permission.[20] It appears that he obtained satisfaction. Thus it seems that the sole purpose behind the renewal of the 'anti-Jewish' bull of Nicholas V in May 1456 could have been only to accelerate payments by the Jews. Well rooted in custom, the system thereafter only underwent small refinements in detail. It is interesting to notice that the Renaissance popes did not publish *Sicut Judaeis* bulls which, in these circumstances, had become pointless.

A fact drawn from the archives at Mantua illustrates the significance for Jewish lenders of papal concessions, a necessary though sometimes inadequate condition for the peaceful practice of their profession. On 13 August 1462 the brothers Leone and Jacob de Nursia [Norsa] wrote to the marquis, with whom they were on excellent terms, to complain of the bishop of Mantua, Monsignor da Cervia. He *non obstante . . . certe bolle papale*, had made a judgment against them, condemning them to a heavy fine, which might force them to make a journey to Rome and thus incur even higher costs. This was perhaps the same bishop who excommunicated the inhabitants of the little town of Quistello in spring 1464 because they had concluded an agreement with Salomone da Padova. Salomone explained his difficulty on this occasion to the marquis: 'This Easter Day,' he wrote, 'the men of Quistello and its parish have been publicly excommunicated and driven out of the church, particularly those to whom I have lent money. I do not know whence this comes: from the priests of Quistello and Nuvolaro, or from Monsignor [the bishop of Mantua]'. Whatever the ecclesiastical pressure which had necessitated a boycott of the Jewish banks, the measure could not but be fairly effective, as we know.[21] In his own State, it was the pope himself who sometimes excommunicated certain towns or certain municipal administrations when the agreement concluded with the Jews did not suit him.

Under Sixtus IV, at the time when the Jews' *vigesima* or twentieth (which turned into a permanent tax) was levied, the appearance of a new official of the Curia can be noted: Pellegrino da Lucca, 'commissioner to the Jews for all Christendom'. In February 1478 we see him sending one 'Master Moses, a Hebrew', as a delegate to Lorenzo the Magnificent to explain to the master of Florence the wishes of the Apostolic See by word of mouth.[22]

It is not known whether the responsibilities of this commissioner with the descriptive title also included concessions to lending banks. It would not seem so, for his name does not figure on any of the known concessions. Moreover, at the end of the fifteenth century, the system of individual concessions was modified or simplified, individual concessions in future being issued by the pope directly to the Jewish financier in the form of a sort of patent, without passing through the hands of the temporal prince. The first known document of this type was issued in 1489 by Innocent VIII to Leone Norsa of Mantua. The patent was granted because of the need to tolerate the Jews so that they could be led to the true faith, the jeopardising of souls by Christian usury and Mantua's special circumstances, all related in full. In 1499 a contract concluded between the town of Cremona and the Venetian Jews specified that it would be incumbent on the Jews to obtain apostolic letters at their own expense, 'so that the community of Cremona and the citizens of the aforesaid city be free, exempt and preserved from all contagion of sin and interdicts and excommunications, and from all other ecclesiastical censures.'

Basically, it was logical to issue the patents direct to the main interested parties, and to charge them with the task of diverting the ecclesiastical thunderbolts from the heads of their Christian partners. In their definitive form, in the sixteenth century, the patents of the *banchieri*, stereotyped (but with slight variations), talked about Jewish blindness to the 'comfort of the Christian poor', which it was important to remedy, and declared that, swayed by entreaties from the Jews, the Apostolic See absolved the prince, judges, officials, etc., from all ecclesiastical censure that they could have incurred from the toleration or privilege they had accorded the petitioners.[23]

It should be noted that in the sixteenth century—at least after 1530—these patents were no longer granted in the name of the pope, but of the cardinal camerlengo whose office must consequently have had additional revenue at its disposal. The first known patent of this type was issued by Agostino Spinola to a Jew of Ferrara in 1530. In the seventeenth century the Roman Inquisition questioned the validity of certain patents previously issued by the cardinals camerlengo, and the Jews themselves sometimes tried to obtain confirmation of them from the sovereign pontiff in person—this happened in the duchy of Milan in 1541. From the papacy of Paul V (1605–21) on, they were again granted by the popes themselves.

In about 1587 Sixtus V reorganised the protection of Jewish banking and introduced a system of registration which enables us to obtain more precise knowledge of the way it worked, as well as of its territorial extent. The registers opened at this period, according to Ermanno Loevinson, show a considerable increase in the number of *banchi* in Rome and Ancona; there were seventy in the town of Rome alone at the end of the sixteenth century. This proliferation is certainly explained by the profits which the cardinals camerlengo derived from them. The Jewish communities and the rabbis, on the other hand, were trying to limit the number of banks, as will be seen. In Responsum no. 88, dating from about 1625,[24] Leon da Modena draws a distinction from this point of view between the *condotte* from the princes, and the *toleranze* issued by the pope in his own State, inferior [of less value] to the *condotte* from the lords, for, in the case of a *condotta*, the prince cannot grant privileges to other bankers without the agreement of the titular concessionary. The pope, on the contrary, always reserved to himself the right to satisfy the petitions of other Jews applying for a *toleranza*.

In the Papal States, it seems that the price of a banker's licence in about 1600 would have been 250 *scudi*, which was its actual true market value. As far as the other Italian states are concerned, the price of a papal bull of toleration granted to the Jews of the principality of Montferrat is known by the chance survival of commercial correspondence dating from the middle of the seventeenth century. It covered a period of twelve years and cost 240 *scudi* (this price would seem to have included the licences of the *banchieri*) and, in addition, Vita Corcos, the rabbi of Rome, received a gratuity of 50 *scudi* for his representations.[25]

It can therefore be seen that, contrary to persistent legends, neither the increase in the number of Monti di Pietà, nor the strict measures the Counter-Reformation popes took regarding the Jews, had any notable influence on the practice of Jewish banking, at least in the short term. In about 1670 or 1675 an anonymous adviser noted: 'Zealous popes who punished the Jews harshly— like Paul IV, who shut them up in a ghetto, and Pius V, who expelled them from the ecclesiastical State, as well as others who issued strict decrees against them—have all positively permitted the use of banks.' In fact, it was not until 1682 that the papacy, on this point at least, succeeded in reforming customs dating from the fifteenth century, while the impersonal interaction of economic forces finally permitted the Franciscans' old dream to become a reality even in the Papal State itself.

PART TWO

# The Techniques of the Jewish Money Trade

# CHAPTER VI

# *The* Banchi

The registers set up under Sixtus V show the existence of 279 Jewish banks in 131 places in Italy in about 1600. In fact, there were certainly considerably more. In the first place, it would seem that a certain number of banks were operating without papal authorisation. This emerges particularly from the 'absolutions' which, together with patents proper, the cardinals camerlengo were issuing *post facto* to banks which were already in operation. But above all it can be concluded that in certain cases a single entry in the register or on the patent was sufficient to cover the functioning of a whole group of banks. In the majority of cases, it is not possible to know if the entry corresponds to a single bank or to several.

The system of organisation of the Jewish banks was indeed very complex, and rights of ownership most frequently confused. The general structure was obviously affected by the fact that the existence of the *banchi* was always under threat of non-renewal of the *condotta*, or of expulsion of the Jews, or more simply of plundering in the wake of disputes or popular agitation. An example of this can be found in a ruling by Rabbi Joseph Colon on a lawsuit between the former holder of the *condotta* in Colorno and another Jew to whom the ducal government had granted the monopoly of pawnbroking, after the annexation of the town by the duchy of Parma. Colon's opinion was that the former

85

holder had no right to any indemnity, for, according to the famous Talmudic maxim, 'the law of the country is the law.' It was certainly to reduce the effects of these local blows of fate as far as possible, and to spread the risks, that financiers at an early date adopted a system of networks or chains of businesses, and of multiple participation. Moreover, this is not unlike the 'decentralising' tendencies of the large Christian firms of the period.

For example, one of the principal members of the group which acquired the concession at Florence in 1437 in the name of Abramo di Dattilo da San Miniato was the Padua banker Jacob ben Jekutiel, son of the communal treasurer Jekutiel ben Emanuel of Padua mentioned above. At the same time, this Jacob ben Jekutiel held the pawnbroking concession in Siena in his own name. Umberto Cassuto, who studied the genealogy of the da Pisa family—probably the most important of the Jewish banking dynasties—has noted that in about 1450 it owned businesses at Pisa, Lucca, San Gimignano, Monte San Savino, Rimini and Forli, and shares in businesses at Florence, Venice, Siena, Arezzo and Prato. This sort of financial policy was facilitated by the closeness of family ties, by matrimonial alliances concluded as a result, and by characteristically large families—this will be mentioned again in the next chapter.

The various branches were administered by managers who were not necessarily related to the owners. The beginning of the first chapter of *The Book of the Lender and the Borrower* is a good instance: 'The principal director of the bank, whether the capital belongs entirely to him in his own right, whether he has a partner, or whether the capital belongs to a patron, must be a humble and modest man . . .', etc. The whole of chapter X of *The Book* is devoted to the way in which the annual reckoning between owners and managers took place. Quite complex forms of organisation—which Gino Luzzatto thought comparable to modern mixed liability companies—were therefore involved.

In short, the total number of Jewish banking establishments at the time when the papal registers were opened, certainly—as Milano assumed—approached five hundred; perhaps it was even higher. And this was in a territory which altogether corresponded to only half of contemporary Italy, since the Jews had been expelled from the kingdom of Naples in 1540, and Jewish banking seems to have disappeared from Tuscany in 1570 or 1571.

## EXTERNAL APPEARANCE AND ARRANGEMENTS: THE SECURITY DEPOSIT

I was at first doubtful about applying the term 'bank' to the counting-houses or offices of the Jewish lenders—labelled 'usurers' not only by their Christian customers but also by many modern authors. These doubts were given extra weight by details which at times were not entirely devoid of an element of the graphic—such as the obligation, stipulated in some *condotte*, to keep cats in the security deposits to keep the mice away. However, closer study of the activities and techniques of the *banchieri*, and especially of the light certain rabbinic decisions throw on them, convinced me that the term 'bank', in the broad sense of the word, was here entirely justified.

How was a *banco* built and equipped? We have seen from *The Book of the Lender and the Borrower* that it had to be constructed from hard stone and its windows protected by a grille in order to thwart any break-in or burglary. Obviously, this is not to say that it was always thus. In particular there was an assortment of movable branch establishments of simple wooden scaffolding that would have resembled pedlars' stalls in the market. But the permanent centre, where the security deposit was set up, was certainly built of stone. In July 1551 the council of Ascoli Piceno (probably in anticipation of a threatened famine) placed local Jewish *banchieri* under the obligation to acquire 100 *salme* of corn and to store it carefully in a *fondaco* to which they held one of the keys. It can be assumed that this *fondaco* was nothing other than the 'strong room' or 'upper room' of a bank, which *The Book of the Lender and the Borrower* mentions as follows: 'In the upper room, the security deposit must be set up. It must be built of stone so that light does not enter therein, dust does not infiltrate therein, and that thieves climbing up cannot see therein.' It is interesting to note that the Lombards of Bruges also use the term 'upper room' to designate this place. As we saw in chapter III, *The Book* also supplies other details about the arrangements and location of the bank, notably the existence of a 'curtain . . . blue in colour', over the entrance. This is the traditional pawnbrokers' curtain which Davidsohn mentioned in connection with fourteenth-century Florence. In 1521 the *banchieri* of Mantua were prosecuted for having no curtains hung over the entrance to their establishments.

In 1488 a Brescia banker was prosecuted (wrongly it may be thought, since he was acquitted) for keeping securities in his apartment and not in the deposit.[1] Section VI.3 of *The Book* specifically warns against such negligence.

The *condotte* contained stipulations about keeping the pledges in good condition, about their periodic dusting or cleaning and their protection against rodents and insects. *The Book* also holds forth at length on this subject and is a source of information on the care and proficiency needed to keep a motley collection of articles, valuable in their day, in good condition and good order. In a passage in sermon 43, Bernardino da Siena gives a further reason for warning his audience against usury: as one of its pernicious consequences, the saint includes the deterioration of clothing or fabrics given as security. Concerning precious stones or metals, among the motives which the marquises of Mantua mentioned in justification of their decision to re-establish the Jewish banks in 1557 (after trying to abolish them in 1547) was that Mantua was slowly being emptied of its treasures, which were finding their way to neighbouring principalities. Regarding Rome, a biographer of the Fugger family shows that, after its capture by the Constable of Bourbon in 1547, the inventory of the treasures the Welsers entrusted to the Fuggers' counting-house included 'an interminable list of precious stones, some of which still had the pawn tickets attached', and which could therefore have come only from Jewish lending banks.[2] In the absence of numerical data, such details are a source of information on the important role of pawnbroking in the framework of the 'expenditure pattern' of medieval Italy. It can be assumed that the variety of objects kept in Jewish bankers' deposits constituted a not inconsiderable portion of the country's personal wealth. The fact that the annual number of transactions in the large towns was approximately equal to the number of inhabitants[3] is also interesting and relevant. This statement is even more striking when we know that the total number of pawn transactions at the Crédit municipal in France in 1959 was 380,038, and in Algeria 172,406. Without wanting to compare 'underdeveloped' Algeria with Renaissance Italy, I think it can be concluded from these figures that the popularity of pawnbroking in Italy not only corresponded to the lack of accumulated capital, but also to a way of life in which such a method of obtaining ready money was usual and widespread, through either necessity or whim. Perhaps it was not only ready money which was involved—in fact the question arises whether credit sales of clothing to individuals (which the Jews of Rome carried on at the end of the sixteenth century, as archives executed and authenticated by a lawyer show) may not also have occurred in other Italian towns. In any case, in a situation such as this, it is easier to understand the exaggerations of a man like Bernardino da Siena when he expressed the fear that the major part of the country's capital was becoming dangerously concentrated in the hands of the Jews. It was, Bernardino said, like the natural warmth of the body which leaves the extremities and surface to flow towards the heart and viscera, bringing danger of 'imminent death' to the entire organism.

The fact remains that the security deposit, bursting with property of every type, probably stimulated popular jealousy and its consequences in that it was conspicuous; hence the security measures advocated in *The Book of the Lender and the Borrower.* When the Jews of Mantua were threatened with being shut up in a very confined ghetto, one of their allegations was that there would not be enough room for the *banchieri* to set up their shops there. A similar problem was posed by the first Monti di Pietà. The value represented by the mass of securities also emerges from the efforts made by the commune of Reggio Emilia in about 1450 to obtain the grant from the local banker of a right of pre-emption which would permit it to buy back unredeemed securities before they were put up for auction. According to Andrea Balletti, who set out to reveal the significance of these dealings, the transaction promised to be quite lucrative.[4]

Securities not redeemed within the statutory time (twelve, fifteen or eighteen months, according to the case) and not renewed were put up for sale, either by auction or by private contract. Judging from *The Book*, which prescribed the use of a special ledger to enter receipts from these sales, this seems to have been quite a frequent occurrence. In the case of the Banco dei Quattro Pavoni at Florence, it is known that out of eighty securities, seventy were redeemed by the borrowers and ten sold. As a result, pawnbroking led to Jewish trading in secondhand goods. Moreover, wherever they were left the opportunity, the *banchieri* engaged in other types of trade as well as banking. Authorisation could be specific—for example, a silk and tapestry shop as in the Cremona *condotta* of 1499—or general, 'to stay, come, spend the night, deal, trade and lend as they wish', as in that of Mortara.

## THE CLIENTÈLE AND TYPES OF SECURITY

The ledgers which have been preserved (I know of three, and also two inventories) confirm the importance of the pawnbrokers' function in the everyday life of Italian towns. His clients belonged to every class of society; rich and poor, laymen and ecclesiastics, townsmen and country-dwellers, all took the road to the *banco* for the same reasons. One comes across famous names in the documents: for example, Paolo Norsa has noted that Ariosto frequented the bank his distant ancestors had kept at Ferrara; I myself have noticed among the customers of the Jewish bank at Rome the names of the Orsini and the Colonna, Cenci and Ludovisi, Charles of Luxemburg, count of Brienne, Prince Zamoyski, 'Count Dudley' and many others. The bustle which prevailed in the *banco* of a large town is evoked in a letter Salomone da Montalcino, manager of an establishment at Florence, wrote to a relative or friend: 'the town is vast and full of business: with the result that from morning to evening, until eleven o'clock or midnight on working days, people never stop coming asking for money, and one would not believe it if one did not see it with one's own eyes, as I am seeing it.'[5]

A remarkable characteristic of contemporary customs is the frequency of short and very short term loans: for less than one month, sometimes even for the same day. Lodovico Zdekauer, who studied this latter case,[6] sought to attribute it to the excitement of speculation, and in fact there seems no other explanation for a debt paid back on the day it was contracted. Together with the fortunate speculators, borrowers at very short term also included devotees of festivities. In its very individual way, *The Book* mentions clients who borrow on Easter Saturday to make repayment the day after the festival, and advises against rendering this service free to Christians.

If such practices were evidence of the spending habits of the Italian Renaissance, the *banchi* also numbered artisans amongst their clientèle, who 'pawned what they found within arm's reach in their shop', writes Zdekauer vividly: 'the tanner, his leather; the weaver, his cloth; the jeweller, his pearls'. Stocks of merchandise appear on three occasions in the categories of securities listed in *The Book*. It would not be wrong to assume that advances on such merchandise went beyond the framework of the consumption loan and constituted interest-bearing commercial credits. Clients of the Viterbo bank at Rome included one Coriolano Colombi who opened a credit account of 6,000 *scudi* guaranteed by several lots of fabric—which were put up for sale after he went bankrupt in 1603. Equally interesting are the recommendations in *The Book* on the choice of place to open a bank: it should be in a market town with at least a dozen food shops. 'This town should be a commercial centre and a transit point.'

The author of *The Book of the Lender and the Borrower* does not bother to make explicit distinctions between different categories of clients. The most he does is to divide them into 'poor' and 'rich', and of these he clearly prefers the latter. A typical passage recommends that the windows of the bank be papered or painted over, 'because of the poor' (i.e. so that the poor cannot look inside;

for fear, it must be supposed, that they might be tempted to rob the bank). Similarly, it is with an eye to the rich that he advises a Jewish banker to take care about his appearance, and counsels against setting up the bank in the main street—'lest the rich be ashamed to go there'. Such tones are well in line with the political sympathies or attractions the *banchieri* felt for the well-to-do and the establishment. Elsewhere, the author recommends lenders to be realistic, not to bother about knowing whether the borrower is rich or poor, not to let themselves be moved by clients' supplications. But in reality, the primary concern here seems to be with considerations of distributive justice (cf. Exod. 23:3: 'Neither shalt thou countenance a poor man in his cause'), not expounded without a subtle humour.[7] Such precepts, however interesting, are hardly informative on the social distribution of the clientèle of the *banchi*.

In his work on the Lombards of Flanders, de Roover emphasises the predominance of short-term credit for the benefit of a needy clientèle. My impression is that in Italy such a predominance was less pronounced. Unfortunately, precise data are available only for two or three important centres; for banks in small towns and larger villages, we are reduced to conjecture.

According to the ledger of the Banco dei Quattro Pavoni studied by Cassuto, 202 articles were pawned for a total sum of 1,887 lire at the beginning of October 1473. The average sum advanced on each security was therefore more than 9 lire. At the Brescia bank in the last week of October 1488, eighty-six articles of clothing, thirty-five belts, twenty jewels and valuables and twenty various securities were pawned. The third case, really quite exceptional, concerns a Padua *banchiere* who took advantage of a dispute between his colleagues and the town council in 1433–47 (in the course of which the banks had closed) to receive his clients at Este and Pieve di Sacco. The average of his loans, sometimes expressed in ducats, sometimes in lire, is 53 ducats (from sixty-eight transactions) and 125 lire (from forty-five transactions). A hand-picked clientèle from very fashionable society was therefore involved here; the marquis d'Este himself, several professors from Padua and gentlemen, but also merchants.

The importance of jewels and valuables as securities again emerges, not without an element of the picturesque, from the debates of the Reggio Emilia council, when it decided to set up a Monte di Pietà in 1494. It was said that Jewish usury 'absorbs and consumes valuable jackets, necklaces, ornaments, gold and silver belts, shields, gems, rings, goblets; all the delights we say, of the city.' A fine picture of the wealth of fifteenth-century Italy!

But there is no sign either at Florence, Brescia or, of course, Padua, of the tools of crafts or agriculture being pawned. Similarly, *The Book*, so detailed in its lists of the different categories of securities, makes no mention whatever of such implements. As far as the peasant clientèle specifically is concerned, *The Book* mentions its existence only in one place: 'One prefers lending to people who are from another town, and to peasants rather than to townsmen'. What this refers to, I think, was a higher rate of interest that could statutorily be extorted from them. On another score, in all the sources, I have found only one solitary mention of lending seed corn, so frequent in other countries. According to an edifying anecdote reported by Sanuto, a peasant's fields sown with corn borrowed from a Jew, brought forth an unnatural vegetation as a punishment to the peasant. Finally, *The Book*, which lists foodstuffs such as wine, oil and even fruit amongst the different categories of securities, has not a single reference to corn. From all this I think it can be concluded that the peasant clientèle occupied only a very secondary place in the business of the Jewish *banchieri*. But the business of the *banchieri* was not restricted to pawnbroking—far from it, as will be seen.

## THE INTEREST RATE

The annual interest rate, which was generally specified in the *condotte*, naturally varied from one period to another and from region to region. Although it was not scrupulously adhered to in every case (a Responsum by Leon da Modena gives an interesting piece of information on this subject),[8] this statutory rate must most frequently have been observed. Otherwise there would be

D*

no explanation for the lengthy haggling when *condotte* were drawn up, or for the strikes by bankers when there were attempts to impose too low a rate on them. It was not therefore a question of specifications which remained dead letters—far from it.

At Rome and Mantua the slow fall in this rate can be followed during the sixteenth and seventeenth centuries. At Rome, where it was 30 per cent in the first half of the sixteenth century, it was lowered to 24 per cent under Pius IV (1559–65), to 18 per cent under Gregory XIII, and to 12 per cent under Clement X (1670–6).[9] It fluctuated at Mantua between 25 and 30 per cent (40 per cent for foreign borrowers) between 1418 and 1540, was fixed at 25 per cent in 1540, and at $17\frac{1}{2}$ per cent following a closure of the Jewish banks which lasted from 1547 to 1557.[10] As we have seen, while the Jewish bank was in existence at Florence from 1437 to 1527, the legal rate there was 20 per cent. As a general rule it was the same at Siena, where the Jewish bank was abolished in 1571, which leads to two interesting conclusions. First, at the time of the renewal of the *condotta* in 1457, Jacob ben Jekutiel of Padua agreed to forgo the monopoly of pawnbroking if another *banchiere* would offer to lend at $17\frac{1}{2}$ per cent, from which we can assume that he was not excessively afraid of such an event.[11] Second, in 1505, in the anarchic days of Pandolfo Petrucci's influence, the rate was temporarily raised to 30 per cent. From this I think it can be concluded that if the lower limit of the interest rate was basically determined by the price of borrowing money, following the general laws of economics, its upper limit varied primarily according to local situations and considerations.

An example of the relationship between the statutory rate and the amount of the fee that the Jews paid to the authorities comes from Padua where, in the first half of the fifteenth century, the rate was 20 per cent (as at Florence). In about 1435 the commune tried to lower it to 15 per cent (to 10 per cent, according to de Nevo, but this theologian probably had a tendency to twist the figures to suit the requirements of his thesis, whereby under no circumstances was it necessary to deal with Jews). The *banchieri* refused, closed their banks and threatened to leave town, so that Paduans seeking money had to go to neighbouring towns.

Finally, after lengthy negotiations, the rate was kept at 20 per cent, but the Jews had to pay the commune 15,000 ducats.

The range of variation in the interest rate is in its way reflected in the following passage from *The Book of the Lender and the Borrower* (IV, 2): 'One can always lend a sum equivalent to half the value [of the security] if one lends at 30 per cent or more, but one can never do so in any case where one is lending at 15 per cent or less.' In reality, the amount of the sums lent on securities of a given value also varied according to the quantity of liquid cash available.

In some towns, the legal interest rate varied according to the sum lent. The variation was sometimes in an inverse ratio, as at Fano—where the rate was 30 per cent for loans of less than 1 ducat, 25 per cent from 1 to 3 ducats, and 20 per cent for anything higher—and sometimes in a direct ratio, as specified in the *condotta* granted at Mantua in 1430 to one Calimano fu Consiglio: 10 per cent for less than 10 *soldi*, 15 per cent for 10 to 20 *soldi*, and 25 per cent for a greater sum. According to the case in point it was therefore either the purely commercial function of the Jewish bank or, on the contrary, its 'public service' character which determined the regressive or progressive nature of such scales. Mantua also offers an example from 1567 of a system of rotation. After 1567, each of the eight local banks in turn had to lend at the specially favourable rate of 15 per cent ($12\frac{1}{2}$ after 1626), the general rate for the other banks remaining fixed at $17\frac{1}{2}$ per cent. It has already been noted that at Venice the 'public service' character was taken to its logical conclusions. In the second half of the sixteenth century the Jewish pawnbroking banks were transformed into 'Banchi dei Poveri', lending at 5 to $5\frac{1}{2}$ per cent.

Whether it be 15 or 30 per cent, a rate within this range seems exorbitant and excessive to twentieth-century man who usually is unaware that he himself is paying between 25 and 30 per cent interest on the car or television set he is buying on credit, and does not even appear to be especially anxious to know. Dr Ernst Dichter, the author of the study on the psychology of lending at interest mentioned earlier, thought it legitimate to conclude that normally, and whatever they said, borrowers were less concerned about the interest rate they had to pay than about the unpleasant state of dependence in which they found themselves in relation to the lenders, and that their attitude was consequently determined by emotional reactions much more than by rational calculation—hence a relaxation of critical faculties, a tendency to believe every sort of fable and nonsense; in short, a malevolent credulity which in the case of the Christian clientèle of Jewish financiers in the middle ages, not surprisingly knew no bounds. Typically, the myths which circulated about them likened money to *blood*. Accusations of ritual murder multiplied, and the metaphor of the contaminated blood circulation used by Bernardino da Siena has been quoted above. Another form, perhaps more typical of the rational Italy of the fifteenth century, was the 'logarithmic legend', where an attempt to make the myth more plausible cloaks it in the semblance of rationality by means of a bogus mathematical proof. According to this legend, Jewish fortunes were growing *ad infinitum* as a result of the automatic action of compound interest, since 100 ducats invested at 30 per cent would be transformed into 50 million in fifty years. This piece of reasoning, seemingly first put forward at the end of the fifteenth century, has been revived by various recent writers and, in the latest instance, by the author of a treatise on the institutions of pawnbroking published in Paris in 1939![12]

In his study of the Lombards of Bruges, de Roover has provided a realistic and sober analysis of the running costs of pawnbrokers' offices. This analysis stimulated this excellent historian, figures at hand, to plead the lenders' unpopular cause[13] (it should be explained that in Flanders the legal interest rate was 43⅓ per cent). It is remarkable to compare the almost exact coincidence of the expenses de Roover lists with those given in *The Book of the Lender and the Borrower* (X, 8):

> everything the manager could have spent on the requirements of the bank; his salary and those of his assistants; all duties and taxes, municipal and otherwise; expenses of announcements and publicity; tax on books; office furnishings; alms he has distributed; gifts he

has made and entertainment allowance; maintenance expenses of the bank; rent . . .

There is therefore no risk of error in applying de Roover's conclusions to the *banchieri* of Italy.

Trying to determine the net profit of the money-dealers, de Roover lists the following categories of expenses:

*Rent*: as we know, the *banco* in Italy was normally set up in one of the best buildings in town. In one case—Siena in 1391–6—we know the rent was 40 florins a year.

*Salaries*: De Roover assumes that several people, book-keepers or warehousemen, were permanently employed in an office of any size. In the case of the Italian Jews, it has been seen that the establishment was most frequently administered by a salaried manager and, as a general rule, quite a large household of Jews gravitated to it (see the following chapter).

*Canvassers* who visit homes to recruit clients: I have found no trace of such a custom in Italy, where perhaps it was not justified, given the deep-rooted pawnbroking tradition. However, paragraph X, 8 of *The Book* mentions 'expenses of announcements and publicity'. I do not know what is meant by this: publicity for auction sales or something else.

*Judicial costs*: Lawsuits were not infrequent and were particularly expensive, including payments to the judges.

*Alms and offerings* which, it is known, were considerably important in the middle ages. Traditional Jewish solidarity and mutual aid could only increase the relative size of this category; moreover, legacies and gifts made to Christian charities and institutions are also recorded. Above all, the Jews' communal self-taxation should be mentioned at this point, the major part of which was borne by the *banchieri*.

*Idle capital*: The lender always had to have liquid cash to hand, which did not produce interest while it was thus immobilized. The yield on total capital was thus correspondingly diminished.

A Responsum by Rabbi Joseph Colon shows that 'idleness' of money was quite common and could lead to other difficulties. The dispute submitted to Colon concerned the doings of a *banchiere* who, unknown to his partner, had granted loans out of

97

his own capital and not the company's. Colon's judgment was that he must be held responsible for losses the bank suffered as a result, for if he had not put his own money into circulation, 'the company's money would have been lent instead of remaining idle. Certain securities having been found to be of poor quality [of insufficient value], this is perhaps due to the abundance of money: for it is the custom of bank managers, when they see a great deal of money lying idle, to lend more, even on poor quality securities.' Colon consequently condemned the erring partner to make good the bank's losses.[14]

*Interest paid on funds lodged with the lender*: De Roover notes the existence of such deposits in the case of the Lombards, but he thinks that they primarily worked with their own money. As for the Jewish *banchieri* of Italy, it has been seen that the practice of investing funds with them had expanded considerably in the second half of the fifteenth century; the interest paid to Christian financial backers on such money is not known. Later, in the case of Jewish sleeping partners, it can be put at 12 per cent, probably in Venetia in the middle of the sixteenth century, and 10 per cent at Mantua in 1601.

*Losses* that could be incurred:

a. By the debtor's insolvency in the case of unsecured loans. The extent of this risk is confirmed by the insistence with which *The Book of the Lender and the Borrower* advises against lending otherwise than on securities. But, as will be seen, such loans were frequent and, in the case of important people in high places, probably difficult to refuse.

b. By every variety of swindle, particularly the pawning of imitation jewels, counterfeit money, etc.—dangers against which *The Book* constantly warns.

c. By 'losses', writes de Roover, 'due to a fall in value [of the security], to its deterioration, to lack of necessary care, or to an error at the time of valuing the security'. Here again, the first ten paragraphs of chapter IV of *The Book* confirm and illustrate the opinion of the eminent Belgian historian.

d. Losses caused by burglary, pilfering and different forms of extortion (de Roover omits to mention these). These were not the least significant, in my opinion, and nearly all chapter II of *The Book* is very informative from this point of view.

*Cost of licences*: 'As we have seen', writes de Roover, 'the cost of licences was very far from negligible, and certainly contributed to raising the rate of interest at which the Lombards could lend with a profit.' I even think it was the main factor in fixing the level of this rate and that its importance justifies the classic image of the Jews as 'sponges' to be squeezed by the hand of authority at the requisite moment to discharge the money they had attracted. This concept of the 'cost of licences' must, however, be under-stood in the wide sense of fees paid to the authorities; more precisely, to the different types of authorities, their agents and representatives. In this way the concept tends to become fairly elastic and, at the extreme, to become confused with the 'different forms of extortion' mentioned under the preceding heading of 'losses'.

The cost of licences, or permits to operate—in the strict sense of the word—could not have been more varied. At Florence, for example, no tax was imposed on the *banchieri* when the first concession was granted in 1437; the commune even prided itself on drawing no material advantage from the agreement. But an annual tax was imposed on them in 1459; the actual amount at that time is unknown, but in 1471 it was increased to 1,200 florins.[15] The annual tax of Siena was 1,500 lire in 1420, but only 600 lire in 1457 and 1477.[16] For the duchy of Milan as a whole, it was 3,000 lire in 1463 and rose steadily until it reached 20,000 lire at the end of the fifteenth century.[17] No annual fee is mentioned in fifteenth-century *condotte* for Mantua. It was 500 *scudi* in 1567 and over 2,000 *scudi* in 1587 and 1597.[18] Such disparities make it possible to assume that the amount of the official tax has no real significance and that the fees specified in the *condotte* might have been only a fraction of the sums actually levied on the Jewish bankers by the various custodians of power.

These charges, it must be reiterated, varied considerably. The Siena archives produce two further examples. First, the Sienese offered 6,000 florins (or over 30,000 lire) for the crusade planned by Pius II and, as a result, created a new land-tax and taxed various charitable works—as well as the Jewish *banchieri*; the latter to the tune of 9,000 lire or fifteen times the sum total of the annual tax they had to pay. Second, it emerges from the papers of a Siena lawsuit in 1480 that, to obtain the renewal of his *condotta* in 1477, the banker Isaac di Guglielmo promised a gratuity of 125 ducats to the *Capitano del Popolo*, Jacopo di Ser Minaccio (or a sum greater than the total of the annual tax). Isaac had refused to pay, on the grounds that Jacopo had given up his appointment before the renewal of 1477. This was the basis of the case, and it is significant that the communal official did not hesitate to take it up. The considerable role played by bribery in the life of the times has not perhaps been sufficiently studied. Even in 1663, a memorandum formulated by that learned theologian Cardinal Lugo considered such practices to be perhaps not particularly commendable, but legal and to some extent natural.[19] This suggests the extent to which bribes as an item must have burdened the running costs of Jewish banks. Furthermore, two decisions by Joseph Colon show that, in rabbinic jurisprudence, the payment of duly accepted bribes constituted a legal title to the *condotta* in case of dispute between two bankers for the local concession.

Among the charges of this type that the Jews had to bear was the picturesque custom of gifts solicited by the princes themselves, who used to depart on New Year's Day to 'seek their fortune', and had to be offered refreshment by those of their subjects whom they honoured with a visit. It can be assumed, and the documents confirm this, that the Jews welcomed such illustrious spongers 'in order to gain even more of the marquis's favour', as the chronicler of Mantua wrote.[20]

But perhaps the most important item, and that which seems best to justify the metaphor of 'the Jews as sponges', was that of extraordinary taxes and fines. The two fines imposed on the *banchieri* of Florence already mentioned (p. 60)—21,000 florins in 1441 and 22,000 florins in 1461—are good examples. A detailed study of the first[21] has shown that the commune needed this money to pay Pope Eugenius IV for the price of purchasing Borgo San Sepolcro and that the informer who suggested the judicial pretext for the fine (namely, that the banker Salomone da

Terracina was himself the manager of a bank for which the concession had been granted in the name of his infant sons) collected a premium of 1,000 florins. There is also the case, familiar to historians of fifteenth-century art, of Mantegna's 'La Madonna della Vittoria', painted at the expense of the *banchiere* Daniel Norsa, whose house was expropriated at the same time and on the same pious pretext.[22] But the two most frequent pretexts for exacting payment from a Jew flowed directly from his specific status as a Jew: the absence of a distinctive badge in a place where it was obligatory to wear one, and sexual relations with Christian women. At Florence a certain Sabato, a banker from Pistoia, was sentenced in 1463 to pay 6,000 florins in eight years for the latter offence. Elsewhere, it was sometimes punished by death and occasionally pardoned beforehand. These questions will be discussed later. One must admit that in cases like these it is hard to draw the line between tax, fine, and extortion pure and simple.

More or less forced loans can be included in the same category. One of Joseph Colon's pertinent and interesting decisions involved a dispute between a group of *banchieri* and the Jewish communities in the duchy of Milan. Duke Galleazzo Maria Sforza had borrowed 5,000 ducats from these bankers. After his assassination in 1476, Duchess Bianca Maria allowed the communities to deduct this amount from a sum of 13,000 ducats they owed as taxes. The bankers, who had been ruined in the interim, asked the communities to reimburse them. They refused, and Colon settled the dispute in their favour on the grounds that, in his opinion, the bankers had practically no hope of being reimbursed by the duke. 'To get something back from a prince is like getting something back from a lion', he concluded, quoting the Talmud.

Confronted with such an accumulation of charges and costs which were collected by the greatest variety of recipients, it might almost be asked how the *banchieri*, who were certainly not philanthropists, managed to survive by charging only an average interest of 20 to 30 per cent. Could this rate have been theoretical?

Did not the various types of expedients always used by bankers enable them to increase their real profit considerably?

Unfortunately, we possess only a single extract from a Jewish banker's ledger (translated from the customary Hebrew into Italian for the requirements of the law) which actually indicates the 'usury' charged and this extract cannot be regarded as typical. The book concerned belonged to a Paduan lender who took advantage of one or more strikes by his colleagues in about 1435–50 and started operating at Este and Pieve di Sacco. I think that this explains the abnormally high average of the sums advanced, since only loans of some size could have justified his customers' journey from Padua. Later, the rectors of Padua tried to pick a quarrel with this lender for lending money to Paduans in the absence of a regular concession. A court case followed in 1450 and a legal translation of the ledgers—which accounts for the preservation of the extract. Having said this, let us see what information the document conveys.

The extract involves some eleven transactions,[23] sometimes expressed in ducats, sometimes in lire, described with customary precision. In four cases—a loan for a period of a year, another for two years, and two for three years—the transaction is clear and simple: a rate of 20 per cent, no compound or accrued interest.

In the case of two simultaneous loans repaid in nine months and eleven days, the rate is nearly 25 per cent. For a loan for three months it is 30 per cent. It is not possible to determine the interest rate for three other transactions, which are complicated by exchanges and the sale of part of the securities. Finally, for a loan of 10 ducats for two months, the *usura* shown is 3 lire 7 *soldi* (this is the only case of such a disparity)—the rate would therefore have been 40 to 50 per cent.

This does not take us much further forward. Nevertheless it can be concluded that the real interest rate seems to be in inverse ratio to the length of the loan, and that when the opportunity occurred, profit could be increased by manipulating different types of money. Careful study of the *condotte* and *The Book of the Lender and the Borrower* confirms this and adds to our knowledge of the various methods whereby profit could be systematically increased.

The most important were:

1 *Rounding off a month already begun to a whole month, or a fortnight already begun to a full fortnight*

Most of the *condotte* granted bankers the right to charge interest for the whole of the first month, whatever date the pawn transaction took place, or, at least, for the whole of the first fortnight. At Rome, the 'full fortnight' rule was abolished only in 1670, at the same time as the interest rate was lowered from 18 to 12 per cent. At Siena and Fano, the 'whole month' rule is found in the fifteenth century; at Cremona, the 'full fortnight'. This procedure obviously raised the real rate, particularly for short-term loans, and had the added advantage of simplifying its calculation. Too few data are available to determine the average length of loan with adequate precision. On the basis of two cases at Pistoia and Florence for which the ledgers exist, a very approximate length of three months can be obtained giving a rate of accrued interest of $\frac{1}{6}$ when rounded off to one month, and of $\frac{1}{12}$ if rounded off to a full fortnight. In the case of a rate of 20 per cent, his producest true rates of 23.33 and 21.66 per cent respectively.

2 *Rounding off to the highest half-lira*

The right to round off to the highest half-lira when calculating interest is found in the *condotte* of Siena (1457) and Cremona (1499). Elsewhere it is not mentioned but it was perhaps widely tolerated as a means of simplifying calculations which would otherwise have been interminable. Moreover, in the case of very small loans, it did not make much difference to the rate.

3 *Profits on exchange rates and different grades of currencies*

It can be assumed that this involved a far from negligible source of additional profit, but it is obvious that no real estimate can be made. These types of profits are described in *The Book*; not without lively detail, as the following extract shows: 'Pious men of yore were able to anticipate the future and were men of action. That is why they lent either currency or gold coins depending on fluctuations in their rates. Impeccably minted coins are not ent for the profit is the same whatever the alloy' (IV, 12). 'Should the occasion arise, the lender must convert gold into silver at a very low rate and carry out the reverse transaction at a very high rate' (VI, 16). 'One gives him copper coins and sees that one is paid back in gold, as it is said (Isa. 60:17): "For brass I will bring gold"' (VI, 17). 'If he [the banker] receives gold coins, he must collect a profit on the deal . . . if he is brought a foreign coin, he must declare that he does not know its exact value, and should accept it only if the other accepts a reduction' (IX, 4).

### 4 *Fixed commission*
This is mentioned in *The Book of the Lender and the Borrower* in the following cases:

Exchange of one security against another (VI, 8)
Very short term loans, on the occasion of Christian festivals (VI, 9)
Unpacking and packing of securities (VI, 15)
Commission charged on the pretext of absence of ready money (VI, 17).

*The Book*'s comments on the matter are fairly typical of age-long Jewish tradition: 'All this applies in the case when the client consents with good grace, but he must not be forced, for persuasion is permissible but coercion is forbidden' (VI, 18). No statutory rights authorising the *banchieri* to charge were therefore involved, and I have not found references to them in any *condotta*.

### 5 *Exceeding the statutory rate, and other types of cheating*
It is natural to assume that this took place, and a Responsum by Leon da Modena quoted earlier refers to something of the sort. He also reports that in the event the profit remained in the pocket of the *banco* manager. *The Book*, particularly the last chapter which abuses unscrupulous managers, is very relevant. Elsewhere (VII, 21) it states that in a similar case the additional profit realised by the manager must go to the owner.

The last chapter of *The Book* also describes other types of cheating, and other sources supply further examples, notably frauds carried out at auction sales of securities (bidders forming a consortium, the substitution of one security for another, etc.).

Thus, by employing a great variety of expedients, the *banchieri* succeeded in increasing their profits. But speculation on the average rate of true interest collected in these circumstances is fruitless.

While this attempt to elicit the facts about the profits and losses of the *banchieri* has so far talked only about pawnbroking, their most regular and most visible activity, this was by no means the only side to their business. We will now turn to a different type of transaction, and one of considerable extent.

## JEWISH BANKERS AND PUBLIC CREDIT

*The Book of the Lender and the Borrower*, as has been seen, formally advises *banchieri* against lending otherwise than on security. This constituted the real guarantee for the loan, and it is not hard to imagine the difficulties lenders could have had in attempting to recover their money in the absence of a security, particularly from highly placed and influential borrowers. It could also happen that the public authorities refused a helping hand to Jewish creditors for unsecured debts. This did happen at Mantua in the middle of the sixteenth century, as emerges from Responsum no. 39 by Rabbi Meir Katzenellenbogen, who expressly says that he decided against the plaintiff because the latter could have avoided the losses he sustained by not lending except against security. It is typical that in some *condotte* Jews expressly reserved the right to refuse loans in the absence of security. The importance of security as an instrument of credit has struck historians, particularly legal historians, for a long time, and Zdekauer even went so far as to hazard the suggestion that the security was historically at the origin of credit, not only in its role as its guarantee but also as a material *proof* of the existence of a contractual obligation as required by procedure in the early middle ages. Armando Sapori criticised this idea but he also seemed to think that the security as a guarantee of credit was practically indispensable, even in the thirteenth century. I think it important in this context to make a distinction between 'private credit' and 'public credit'. It is true that in the case of private credit, a security practically eliminated any risks of insolvency or ill will on the part of the debtor. But where public credit was concerned, loans which were financially risky without real guarantees and with a profit which could be as mediocre as it was uncertain, in return assured Jewish financiers of the guarantees necessary for the practice of their profession and the security of their residence.

Once again it is Gino Luzzatto who has provided the most interesting comments on this subject. Examining the finances in the thirteenth century of Matelica, a small town in the Marche, he wrote that, when financially embarrassed, such communes were left with 'only two choices: either obligatory loans imposed on the citizens, or voluntary loans and contracts with local or foreign capitalists.'[24] At Matelica (which could not have been unique), these capitalists were first of all Tuscans and then Jews. Luzzatto gives the following summary of the reasons why Jews gradually replaced the former:[25]

> In their very special position [as a religious minority] must be sought the principal reason why medieval republics and princes to a large extent turned to Jewish bankers and granted them ample help and privileges at a time when people had not yet acquired the habit of regarding credit as a public function, just as governmental bodies today are doing their best to introduce public credit institutions indispensable for the development of all types of industry and trade.

However, this very accurate observation does not sufficiently bring out the vital importance of the 'help and privileges' granted by the authorities to the Jews. Furthermore, it should not be confined, as Luzzatto does, to the middle ages, since it often is valid right up to the nineteenth century. Only after the emancipation of the Jews did the combined effect of the canonical prohibition on lending at interest (to which papal protection of the *banchieri* was a curious corollary) and of the exceptional sociolegal position of Judaism begin to decline.

There is also a third interesting observation by Luzzatto which should be mentioned. At Matelica in the thirteenth century the Jews lent money to the commune, and thereby fulfilled what would now be considered a 'public credit' function which enabled them to obtain privileges and to pursue various commercial activities. But they did not go in for pawnbroking. Studying the oldest agreement between Jews and commune authorities, I myself stumbled upon a similar state of affairs at Orvieto and Todi which led me to write (p. 53): 'at the end of the thirteenth century . . . they are not as yet the classic type of *condotte*, or specifically loans on security.' It would seem therefore that a sort of rudimentary public credit is to be found at the source of the Italian Jews' specialisation in the money trade. A closer study of the situation at Florence is revealing.

When the first concession was granted to the Jews in 1437, the Seigniory gave up the direct financial advantage of levying an annual tax so as not to be an accessory to the 'sin of active usury' (see p. 99). In 1459, at the second stage, this high-principled position was abandoned and in 1471 the tax levied on the Jewish bank was raised to 1,200 florins a year. During the third stage, in Savonarola's day, Jewish lending banks were officially abolished after the setting up of the Monte di Pietà. The Jews, however, who had lent the town 16,000 florins (without interest) in 1496, were authorised to stay and go about their business while waiting for repayment (which, according to Cassuto, they got in 1508 or 1509). It can be seen how the Jews were relegated to the function of 'public bankers', a function that was moreover curiously favourable for the propagation of myths about the omnipotence of Jewish gold (the residue of truth being that, without their gold, the Jews would not have been able to stay in Florence).

From Niccolò Piccolomini and Narciso Mengozzi's detailed study of Siena, it can be seen that when the *condotta* was renewed in 1420, an annual tax of 1,500 lire was agreed. But it so happened that the commune already owed the Jews 10,500 lire, and they succeeded in obtaining the right to recover this sum by annual deductions so that they did not have to pay out anything in tax for seven years. In the event, it is not known whether the debt carried interest or if it was a 'grace and favour' loan (in practice, both types occur equally frequently). Then in 1457 the annual tax was 600 lire, but the Jews undertook to lend the commune 1,000 ducats, which would consequently take some ten years to repay. It is interesting to note that the 1,000 ducats were not paid entirely to the commune. A *condottiere*, 'Cecchone d'India', a creditor of the town but in debt to the Jews, was able to redeem certain objects he had pledged with them without spending a penny, and the commune was debited with a corresponding amount. Later, at the time of the 1495 renewal, the Jews lent money to two charitable foundations, the 'Casa della Sapienza' and the 'Casa della Misericordia', which, in their turn, provided for the needs of the Monte di Pietà which had meanwhile been created at Siena. Finally, in 1526 the commune again made specially advantageous conditions for the Jews, 'per la conservazione della libertà et del presente stato'—according to the council's decision to renew the *condotta*, for the treasury coffers were empty and Captain Aeneas and his 200 soldiers urgently required payment.[26]

We also have some information on activities in other towns which were less spectacular than pawnbroking in the eyes of contemporaries and, consequently, are less well known.

From Balletti's work we know about certain transactions of Zinatano fu Musetto (Jonathan ben Moses), who kept the bank of Reggio Emilia from 1445 to about 1485. In 1445 Lionello d'Este imposed an extraordinary contribution of 2,000 ducats on the town, which, in its turn, demanded an advance of one-quarter of this sum from Zinatano. Finally, a compromise of 400 ducats was arrived at. Over the following years, the commune asked Zinatano to make several payments. In April 1468 the accounts were audited: in capital and interest the commune owed Zinatano over 290 lire. After a lively discussion between the town council and the banker, in the course of which appeal was made to Zinatano's civic sentiments, he, *pro amore patria*, gave up the interest and settled for the capital, that is to say 173 lire 16 *soldi*.[27] Zinatano fu Musetto was thus the official banker to the commune, advancing funds to them and settling all types of payments on their behalf.

At Pavia, at the same period, this office was filled by one Manno fu Averlino. Carlo Invernizzi related in 1458 that Manno settled various expenses in 1448, including the 200 ducats necessary for sending men and munitions to the camp of Duke Francesco Sforza. He also provided 1,500 lire in 1454 for the subsidy Sforza was demanding for the construction of a fortified castle, and 2,000 lire in 1457 for the expenses of repairing the dikes on the Ticino. We know that all these sums carried interest, and the 1448 advance was guaranteed by 600 ounces of worked silver. Moreover, it can be assumed that Pavia's good graces were much less important to Manno than the duke's, on whose behalf Manno collected the quota due from all the Jews of the duchy of Milan, and a letter written by the duke mentions certain services he rendered. These, too, probably involved loans of money.

The financing of various Monti di Pietà by *banchieri* will be discussed later. In their plea to Ferdinand of Aragon in 1478 for authorisation to open a bank at Cosenza, the Jews stated that such a bank would be inestimably useful 'for supplying the needs of the poor, particularly so that they can pay the taxes'.[28] There was also a transaction in 1481 when the clergy of Faenza gave a gold rose belonging to the cathedral as guarantee for a loan designed to pay off the tithe. In Vigevano in Lombardy, at almost the same period, Jews were advancing funds for the construction of a communal brothel.

Sometimes it was stipulated in the *condotta* itself that the bankers had to lend a certain sum to the commune without interest. This was so at Fano in the duchy of Urbino, where the 1464 *condotta* specified that when it was finalised they had to lend 100 ducats without interest 'for six months and, after repayment, whenever asked', 50 ducats (in 1492, this sum also was increased to 100 ducats). Luzzatto, who studied the operations of Jewish banking at Fano and Urbino, points to the frequency of unsecured loans in the latter, not only to the commune and nobles, but also to merchants. These loans obviously carried a much greater risk and were therefore made on much more onerous conditions, not only because of higher statutory interest, but also because of covering-up operations which seem to have been quite common. The *banchieri* sometimes reserved the right to refuse unsecured loans. (Needless to say, a refusal was not always possible. An example of an extorted loan can be found in the popular poem *Il Piccinino*, which describes how Emperor Sigismond obtained 1,000 ducats from the Jewish bankers of Lucca in 1431 on the grounds of his sovereignty over them.)

Luzzatto's book makes some pertinent comments on the wealth of the Jewish *banchieri*: he notes that at Fano they did not figure among the most heavily taxed taxpayers of the town. In this context, he outlines some general observations on the relatively modest size of Jewish capital which are completely borne out by internal Jewish sources published since, and which will be discussed in the next chapter. Also, from the point of view of banking techniques, if Jews did originate the techniques of pawnbroking, later taken over by the Monti di Pietà, they contributed nothing to those of international exchanges and transfers and other functions of modern banking which are attributable to the great Christian bankers.[29] However, it can be noted that this capital, because of its investment at short and very short term loans on security, circulated faster than the capital of Christian businessmen and so played a relatively more important role in financial life generally. It remains to be noted that pawnbroking was by far the Jews' most visible activity, the one which was familiar to all levels of the population and consequently the one most reflected in every sort of document. Financial transactions of a different type, often quite considerable in extent, can more easily be overlooked. The Jew was by definition a pawnbroker; the Christian banker seems to have benefited from the contrary presumption.[30]

This part that the Jewish bankers played in public credit and, more generally, in the large and medium scale money trade, continued to diminish as the Monti di Pietà supplanted them in transactions involving lending on security, which in the event seem to have served as an indispensable sliding regulator for all types of banking transactions. The period of this decline varied according to the place and the country and will be discussed later. Where the princes traditionally showed the Jews great favour and did not confine them to pawnbroking but gave them the opportunity to engage in all types of commercial activities, Jewish banking continued longer (this was particularly the case in Mantua, Ferrara and the kingdom of Savoy). But in the fifteenth century and to a large extent in the sixteenth, the Jewish financier had his place in every centre of any size and carried out the most varied transactions. A few more examples follow of the transactions, both large and small, revealed from a selection of documents.

In 1435 the banker 'Salomone di Gallis' opened a business at Vigevano, a small town in Lombardy, on payment of an annual fee of 25 lire to the commune. In 1450 Duke Francesco Sforza called on the councillors of Vigevano to buy the possessions of a certain Silva, so that Silva could repay the ducal armourer Delpiglio the 300 ducats he owed him. The commune protested its 'poverty and lack of resources' in vain; the duke did not want to hear; the money had to be found. They therefore turned to the Jew, threatening him with the most severe punishments if he refused, and offering him ownership of Silva's lands if he granted the loan. He consented; repayment, judging by very fragmentary documentation, took several years.[31]

In 1557 Cosimo I asked Jacob Abravanel, son of the financial adviser to the viceroy of Naples, to repay on his behalf the 5,000 *scudi* he owed to the duke of Ferrara, and promised to return this sum at an 'exchange fair' of his choice.[32] Such transactions make it easier to understand how Jewish businessmen, without belonging to the tight circle of sixteenth-century European high finance, were accurately informed of its techniques. Yehiel Nissim da Pisa, a member of a great banking family, has left a remarkable description of these techniques in *The Eternal Life*.

From 1620 until the second half of the eighteenth century the Jews of Mantua were responsible for advancing funds for the upkeep of the duchy's irrigation system and the repair of the dikes on the Po. This obligation previously devolved directly on the riverside residents but, as bankruptcies were frequent, the Jews had to replace them. Their advances were then settled through the intermediary of the 'Camera Ducale dell'Acque'; when necessary, the debtors' personal property and land served as security.[33]

# CHAPTER VII

# *The* Banchieri

In his introduction to *The Eternal Life*, Yehiel Nissim da Pisa wrote:[1]

> Indeed its purpose [the purpose of this treatise] will be to deal with the problem that in these lands, the practice of lending money to gentiles is more widespread than in the rest of Israel's diaspora . . . Since in their [the codifiers'] days, this illegal practice was not so widespread as to merit special treatment, they merely included it among the other precepts. But in these days and in these lands, since the matter of loans has become the common vocation of the people and the chief source of their livelihood, it became essential to compose a short treatise that would, as best as possible, include in it all the laws of interest . . .

According to the famous rabbi Joseph Colon of Pavia also, the money trade had become 'the fundamental occupation of the Jews in these countries'.[2] It can be seen that it was not solely Christian authors and Christian polemicists who were propagating the idea that every Jew in Italy was engaged in usury. While it is obvious that not all the tens of thousands of Children of Israel living in the peninsula at the end of the middle ages or during the Renaissance were managers or employees of the *banchi*, it is reasonable to suggest that, in a certain sense—in the very literal sense of the words—they all 'earned their living' as Jews (in other words, maintained their existence as such) thanks to the money trade, which, as has already been pointed out, was important for the consolidation and maintenance of Judaism.

Economically powerful, the *banchieri* exercised a function of control and leadership within the bosom of the Jewish communities which was essential for the cohesion and survival of the group. This state of affairs makes it easier to understand the turn of phrase used by men such as Yehiel da Pisa or Joseph Colon. We have already seen how, particularly in northern Italy, the *banchieri* were the pioneers of Jewish colonisation and how, once they had established themselves in a place, they helped coreligionists to settle there, if only to comply with the requirements of Jewish worship. It could happen that they were exempted in a period of expulsions, as happened at Florence in 1477, in the kingdom of Naples in 1510 and at Alessandria in the duchy of Milan at the end of the seventeenth century. A typical distinction is to be found in certain lists or tax registers which summarily divided the Jews into 'Hebrews who do not bank' and 'Hebrews who do bank'. The latter, most frequently statutorily excused from wearing the *rouelle*, on the whole enjoyed a very satisfactory and even honourable social position. It would be quite wrong to imagine them in Italy in the conventional guise of the 'despised usurer'. The greatest contempt for the Jews was felt towards the poor man, the one compelled to wear the *rouelle*, and this sort of situation recurs throughout Jewish history.[3] It does bear some similarity to the conditions described by specialists in race relations in Latin America or other areas where discrimination against Indians or Blacks is no longer practised or becomes blurred at a certain income level. The social prestige enjoyed by the *banchieri* will be discussed later.

It is almost unnecessarily to add that the 'Hebrews who do no bank' have generally left much less documentary evidence. Zinatano fu Musetto of Reggio Emilia, a medium-sized banker in a medium-sized town in the fifteenth century, was head of a household of thirty-three. A great deal is known about him and two of his sons. Nothing is known about the others except that they lived under the roof and protection of the *banchiere*.[4] Moreover, before moving on to the main financial dynasties, a few words about Jews who were not bankers seem appropriate here.

I think the idea of an overall statistical evaluation cannot be pursued. A distinction must be made between the old Jewish communities of southern Italy and the Papal State, and the colonies in the north which were formed at the end of the middle ages following the establishment of the *banchi*. In the old communities the range of professions was wider and the crafts in particular much more heavily represented. This was mentioned in chapter V where the Jews in Rome who lived 'under the Pope's wing' were discussed and evidence was quoted from contemporary observers who were impressed at seeing them working with their hands. A document of 1527 makes it possible to give solid evidence for these impressions.

The *Descriptio urbis* of 1526–7[5] gives the names of 370 Jewish heads of households (described as '*hebrei*') and a total Jewish population of 1,750. It is possible that the adjective '*hebreo*' has been omitted in some cases, so that the total Jewish population was slightly higher. The *Descriptio* quotes the profession of ninety-eight of the heads of Jewish households. It is not known to what extent this 'sample' of over 25 per cent corresponds to the overall socio-economic structure. It might be assumed that the information or lack of information on profession depended on nothing but the whim of the clerks. But it is strange that there is only one mention of *banchierus*, although the number in Rome at this period rose to around forty. (Could this have been something to do with the district?) Against this background, let us look at the figures in the *Descriptio* (listed on p. 115).

The Jewish community of Rome, therefore, in the first half of the sixteenth century, according to this more or less fair 'sample', consisted of about 50 per cent craftsmen, 40 per cent traders and 10 per cent members of 'liberal professions'. Then again, it should be remembered that the Jewish colonies south of the Po were primarily made up of Roman Jewish émigrés. It is all the more interesting to compare these data with the information that

| | |
|---|---|
| 21 tailors | 22 secondhand dealers (*veteramentarii*) |
| 1 tailor and dyer | 6 cloth merchants |
| 9 shoemakers | 4 butchers |
| 3 weavers | 2 scrap-metal dealers |
| 3 paper-workers | 1 wine merchant |
| 3 pack-saddle-makers | 1 fishmonger |
| (*bastarii*) | 1 innkeeper |
| 1 mattress-maker | 1 '*charcutier*' |
| 1 farrier | 1 attorney |
| 1 gunsmith | 1 banker |
| 1 furrier | — |
| 1 lantern-maker | 40 |
| 1 '*pollarolus*' | 6 doctors |
| 1 sail-maker | 3 rabbis |
| 1 wool worker | 1 schoolmaster |
| — | — |
| 48 | 10 |

Cassuto gives about Florence in the fifteenth to sixteenth centuries. Here there were no craftsmen at all; in fact the only traders he mentions (excluding bankers) are precious-stone and cloth merchants, as well as a few international businessmen after about 1550. These were Levantines or marranos whose enterprise and initiative later led to the creation of the port of Leghorn. As has been seen, when the Jews became too numerous for the authorities' liking in Florence in 1477, all those who were not dependents of bankers were expelled from the town. Later, in the sixteenth century, the dukes of Tuscany favoured the settlement of Jews who seemed useful to them, big merchants or members of the liberal professions. In fact the impression emerges—perhaps because more is known about them?—that among the Jews who 'do not bank', the artists, scholars and copyists, inventors of all types and, of course, doctors were best able to find employment in Italian towns, thanks to the patronage of both the *banchieri*, their co-religionists, and the princes, nobles and prelates.

Everyone knows, moreover, that such a state of affairs can be found elsewhere and at other times, even today. The internal distribution of Judaism corresponded to specific social conditions which governed the employment of 'marginal men'. This vast subject cannot be treated here, and a few brief indications must suffice.

It is easy to understand why Jews were not represented in the figurative arts in the Italy of the past, although they did figure among the best servants of Euterpe and, oddly enough, Terpsichore. Guglielmo da Pesaro ('ebreo'), one of the founders of modern ballet, on which he wrote a famous treatise, flourished at the court of Lorenzo the Magnificent; the composer Giovanni Maria (a convert) and the violinist Jacopo di Sansecondo, who served as a model for Raphael, at the court of Pope Leo X. The noted Salomone di Rossi was surrounded by a galaxy of minor Jewish musicians at that of the Gonzaga of Mantua. In 1443 the Venetian authorities forbade attendance at dancing-schools kept by Jews. Italian belles-lettres, however, as is typical in Jewish tradition, were primarily the domain of women such as Deborah Ascarelli at Rome or Sarah Sullam at Venice. Any history of Jewish humanism would be incomplete if it omitted the rabbis, exegetists, philosophers and Hebrew masters who taught at the academies and filled lecture rooms. The practice of medicine certainly offered Jews an even greater number of openings, and the times were propitious for seekers after the philosopher's stone and specialists in the arts of magic. Nor was there a shortage of experts in the practical arts; the multiple inventor Magino di Gabriele, glassmaker and silkworm breeder, was the protégé of Sixtus V; Moses of Pavia obtained a patent for a new method of growing rice in 1588; Abramo Colorni of Mantua, even more universal an inventor than Magino, had an infinite store of 'secret knowledge'; the engineer Salomone Giudeo 'specialised in aqueducts and the construction of dikes'. There were also those anonymous 'Jews, saltpetre experts, who know certain new and secret processes', whom Cardinal Giulio de Medici recommended to his cousin Lorenzo duke of Urbino in 1515, urging him to let the city of Florence reap the benefit of their skill. Recourse to the works of Cecil Roth, Guido Bedarida and others would easily provide a list ten times as long, with a multitude of names and vivid quotations.

Finally, and most important to the aspect now under discussion, we must return to the *banchieri*'s 'households'. We must take into consideration that strict observance of Jewish religious ritual as guaranteed by the *condotta* required not only the services of a rabbi, a butcher for ritual slaughtering and a teacher—all of which functions could be combined in the same person—but also the presence at daily prayers of a quorum (*minyan*) of ten Jewish men who had reached their religious majority. Thus at all times the Jewish solidarity prescribed by the Talmud was reinforced, and here too, besides any other considerations, lies the explanation for the almost obligatory existence within the family circle of a *banchiere* of several other families, whatever their occupation, whose heads 'did not bank'.

## THE GREAT BANKING DYNASTIES

Although we know the total number of Jewish *banchi* in Italy at the time of their greatest expansion, i.e. in the first half of the sixteenth century, must have been nearly five hundred, the number of banking firms, as well as the number of great family dynasties of *banchieri*, was infinitely smaller. In the majority of cases, the bank was administered by a manager on behalf of the owner or owners. In fact, the juggling of multiple partnerships and joint ventures, and the tangle of interests which it is impossible to unravel, resulted in the concentration of the major part of the Jewish money trade in the hands of a few family businesses which were truly dynastic syndicates. The Pisa, Norsa, del Banco, Volterra and other families veritably formed a fairly closed class or caste within the bosom of Italian Judaism which was perpetuated, as it were, by means of second-degree inbreeding, thanks to a corresponding matrimonial policy, assisted by the prolificity of Jewish families and by their strict customs. For example, at the end of the fifteenth century and the beginning of the sixteenth, matrimonial alliances can be found between the Pisa and the Norsa, del Banco, Rieti, Volterra and Tivoli families.

In this regard it is interesting to note that the Jewish communal self-administration in the middle ages recognised the franchise principle of three classes of voters. In the 'constitution' of the Rome community drawn up by Daniel da Pisa in 1524 at the request of Pope Clement VII, these three classes were charac-teristically *banchieri*, 'the richest fathers of families' and 'men from the mass of Hebrews, i.e. smaller men'.[6] (Attilio Milano, who has studied this 'constitution', thinks that members of bankers' families who were not in the profession still retained the honorary title of *banchiere*.)

Of course, disputes—even quite bitter disputes—occasionally flared up between the great capitalist families. The Norsa's eviction of their partners the Finzi led to a lawsuit at the beginning of the sixteenth century which became famous in Italian rabbinic annals. The Velletri of Rome, who seem to have had advance knowledge of Pope Innocent X's annulment of all the *banchieri*'s licences in 1682, used it to pull off quite a neat coup at the expense of the Castelnuovo, their colleagues and relations by marriage.[7] One might wonder, however, whether the Jews' pawnbroking monopoly did not take on, regionally at least, and despite internal rivalry, the form of a single collective monopoly, by virtue of a socio-religious and financial solidarity which led to a *de facto* legal solidarity.

All that is available on this subject are merely a few indications, and only a hypothesis can be sketched out. Yet it is interesting to discuss it because it helps to clarify certain generic features of Jewish banking, found again in an attenuated form elsewhere and at other times, even after the Jews' legal fetters had disappeared and their specialisation in consumption loans had come to an end.

The da Pisa family of Rome, which received many proofs of confidence from the Medici and the popes, seems to have played a preponderant role in the trend towards a concentration in this type of banking, and the interest of this family group in a variety of ventures has already been mentioned. In *The Eternal Life*, Yehiel Nissim da Pisa points to some of their other interests at the beginning of the sixteenth century: at Ferrara and Verona, as well as a partnership with the leading Venetian banker Hayim Meshullam del Banco, and 'big business' deals at Padua with Rabbi Judah Minz (a distant ancestor of Karl Marx).[8] According to the *Acta Sanctorum*, Yehiel Isaac da Pisa succeeded in obtaining the expulsion of the anti-Jewish preacher Bernardino da Feltre from Florence in 1488 by bribing Lorenzo the Magnificent. He is said to have intervened in his capacity as doyen (*primarius*) and *director* of all the usurers of Tuscany, and owner of all the *banchi* in Florence. This was probably a Franciscan anti-semitic propaganda exaggeration, reminiscent of the tales about the Rothschilds peddled around in the nineteenth century. None the less, the *banchieri* in their way did tend to practise traditional Jewish solidarity in the face of the Christian world, and Yehiel Isaac was their spokesman at Florence. It is interesting to see how another da Pisa, the scholarly Yehiel Nissim (a grandson of Yehiel Isaac), interpreted the idea of their collective responsibility in Talmudic (i.e. theological-legal) terms in *The Eternal Life*: 'It is obvious and well known to both the individual and the multitude that every Jew is responsible one for another ... just as a sheep who has been wounded on its head or on any of its limbs feels the pain on its entire body ... if one of the people of Israel sins, they all feel it. The reason for this is that the Jewish people are different from all other people in that they are like one body.' These views, current and carefully cultivated by the rabbis in the name of the consolidation of Judaism, recur in many Responsa—a well-known opinion given by Joseph Colon, for example, refers to communal self-taxation on behalf of a community under threat.[9] From documents fortunately preserved, we know in considerable detail how a third da Pisa, Isaac (son of Yehiel Isaac and father of eleven children), did his utmost to get his colleague David da Tivoli out of a hole, with prudent foresight and by appointing himself his guarantor—the fact that David was his brother-in-law and probably his partner considerably diminishes the force of this example. But another one does demonstrate how Christian concepts were akin to rabbinic ideas on the collective responsibility of the Children of Israel. Jews had caused financial losses to a Genoese businessman (whose name and the details of the business are not known), and Pope Leo X, who had set himself up as his protector, introduced a special tax on all Jews under his control in order to compensate him. The tax, of 10 ducats per Jewish bank and 1 ducat per Jewish household, was levied in the Papal State and the duchy of Ferrara from 1515 to 1519. The special relationship between the Holy See and the Jewish money trade thus emerges. The rabbi-banker regarded all the Jews as a single body, and the sovereign pontiff treated them as a single corporation; here, very clearly, the two sources, internal and external, of Jewish solidarity are shown up.

All this, although shedding some light, is still vague. A final example is slightly more concrete.

In 1600 the banker Isaac di Buonaiuto of Modena had gone bankrupt for the sum of 20,000 *scudi*. Subjected to torture on two consecutive Saturdays, he escaped on the third as his colleagues had in the interim clubbed together to settle his debts. Attilio Milano points out that, 'leaving out family ties, the common origin of the lenders' licence to practise helped to cement their interests into a single block', and compares the solidarity the *banchieri* showed at this juncture with the statutory solidarity of contemporary stockbrokers.[10] It seems clear that collective responsibility, in accordance with both the interests of good administration, from the Christian authorities' point of view, and the internal solidarity of Israel, from the rabbinic point of view, could not but be advantageous to the influence and interests of the great families, traditional protectors and spokesmen of Judaism as a whole.

Rabbinic tradition is found even more clearly at the origin of another generic feature of the Jewish banking dynasties which surrounding social pressure could only accentuate: the strength of the marriage bond and, more generally, the whole pattern of family life which found its concrete and, in fact, measurable expression in the well-known prolificity of Jewish families. Unfortunately the data necessary to compare the family trees of the Bardi, Peruzzi or Medici with those of the da Pisa, Norsa or del Banco from this point of view are not available. But I think it can be said that out of the different commandments of the Torah, which were observed with varying degrees of rigidity despite all the persuasive power of Jewish ritual and education, 'be fruitful and multiply' was always one of the best respected. The importance for the perpetuation of a dynasty of entrepreneurs to have a progeny which was numerous and, what is more, patriarchially subject to the law of the tribe, is manifest. The results are expressed in the longevity of the da Pisa family who played a leading role for two centuries, or the del Banco of Venice from whom, according to Cecil Roth, the Warburgs of Hamburg and New York are descended. However, I think the Norsa probably hold far and away the world record in longevity for a family of entrepreneurs, having 'banked' in Italy for over five centuries, passing the business on from father to son. This dynastic strength was obviously reinforced by the Jews' inability to embrace political or other careers or to join the ranks of the Italian aristocracy as did the families of Christian businessmen. It is also clear that the Jewish dynasties showed an exceptional cohesion wherever the ancestral law was observed from generation to generation—but only so long as it was. In modern times, the Rothschilds can be regarded as a typical case. It may be quite true, as Jean Bouvier has stated, that 'the Rothschilds, *in their role as bankers*, appear to the historian to be more bourgeois than Israelite',[11] but from the point of view of family continuity, whose secret lies in the intimacy of the home, they seemed to become 'more Israelite than bourgeois' as one generation succeeded another, to the point where the bankers were disappearing behind the men.

The *banchieri* class tried to defend the positions it had acquired. It has been seen how *The Book of the Lender and the Borrower* protested against enterprising people who offended them—the 'scoundrels in Israel', it exclaimed, because of whom 'the fortunes of the great heads of families totter and fall'. In fact, before the period of decline, the established firms possessed quite an effective means of preventing the rise of such competitors. Most *condotte* contained a clause guaranteeing them a local monopoly of lending at interest. For its part, internal communal legislation based on Talmudic law put the emphasis on provisions relating to 'acquired rights' which were appropriately developed by the rabbis. A Responsum by Joseph Colon shows how these rights seemed to correspond to the interests of the Jewish community as a whole, at a time when the Franciscans' anti-Jewish agitation was raging and when the setting up of a new bank ran the risk, according to Colon, of 'overturning the camel through the weight of its load'; in other words, of being the last straw. In northern Italy in particular, where the communities most frequently owed their origin to the establishment of a lending bank, 'communal administration', as S. W. Baron notes, 'was primarily a family affair',[12] and the admission of new members (i.e. the settlement of Jews in the locality) could not generally take place without the agreement of the titular *banchiere*. A rabbinic conference at Ferrara in 1554 expressed the following resolutions:

> In addition, we enjoin and maintain that no man may without authorisation encroach on the acquired rights of a co-religionist, as far as lending at interest is concerned, in places where such rights have been granted by the lords of the town. We therefore categorically and rigidly declare that no man can lend at interest without the consent of the established banker. This has been decided by the sages of Venice, Padua, Bologna and other [sages] . . .

'But the Jews of the town of Rome and of Bologna are not included in this prohibition,' the text continues. This exception goes to the very heart of the multiplicity of interests in play. On the one hand, the great banking families—because of their dynastic interests, and the rabbis—because of their concern for the position of Judaism as a whole, particularly at the critical period of the Counter-Reformation—sought to limit the number of *banchi*. On the other, the public authorities had a tendency to favour the creation of new establishments as a means of ensuring additional income. Rabbi G. S. Rosenthal of New Jersey, who has specially studied rabbinic Responsa relating to this question, sums up the situation in these terms: 'The local princes and the papacy constantly sought to increase the number of banks for financial reasons; the rabbis and the Jewish communities did their utmost to limit this number for fear of annoying the communities and impoverishing the banks.'[13] To a fairly large extent the rabbis did succeed in imposing their restrictive policy on secular states; but they were forced to abandon it in the papal theocracy, probably in view of the particularly close supervision the sovereign pontiffs exercised over Jewish banking. This state of affairs confirms Vittorio Colorni's assumptions that special regulations were in force in Jewish communities in the Papal State which deprived them of the legal autonomy granted by the temporal powers in other Italian states and the countries north of the Alps.[14]

Moreover, it can be assumed that a provision of the 1429 Jewish conference at Florence, which was devoted to observance of the biblical prohibition on lending at interest between Jews, referred to the same problems. In any case, the aim of the great treatise by Yehiel Nissim da Pisa could not have been better adapted to the interest of his own class, since strict observance of the prohibition would in the first instance have embarrassed managers of *banchi* or other enterprising financiers who were desirous of setting up on their own, and would therefore have constituted an obstacle to the emergence of competitors. Incidentally, it is remarkable how the list of accomplices, guilty of the sin of usury drawn up by the rabbi (the lender, the borrower, the witness, the scribe, the surety of the borrower) is not unlike corresponding lists by men like Bernardino da Siena, for example.[15] The main responsibility, of course, lies with the usurer himself, and the rabbi after his own fashion condemns him to eternal damnation (hence the title he chose for his treatise) as punishment for such a horrible sin. Moreover, his arguments may seem specious by contrast with those which, he says, were currently in use among transgressors (i.e. financial backers). 'If we lend to a Jew and take interest from him, he in turn lends to Gentiles at a higher interest rate; this cannot be considered usury since he merely gives us a portion of what he takes from the Gentiles.' But perhaps what was good for the da Pisa firm was good for Judaism as a whole, so much truth is there in the claim that, from a rabbinic point of view, the hegemony of the old and substantial patrician family firms effectively contributed to the stability and cohesion of Judaism.

The social situation of the great banking families was quite exceptional for the degraded state of the Jews of Europe in the late middle ages and the Renaissance, and is worth examining more closely. In the following chapter an attempt will be made to distinguish the socio-historic factors which combined to bring about such a favourable situation. They are obviously the result of the distinctive character of Italian life and customs before the Counter-Reformation. Consequently Judaism in Italy was wide open to the influences of the outside world and to humanist civilisation. The culture of Italian Jews was a dual culture, both Jewish and Italian, which enabled those who enjoyed the privileges of wealth to imitate the social life of the nobles and the great and even, within certain limits, to have a share in it, without necessarily ceasing to be pious Israelites. The Norsa of Mantua and Ferrara took part in ducal festivities and gaming parties. They had the right to carry weapons. Like the rich Christian bourgeois, the *banchieri* invested part of their money in landed property and built country houses. Meshullam da Volterra hunted deer in his country villa or château on the outskirts of Florence, and presented Lorenzo the Magnificent with the choice cuts. That a Jew should indulge in hunting, an occupation traditionally contrary to the traditions of the Children of Israel,[16] is evidence of his snobbery and of a strong degree of assimilation. It is not known if other *banchieri* followed Meshullam's example in this respect. But we do know that nearly all of them built up libraries, sometimes of considerable size, as is borne out by the numerous manuscripts at present scattered in collections throughout the world. Children's education, traditionally the object of great family attention, was ensured by tutors chosen from among the best Jewish scholars of the day, and some of their pupils became well-known Talmudists. When the Florentine Giannozzo Manetti, one of the very first Hebraists in Italy, wanted to learn the language of the Bible, it was the banker Manuello, the son of Abramo da San Miniato, whom he chose as his teacher; in exchange Manuello received lessons in philosophy. The master of Pico della Mirandola, the philosopher Jochanan Alemanno, was on familiar terms with the da Pisa, who had brought him up in their home. Cassuto, in *Gli Ebrei a Firenze*, provides dozens of other examples of such links between scholarship and banking. Throughout history, the Jews had been drawn towards things of the mind, so that the influence and prestige of the surrounding humanism only strengthened these inclinations.

There is still more interesting evidence on the way of life and relationships of the da Pisa dynasty. Two ambassadors sent by Alphonso V of Portugal to Sixtus IV visited Yehiel Isaac da Pisa to give him valuable gifts from Isaac Abravanel and to pass on a message from him. In this way, the leader of the Portuguese Jews paid homage to the leader of the Italian Jews through the good offices of Christian diplomats—but perhaps one of them was a marrano. Half a century later the famous messianic agitator David Reubeni, in order to obtain an introduction to Clement VII (who, of course, was a Medici), appealed to Daniel da Pisa, the banker whom the pope had charged with formulating the statutes of the Rome community and head of the firm at the time (1524). This is how Reubeni describes the episode: 'I chose a man called [Daniel] da Pisa who had an entrée to the pope and lived near him . . . I said to him; "I see that you are honoured by the pope and all the cardinals. I want you to be an intermediary between the pope and myself, and to advise me".' The intervention of Daniel da Pisa marked the beginning of the support Clement VII granted for several years to Reubeni's plans for a crusade. Reubeni then went to Pisa to Daniel's young cousin Yehiel Nissim, who put him up in his house and took him to visit the Leaning Tower and the main churches in the town. The young rabbi, who was only seventeen at the time, was already showing signs of the scholarship and piety which later drove him to abandon the bank the better to devote himself to his kabbalist and philosophical studies. Reubeni praised him for being 'humble, pious and charitable; his heart cleaves to Jerusalem, the holy city'. The Sienese banker Ismaël Laudadio da Rieti, the da Pisas' brother-in-law, on the contrary, informed Reubeni that he was not interested in the reconquest of Jerusalem, as he felt that he could not be better off than in his native town. In general, Italian Jews do not seem to have shown great enthusiasm for Reubeni's bellicose plans.[17]

*The Eternal Life*, which Yehiel Nissim wrote some thirty years later, shows that his scholarly research did not prevent him from being alive to the financial problems of his day. The penultimate chapter, which is devoted to a clear and detailed description of the functioning of the great exchange fairs, was apparently written before Davanzati's treatise of 1560–81. Another interesting passage in *The Eternal Life* praises the Monti di Pietà, and holds them up as an example to Jews who lend at interest to co-religionists, as I will discuss later.

All the evidence seems to confirm the impression that the specific role the da Pisa played within Italian Judaism was matched by more financial power than that of other great families—at least before 1570, the year of the closure of their banks in Tuscany —but we lack the data to estimate their fortune at the different periods. Meshullam da Volterra assessed his family's wealth at 100,000 ducats in about 1460, not counting landed property. The da Pisa fortune must have been greater—unfortunately, even the dowries they gave their daughters are unknown, although in some other cases the amounts are known from marriage contracts.[18] What information there is confirms that the great Jewish fortunes remained well below the principal Christian fortunes. The amount of the Jewish *pro rata* contribution in cases of extraordinary taxation points to the same conclusion. In about 1520, according to the Venetian rabbi Axelrod ben Eleazar, the richest Jew in Italy was Hayim Meshullam del Banco of Venice.

# CHAPTER VIII

# The Jew in the Italian City

The external manifestations of popular attitudes to the Jewish infidel in Italy, as in the other Christian countries, stimulated by age-long indoctrination from the height of the pulpit, took the form of both spontaneous violence and the usual variety of provisions designed to emphasise the degradation of the Children of Israel and to exclude them from Christian society. Some of the Counter-Reformation popes introduced the same type of legislation against the Jews as against prostitutes.[1] But people had been putting this identification into practice for a long time, as is shown by customs such as the famous 'races'—the best known of which took place at the Roman carnival. Equally typical is the prohibition certain communal statutes placed on touching food products on the markets by hand. And the ghettos set up officially in the sixteenth century were foreshadowed from the fourteenth by the prohibition on living in good districts in certain towns. As elsewhere in Europe, it was therefore a question of a permanent interaction between theological doctrine and the aggressive instincts of the masses which were seeking fulfilment under cover of this doctrine. But the fact remains that at least before the Counter-Reformation the social and judicial conditions of the Jews in Italy had not sunk anywhere near the level of degradation they reached elsewhere. Moreover, the Jews' everyday relationships with Christians were often imbued with a cordiality which past generations of Jewish historians liked to attribute to the good nature of the Italian national character or to their superior culture. Can more precise features be detected behind these verbal formulae?

To obtain a clearer view of the problem, it is worth looking more closely at the humiliation measure *par excellence*, in other words, the wearing of a distinctive badge. The powerful symbolism of this lies in the fact that it *distinguishes* the Jew, expresses his disability and goes right home to the attractions and repulsions, sexual in nature, which serve as stimulants to religious hatreds and form perhaps their final motivation.

Two relevant examples are of help in putting the problem in context. In 1449 at Recanati, at the time of the anti-Jewish agitation by Giovanni da Capistrano, a *fraticello fiorentino* had offended some Christians whom he had taken for Jews. The town council debated whether to introduce the *rouelle* in order to prevent the inconveniences which resulted from such confusions.[2] In 1523 the council of Cremona contemplated this measure because of numerous mistakes which could occur, as experience had shown, such as Christians respectfully greeting Jews who were too well-dressed and allowing them to pass before them. It was therefore a question of preventing Christians being bullied as Jews, or Jews being honoured as Christians; in other words, of relegating Jews to their canonical place as a despised minority. Moreover, Jews in every Christian country were making very great efforts to avoid wearing the badge. At the end of the middle ages they had had to accept it everywhere, apart from individual exceptions. It was only in Italy that the breaches, by becoming more widespread—as has been seen in the case of the *banchieri* and their dependants (as well as doctors and certain other protected persons)—appear to have been more common than the observance of the rule. The first reaction is to interpret this as a privilege granted to the rich, as homage paid to wealth, against a background of urban and bourgeois civilisation which cared little for the feudal type of religious hierarchy. But the spread of dispensations in its turn led to an increase in the transgressions, both major and purely symbolic, which the wearing of the *rouelle* was intended to prevent. The frequency of sexual relations between Jews and Christian women (or *vice versa*, but this was rarer) is borne out by the frequency of sentences, generally fines—some of which were very high—pronounced as a result (thirty-four cases at Florence in the fifteenth century, out of eighty-eight known convictions of Jews). Even better corroboration seems to be provided by the existence of *condotte* excusing Jews from all punishment for this offence (for example, at Ferrara in 1473 and at Castelgoffredo in 1558).

Carnal commerce between Jews and non-Jewish women (to which rabbinic tradition did not attach great importance) can be considered—as an everyday phenomenon—as the extreme case of a familiarity between Christians and Jews which, in Italy, lasted until the dawn of modern times. The measures which the Church in the Counter-Reformation took to put an end to it, and to limit contacts between them strictly to business matters (productive of hostility, not friendship), will be discussed later. In the Papal State, the ghetto wall generally produced the intended result, but in other Italian regions at the end of the sixteenth century an example of the state of affairs is shown by a report from the Holy Office at Reggio Emilia in 1598:

> In this land of Scandiano a very great familiarity exists between Jews and Christians; the women visit each other as if they were related; the young people play together as if they were brothers, and argue thoughtlessly about things of the faith; great blasphemies by Jews against the holy Christian faith are to be heard; Christians go to circumcisions of Jews, who give them good feasts; unleavened bread is offered them; some Christian women live as servants in Jewish houses, without going to confession or taking communion at the requisite time; they go only rarely to Mass, and a Jew from this place said publicly that the preacher who censures such abuses is an ignoramus and a fool.

Elsewhere in Europe such intimacy, which a man like Agobard, archbishop of Lyons, described in fairly similar terms[3] in the ninth century, was successfully combated by the Church, and disappeared as feudal society became more hierarchical. Its persistence in Italy would seem to be explained by peculiarities in the country's social structure. But this explanation would be incomplete (if not tautological), without going further back into the past: i.e. to the distinctive features of Italian history which are related to the origins of both the structural forms and the position of the Jews.

It is important in this context to bring out the role of local particularisms and of the feeling of belonging to a community, which counter-balanced the unifying effect of medieval civilisation and contrasted with the progressive isolation of the religious minority within the universal Christian city. This advantage of 'belonging' makes it permissible perhaps to talk about the 'patriotism' of Italian Jews in the Italy of the communes. Unlike the Jews in countries north of the Alps, who early on were regarded as non-naturalised aliens, those in Italy enjoyed full citizenship, as Vittorio Colorni has shown. The frequent occurrence of the terms *'judaeus de urbe'* or *'cives de urbe'* in twelfth- to fourteenth-century sources, and the fact that Italian Jews described themselves as *'romaneschi'*, are evidence of the value they attached to this citizenship. Here a more local factor in their favourable position can thus be seen taking shape, linked to the strength with which classical recollections persisted in Italy; in this sense, it is possible in reality to talk about the 'superior culture' of the country.

For the Jews, such traditions were nourished on the memory that their settlement went back to the pre-Christian era, which enabled them to maintain that their ancestors had not taken part in the crucifixion. The cycle of legends of the Rome ghetto mentioned earlier expressed in its own way the deep roots the Jews of the old Roman stock had laid down, as well as their particular relationship with the sovereign pontiffs. It was, one might say, a good reciprocal arrangement.

Historians have not, as we know, attributed these Jews to either the 'Sephardi' or the 'Ashkenazi' branch. They form a *sui generis* group of 'Italian Jews'. Their Italian-ness (or, in other words, their 'assimilation') is borne out by certain details of customs which are not found in the same form in any other European Jewry in the middle ages. These include the use of a hybrid system of dating (Jewish year, Christian months and days) and of two forenames, one Jewish, the other Italian, in which, to use Cassuto's well chosen words, 'the Jewish consciousness and the Italian consciousness, superimposed but not blended, each found expression.' This participation by Italian Jews in the culture around them, their familiarity with the work of men like Dante, Petrarch and other objects of national pride whom Renaissance rabbis quoted in their sermons, conspicuously widened their areas of contact with Christians and contributed to reciprocal affinities, particularly at the top of the social ladder. The philosopher Jochanan Alemanno, who belonged to the da Pisas' circle, was the author of a vindication of the Florentines, whom he praised first and foremost for their patriotism and devotion to public duty which he, for his part, did his utmost to inculcate in his pupils. When the rabbi-banker Yehiel Nissim took David Reubeni round the public monuments of Pisa, it has been seen that he did not hesitate to lead him into the churches so that he could admire the pictures, 'so beautiful that they are indescribable'. This state of mind was not limited to Florentine circles. The archives of Reggio Emilia provide a further instance which refers to a business discussion, and, because of this, is an even better example.

Chapter VI mentioned Zinatano, the local banker, who in 1468 refused remission of accumulated interest on a debt, and the town council appealed to his patriotism as well as to his loyalty to the city in which his sons had been brought up. Zinatano, the official report continues, remained for a moment *'suspensus et cogitabundus'*; then, yielding to the 'prayers of so many illustrious personages', agreed in the name of love for his city to give up the interest, while asking the officials not to show ingratitude later.[4]

In a general way, the image of the Jew which emerges from Italian literary documents of all types only remotely recalls the dreadful archetype of the traditional imagery on the other side of the Alps. As Emilio Re has pointed out,[5] the Jew of the Italian theatre and novel is above all the exact reflection of reality. Secondhand dealer or usurer, he is a character from everyday life. Whether a passive victim of persecution or astutely evading it, he is primarily a comic character. With certain exceptions, he is devoid of the satanic dimension which medieval folklore attributed to him elsewhere. He can even be used to poke fun at the Church, as in Boccaccio, or at bad Christians in general, as in Franco Sacchett'is writings in the fourteenth century.

The great exception remains the anti-Jewish agitation of the Franciscans. In the second half of the fifteenth century particularly, northern Italy was the centre of campaigns which spread throughout Europe in the form of ritual murder accusations. Their methods and effects, as far as they directly concerned the practice of banking by the Jews, will be examined later.

The great persecutions of the Iberian peninsula also had unfavourable repercussions on the position of Italian Jews. The expulsion of the Jews from Spain in 1492 was extended to those in Sicily in the same year. In the next century Jews in the other Spanish possessions in Italy met the same fate: Naples in 1510 and 1540; Milan in 1597. It was a good argument for anti-Jewish agitators, with the spirit of imitation also playing its part. On the other hand, some of the refugees took the road to Rome and northern Italy, swelling (it is not known to what extent) the populations of native Jewries, and here and there giving rise to dangerous competition with Christian merchants. It is known, however, that the number of Jews expelled from the Iberian peninsula has often been exaggerated. According to the estimates by Yitzhak Baer,[6] it did not exceed 150,000, of whom only a fraction emigrated to Italy. As early as April 1494 the Brescia council was demanding that the Venetian government dismiss the Jews, on the pretext of their increase in the town as a result of expulsions 'from other Christian kingdoms and dominions'. Anti-Spanish feeling in sixteenth-century Italy should probably be taken into consideration when discussing the issue. At a time when all Spaniards were suspected of Judaic heresies, as Benedetto Croce has shown,[7] even if they were not actually identified as Jews, a public opinion already unfavourably disposed towards the Jewish refugees from Spain was to that extent becoming sensitive in respect of Judaism as a whole. Typically, it was also reflected within the Jewish microcosm itself.

According to an oft-quoted anecdote, certainly true as far as the state of mind it depicted was concerned and perhaps factually true as well, the Jews of Rome offered Pope Alexander VI 1,000 ducats if he would refuse to receive the refugees from Spain into the Papal State. The pope declined the deal, and imposed a fine of 2,000 ducats on them for their lack of religious solidarity. At the beginning of the sixteenth century, Rome became the scene of considerable Jewish immigration: refugees from Spain and Portugal (practising Jews or marranos) were joined by refugees from Sicily and even Tripolitania. The resulting tensions between natives and foreigners were reflected in the 'Constitution' of Daniel da Pisa who, together with an electoral division into three 'classes', also introduced a distinction between Italian and ultramontane 'nations'. This sort of division became common in the sixteenth century, particularly in great commercial centres like Venice and Leghorn where rich merchants of marrano origin, loyal to their Spanishness, ruled the roost and avoided mixing with poverty-stricken Italian Jews, or else lorded it over them. Thus the Jewish migrations combined to achieve the same effect as the segregation of the ghettos imposed by the Counter-Reformation. The *seraglio* walls erected by Paul IV and Pius V were strengthened in places by a linguistic and cultural moat. It was in these circumstances, and with the help of these diverse factors, that the very individual character of the Italian Jews proper, with their centuries-old roots in the country, grew blurred and one might speak of their gradual 'alienation' in the dormant Italy of the baroque. That at the same period the Low Countries, the new masters of international trade, should have become the paradise of the Jews of Europe and that, later on, the Anglo-Saxon countries should have been the sole large cultural area in the West to prove resistant to anti-semitic agitation, tell their own story about the relationship between the state of Judaism, an outlook receptive to new ideas and socio-economic structures.

As the sixteenth century was marked by great demographic upheavals within the Jewish population of Italy, a few words on the subject are appropriate. Dealing with the general growth in the population of the Mediterranean countries in the sixteenth century, Fernand Braudel related the expulsion of the Jews, beginning with the Jews of Spain, to this increase:[8]

> Proof of the overpopulation of Mediterranean Europe after the end of the fifteenth century is the frequent expulsion of the Jews . . . In countries whose population was too great for their resources, as the Iberian peninsula under Ferdinand and Isabella may already have been, religion was as much the pretext as the cause of this persecution.

In its broad outlines, the situation in Italy might be regarded as another illustration of this theory. In fact, between the end of the fifteenth century and the beginning of the seventeenth, the Jewish population there declined by at least two-thirds. This decrease is consequently of the same order of magnitude as that in the Iberian peninsula if we take account, as I think we should, of those Spanish Jews who chose 'internal emigration', in the form of conversions of varying degrees of genuineness, so as to be able to stay in their own country. In 1495 the majority of the Jews of Provence, faced with the same choice, seem to have converted. More precisely, the only spectacular and global expulsions in Italy were in the Spanish possessions: Sicily, Naples, the duchy of Milan. Most of them emigrated to Turkey; a minority joined the refugees from Spain to swell the Jewish populations of other lands. It was only after the persecutions unleashed by Paul IV and Pius V that the number of Jews in central and northern Italy began to fall in its turn. There remain the inevitable differences in viewpoint which lead historians of Judaism to place the emphasis on the immediate and specific causes of Jewish migrations. They lay the stress on religious passions rather than long-term causes such as a general demographic increase which, needless to say, does not inevitably cause an outburst of fanaticism—and this fanaticism itself can operate at the expense of groups or minorities other than the Jews. They then ask why these religious passions led to expulsions in certain cases, and to incarceration in ghettos in others.

To conclude, it should be added that knowledge is still far from complete of the full consequences of the crises within the Jewries caused by the persecutions and expulsions. To some extent, in accordance with prevailing principles, these crises left the choice between conversion and exile, or conversion and the ghetto, to the individual conscience. Inasmuch as this was so, did this sifting —in other words, defections by 'converts'[9]—mark the beginning of a process of natural selection? This would apply whether the defections were unexpected and on a massive scale, as in Spain, or spread over generations, as in Italy. What were the actual psychological (if not psychosomatic) effects on the group remaining loyal to Judaism of the persuasive measures intended to convince them—especially after the Counter-Reformation—of the falsity of their beliefs and the superiority of those of their persecutors? Was a certain ethno-biological individualisation of the Jews beginning to operate, or was it accentuated in the seclusion of the Italian ghettos, as recent research seems to indicate?[10] Probably such questions can be correctly answered only through information which neither social psychology nor anthropology and genetics is yet able to supply. It is interesting that one of the points upon which these questions converge should be the old debate on human liberty. In fact—and this is not the least fascinating aspect of the subject—if Jewish history is not the affirmation of this liberty, as well as an enquiry into the meaning of destiny, it runs the risk of being no more than the pointless chronicle of a people chained to its ducats or revelling in its misfortunes. In a word, it degenerates into the record of a superstition.

PART THREE

# The Decline of the Jewish Money Trade

## CHAPTER IX

# Franciscan Propaganda and the First Monti di Pietà: The Expulsions from Naples and the Duchy of Milan

## FRANCISCAN PROPAGANDA

The relationship already noted between the toleration of the Jews and the toleration of 'Jewish usury' by Christian society could not have been closer, but this does not make it possible to claim that 'the Jews were tolerated because of their usury' or, on the contrary, that theological toleration lay at the origin of economic specialisation. There is probably some truth in each of these propositions. In medieval thought, neither the existence of Judaism nor the practice of lending at interest was in itself justified. Both were attributed to the obduracy of the human heart; they were both endured or borne, in the etymological sense of the term 'toleration'. Moreover, social criticism which protested against the imperfections of the world quite commonly lumped them together in the same disapproval.

The classics of Jewish history mention the systematic hostility shown by the mendicant orders towards the Jews. There is nothing surprising about the fact that institutions created to combat heresies and strengthen the Christian faith should have adopted such an attitude. Unfortunately, apart from general statements occasionally supported by a few examples, there is an absence of serious works devoted to these questions—with one partial exception.[1] It would first of all be important to know to what extent anti-Jewish activity or propaganda by Dominicans and Franciscans was as constant, at all periods and places, as historians such as Graetz and Dubnow and, more recently, Yitzhak Baer suggest.

It is obviously not possible to undertake such research within the framework of the present book. It is even less possible to examine a far more interesting question which demands not only the requisite scholarship but also a very firmly based theological sense. This is to find out whether the anti-semitism of the mendicant orders was fed by some esoteric tradition, inherited perhaps from former heresies which advocated gnosticism,[2] or whether it was more simply due to their social connections within medieval society and to their specific mission of battling against heterodoxies.

Originally, within the framework of their general mission of conversion, the Dominicans seem to have been the most zealous adversaries of Judaism. The forced conversions of Jews in southern Italy at the end of the thirteenth century were mentioned at the beginning of this book. The Dominican Fra Giordano da Rivalto, who took an active part in them, laid the traditional myths of ritual murder and profanations of the Host at the door of the Children of Israel in sermons which he later delivered at Florence. But no word of usury is to be found amongst the criticisms he piled up against them, although he did not fail to preach vigorously against lending at interest in general. When the Jews later specialised in the money trade, this theme naturally moved to the forefront of anti-Jewish sermons. But it can be seen from this that what was involved was not only a pretext but a cause, and an already inveterate hostility.

Moreover, it is a fact that it was precisely at Florence that the question of interest was the subject of fourteenth-century polemics between Dominicans and Augustines on the one hand, and Franciscans on the other, about the interest of 15 per cent paid on municipal forced loans. This payment was contested by the first and justified by the second, who finally won the day. This, according to John T. Noonan,[3] was the first ever open breach in the wall of the canonical prohibition.

Perhaps a comment by Jacques Heers[4] about the recruitment of Franciscans which was carried on at Genoa within the merchant class—the 'new aristocracy'—clarifies the respective positions taken up. While 'the nobles dispose of responsibilities and benefices,' he writes, 'the convents [of the old orders?] and the bishoprics are to some extent their property.' At Milan, at the same period, the famous usurer Tomaso Grassi chose the order of St Francis on which to bestow his acts of liberality.[5] In a study of the mendicant monks of Italy, Hermann Hefele[6] once spoke of their 'petit bourgeois mentality', 'the product of their wandering apostolic life'. Yet various authors have emphasised the great understanding shown by men like Bernardino da Siena of the requirements of economic life: in particular, he is said to have considered an interest rate of 10 per cent as legitimate. Surely this is another illustration of the formation of alliances, if not of the common interests mentioned above: regular clergy as well as princes and old aristocracy, on the one hand; rising bourgeoisie and preaching friars on the other? Of course, these categories are blurred and approximate, and at the time of the great quarrel about the Monti di Pietà at the end of the fifteenth century, Dominicans and Augustines reappear amongst their advocates. But as early as the beginning of that century, the Franciscans were becoming undisputed leaders of anti-Jewish propaganda.

In the first half of the fifteenth century the two leading figures of the order were Giovanni da Capistrano and Bernardino da Siena, two preachers differing greatly in temperament, but professing similar views on the subject of the Jews. As has been seen, the former fought them with the weapons he commanded in his capacity as inquisitor; nor did he spare them in his sermons, which, as was the custom of the time, the Children of Israel were obliged to attend. 'You are far worse than pagans,' he proclaimed; 'because of the crime you committed against Christ, you must be the slaves not only of the Christians but of the Saracens and pagans as well.' Da Capistrano had the reputation of being an incomparable miracle worker: 'wonders and miracles were born in his wake', wrote one of his biographers. It can be noted only incidentally that such gifts often went hand in hand with extreme anti-Jewish feeling.[7] Da Capistrano was also behind various bloody persecutions on the other side of the Alps, the most spectacular being the trial for the profanations of the Host in Breslau, which resulted in the burning of forty-one Jews, and the Jews' expulsion from Silesia.

His master and friend was more kindly a character, content to call for the isolation of the Jews and observance of the canonical legislation. This did not prevent his audience from drawing conclusions of summary brutality from his sermons when the opportunity arose. Franciscan tradition holds that it was Vincenzo Ferrer, according to whom 'Christians should not kill Jews with a knife, but with words', who revealed da Capistrano's vocation to him and appointed him his successor. Warning the Christians against the dangers of usury and without concerning himself with the theological subtleties dear to canonists and Thomists, Bernardino stated that the danger for Christianity was even greater when the usurers were Jews. In his sermon 43 on usury, he argued as follows:

> Money is the vital warmth of a town. The usurers are leeches applied to gobble up delightedly a sick limb from which they draw the blood with insatiable ardour. When blood and warmth leave the extremities of the body to flow back towards the heart, it is a sign of death. But the danger is incomparably more imminent when the wealth of a town comes to be collected and accumulated in the hands of the Jews. Then the warmth no longer circulates to the heart. As in the plague, it runs towards the gangrened part of the body, for every Jew, particularly when he is a lender, is the deadly enemy of the Christians.

Bernardino also warned his audience against Jewish doctors, who, he assured them, tried to kill their patients. To illustrate the wealth of the *banchieri*, he also employed the arithmetic argument mentioned above, particularly suited probably to carry conviction with such serious, sober-minded men as the officials could have been. At Orvieto, the Jews' *condotta* was annulled after his visit.[8] At Vicenza, according to de Nevo, the Jews were expelled after he had called their defenders blasphemers who were basing their arguments on the needs of the people and doubting whether God

would provide for them better than the Jewish usurers. But everything suggests that such decisions, taken under the influence of a
momentary exaltation, fell into oblivion after a few weeks or a
few months—as generally happened with other pious resolutions
relating to prostitutes, gambling or internal unrest.

The tempo increased and the consequences began to become
more serious with the emulators and successors of Bernardino da
Siena such as Jacopo della Marca, Roberto da Lecce, Michele da
Milano, Michele da Carcano, Alberto da Sarzano and very many
other members of the vast Franciscan family. This can be seen as
an indication of a worsening in the position of the poor; but, on
the other hand, anti-semitic propaganda could not have failed to
intensify as the prosperity and number of Jewish banks increased
throughout the fifteenth century. Sermons were often followed
by popular disturbances and acts of aggression against the *banchi*,
which both the lamentations of Jewish chroniclers and the
provisions public authorities decreed for the defence of *banchieri*
confirm. In one sense, the banks were being attacked in the same
way as tax offices in France were burned during the *ancien régime*.
But it was also typical that the majority of these provisions are
dated in the months of February and March, in anticipation of
incidents which would break out in the course of Lenten
sermons, particularly those on Good Friday. While Braudel
compares the 'salutary halt' of the winter calm with the warlike
commotions of the hot season, primitive springtime outbursts, a
sort of carnival fever, and 'the bad habits of those to whom everything appears permissible, and who do what they please' were
probably also involved, since it was the commemoration of
Christ's passion which most frequently gave the signal for these
upheavals. Another distinctive feature was the part adolescents
and even children played in them. A decision by the Recanati
council, which imposed a fine of ten lire on the trouble-makers,
ruled that children below the age of eight should be punished by
twenty strokes of the rod.[9] As will be seen, actual small 'children's
crusades' were subsequently launched against Jewish banks by
preachers such as Bernardino da Feltre.

How much did this agitation hamper the *banchieri* in their

business? The tear-soaked descriptions in Jewish chronicles, particularly in the sixteenth-century *Vale of Tears* by Joseph Ha-Cohen, are not particularly significant from this point of view, since a mournful style, 'the lachrymose conception of Jewish history', as S. W. Baron puts it, was always one of their main characteristics. In *The Eternal Life*, which belongs to a different genre, Yehiel Nissim da Pisa describes a few serious strokes of fate which hit his father at the beginning of the sixteenth century but, judging by his tone, he shrugged them off as the profits and losses of the 'upheavals of war'. Richer in information is Responsum no. 192 by Rabbi Joseph Colon, probably dating from the decade 1470 to 1480.

It was a question of knowing if a new *banchiere* had the right to set up in a certain Italian town. Colon decided that he did not, even if his presence could lighten the burden of communal taxes,

> which would certainly have constituted a valid reason before the preachers of that group [the Franciscans] had multiplied. Up to about some thirty years ago they were not so numerous, but today, when because of our sins there are more of them, they have become 'whips of oppression' for Israel. They preach every day, seeking to destroy us; our bodies and our possessions are threatened and, were it not for divine protection, we would have been swallowed alive and terror would have triumphed. Is it not therefore evident to any impartial judge that the Jews of this town have just cause to prevent a newcomer from setting up against their will . . . if because of him, which God forbid, exile and ruin should ensue in places where there had previously been no trouble—as happens when an additional load is placed on an already heavily laden camel and the animal collapses; he is responsible, for without him the camel would have borne the load . . .

His conclusion shows very clearly that the most serious dangers gathered over the heads of the Jews at the approach of the festival of Easter:

> As I wrote above, on this particular day, because of our sins, the hand of the preachers strikes heavily upon us, and every year we live in fear of this day. It is definite that no man can come and live in a town to lend at interest there without the permission of the people of that town . . .

This is valuable evidence. It dates from a period when Franciscan agitation had assumed its most concrete forms, henceforth redoubling its propaganda in favour of Monti di Pietà, which had been spreading throughout Italy since 1463.

On another count it will be noted that Rabbi Colon, while recommending that the number of banks should not be increased for reasons of public security, did not pass a value-judgment on the practice of pawnbroking as such. I have found no document before the seventeenth century in which Italian Jews themselves openly censured this profession. It was not until the accumulation of their misfortunes, which will be mentioned in succeeding chapters—the expulsions and banishments to the ghetto—that some of their spokesmen adopted critical and openly disapproving tones on the subject of the money trade.

Rabbi Leon da Modena was an exponent of this attitude. In his *History of the Hebraic Rites* (1616), a defence of Judaism for use by Christian readers, he expressed himself as follows on the subject:

> It is very true that in the deplorable state to which their dispersion has reduced them, as they are forbidden to own land almost everywhere and as all major means of trading and making money are closed to them, their spirit may have ebbed and degenerated from the former Israelite frankness . . . For the same reason, they have emancipated themselves enough to turn to usury . . .

He gave his views even more precisely in Responsum no. 88, the problem always being the danger of the increase in the number of *banchi*:

> if new banks are created, the people will be angry and will expel the Jews, for everyone knows how much the people detest usury; and in addition to the good graces of the prince, the Jew needs the good-will of the people, for when the latter have a grudge against the Jews, they send petitions to the prince for their expulsion, God forbid, and the prince listens to them, as has happened, for our sins, in several places, primarily because of usury.

An anonymous chronicler writing in 1660 was much more violent:[10]

> I have already said several times that the expulsions were mainly due to the extraordinary interest that the Jews drew from the people of

the country, eating away at the substance of the inhabitants . . . 'And the children of Israel were fruitful, and increased abundantly, and multiplied, and waxed exceeding mighty' (Exod. 1:7), and the people envied them. The Children of Israel primarily chose this particular profession out of all the professions because it gave them prosperity and tranquillity. Seated on their fat cushions, they earned their living effortlessly and without difficulty, sure of lacking nothing, and that is why nearly all of them chose this profession; and they did not know, they did not understand, that this was the cause of the envy and hatred borne towards them: experience has not taught them that this was the cause of their misfortunes, even the greatest of them did not understand it, with the exception of R. Solomon Ibn Verga . . .

The late date at which such social critics came to the fore probably tells its own tale, for the Jewish money trade was slow to decline.

Let us now examine the direct repercussions of the increase in the number of Monti di Pietà on this trade.

## THE FIRST MONTI DI PIETÀ

The first nineteenth-century historians of the Monti di Pietà were determined to find their antecedents in the middle ages. They referred back to charitable institutions of this type said to have been established in Bavaria in around 1200, or in the Franche-Comté as well as London after the Black Death. Later historians have expressed grave doubts on this score.[11] More reliable and easier to trace is the slow development of the idea of a public office for pawnbroking, at a reduced rate of interest, in the particular atmosphere of the Italy of the fourteenth century. Local chroniclers have put forward the claims of their own cities to the honour of being first in the field. The credit for having definitely established that this honour belongs to Perugia in 1462 goes to Giuseppe Mira.[12] But we have seen that the *condotta* granted to the Jew Calimano fu Consiglio at Mantua as early as 1430 provided for an interest rate of only 10 per cent (i.e., the same as that of the Monte di Pietà in Perugia) for loans of less than 10 *soldi*. As I have already tried to show, in one sense, and to the extent that it is permissible to apply modern terminology to the social facts of the past, all the Jewish banks constituted a public service *sui generis*: the high interest rates should not be allowed to conceal this fact. In this context it can be noted that, before modern times, the institution of the Monti di Pietà was firmly rooted only in economically developed regions where licensed public lenders—Jews in Italy, or Lombards in the Low Countries —had shown the way. On the other hand, it is certain that by attacking the Jews' monopoly, the Franciscans contributed, amongst other consequences, to making money less expensive for the poor at a time when its price was anyway falling generally for purely economic reasons. Thus the slow movement of the money trade out of the hands of Jews back into the hands of Christians, like the reverse swing of the pendulum which had preceded it, was governed by very complex reasons which were far from economic. The most interesting aspect of the question in my opinion is precisely the effect of beliefs or 'ideologies' on economic life in this situation, a many-sided effect varying from period to period and according to circumstance.

When the gradual monopolisation of pawnbroking by the Jewish *banchieri* was discussed earlier on, mention was made of the dual justification for it, moral and theological, given by the powers-that-be in accordance with the ideas of the time; to help the poor and to protect Christians from the sin of usury. The first of these explanations recurs in the arguments advanced by the propagandists and founders of the Monti di Pietà, while the second became 'the protection of Christians from the voracity of Jewish usurers'. The purely moral consideration therefore gave way to the criterion of social efficiency—the 'moralist' to the 'economist', to use a formula coined by Amintore Fanfani in his book *Le Origine dello spirito capitalistico in Italia* (1933). This explains the relaxation of principles on the canonical prohibition on lending at interest.

There is no doubt that this development was greatly accelerated by the appearance of and increase in the Monti di Pietà. But, in fact, a decisive role was played by a handful of preachers, powerful personalities, who exercised a charismatic fascination over the

people: individuals who 'catalysed' the historic processes, according to Fernand Braudel, whose influence is worth clarifying by
examining a few features of individual psychology. It has been
said that the spiritual vitality which animated them lay in an
inextricable mixture of love for the Christian people and hatred
for the Jews, in accordance with the two facets of their slogan
mentioned before. This point can be illustrated by the life and
works of the blessed Bernardino da Feltre.

His biographers dub Bernardino da Feltre the 'St Paul of the
Monti di Pietà'. Heralded, according to Franciscan legend, by
Bernardino da Siena, he began his itinerant preaching in 1469 at
the age of thirty. The examples that have been preserved show
him terrifying his audience with descriptions of the reign of
diabolical councils, of the end of the world, and other 'threats and
fear-inspiring subjects'. Anti-Jewish propaganda figured high
among his favourite themes, and, together with the affair of the
ritual murder at Trento (1475), brought him immense notoriety.
It was only late in the day, in 1484, that he began his activity in
favour of the Monti di Pietà.

Italy had until then been spared the trials for ritual murder
which had made periodic ravages on the other side of the Alps
since the time of the Second Crusade. Under the influence of
Franciscan propaganda, that at Trento, the first of its kind in the
country, was rapidly followed by others. It also contributed
towards the revival of that dangerous myth throughout Europe.
On this pretext, Germany and Spain especially were the scenes
of many very spectacular trials, massacres and expulsions. In Italy
itself, law-suits or lynchings took place in several towns during
the following years. Later on, the legend became one of the main
themes of a specific form of popular theatre, the *giudate*. A
*grida* by the marquis of Mantua on 9 February 1478, informing
the Jews that a Christian child had been lost, that a pogrom might
ensue, and advising them to keep on their guard,[13] is sufficient to
give an idea of the state of mind at the time. It is interesting,
besides, that the original seat of the agitation was the Tyrol,[14] at a
time when the intensive exploitation of the silver mines created
a propitious climate there for social troubles. In a more general

way, the rise in prices and the consequent increase in poverty in Italy at the end of the fifteenth century can also be cited as explanatory factors. Finally, it is remarkable that, like the epidemic of witch-hunting, the Jew-hunt contagion primarily raged north of the Po and halted at the frontiers of the Papal States.

We do not know the circumstances which caused Bernardino da Feltre to supplement the destructive aim of his campaigns with a constructive purpose, the erection of Monti di Pietà, to which Jacopo della Marca, Barnabo da Terni and other champions of his order had already devoted themselves for some twenty years. The first Monte di Pietà attributed to Bernardino's efforts was at Modena in 1484. At Florence in 1488 his stormy preaching prompted the authorities to expel him from the town. Addressing himself to the children, he tried to organise them on a military basis into companies of crossbowmen, cuirassiers and so on, whom he armed with prayers, according to the Franciscan chronicler; but the young crusaders, two or three thousand in number, 'misunderstanding his intentions', launched into an assault on the Jewish *banchi*. Another chronicle describes how the entourage of Lorenzo the Magnificent took up the cudgels for the Jews and sneered at the fanaticism of the plebs, while the people, utterly crushed by Bernardino's expulsion, waited for the worst calamities.

Legend has it that Bernardino founded some thirty Monti di Pietà in the course of his crusade and supplied many proofs of his power as a miracle-worker. His procedure was to go from town to town calling on the people to drive out the Jews, threatening them with dire disasters if they disobeyed. At Genoa, which had received some refugees from Spain in 1492, he exclaimed: 'Soon you will be decimated by plague and warfare for not having resisted this invasion.' At Reggio Emilia, he brandished the same threat because the authorities were slow to establish a Monte di Pietà. He died at Pavia in 1494, and in 1527, besieged by Marshal Lautrec, the town put itself under his protection and vowed to expel the Jews, a vow which could not be fulfilled until 1591—not for want of urgent representations in the interim at Milan and Madrid.

The route of the 'St Paul of the Monti di Pietà' and his colleagues was thus strewn with pogroms and massacres. But if Franciscan preaching threatened the Jews' security and even their lives, it does not look as if it seriously compromised the financial activities of the *banchieri*. On the contrary, the first Monti di Pietà seem to have provided them with the opportunity to handle many new deals. Let us now look at their nature and the way they functioned.

The Italian Monti di Pietà have given rise to an immense body of literature and a great deal of controversy, particularly since the end of the last century. Their latest champion, Giuseppe Garrani, expanding the old theses of A. Blaise (1856) and Father Heribert Holzapfel (1903) in his detailed book *Il Carattere bancario e l'evoluzione strutturale dei primogeniti Monti di Pietà* (1957), writes that, from the economic point of view, 'the modern bank has its historic roots in the Monti di Pietà.' From the social point of view, he says, 'they have helped to arouse and develop the sense of foresight in the working classes.' Finally, psychologically, 'their establishment has brought about a transformation in the collective spirit, insofar as it was still alive amid the torpor of charity.' To their adversaries—outstanding amongst them the scholarly legal historian Lodovico Zdekauer—the Monti di Pietà were purely charitable institutions, with the inherent failings this implies: a premium on idleness, a fertile ground for corruption and the humiliation of beneficiaries. Their history supplies many arguments to support such criticism, but perhaps it would be more accurate to describe them as hybrid establishments, linked to charitable work by a number of their features; indisputably, by virtue of others, heralding the modern credit institution.

In particular, the capital necessary for the functioning of the first Monti di Pietà was collected by the traditional methods typical of the middle ages: religious processions and collections, gifts and legacies stimulated by indulgences and exemptions, and also forced interest-free loans, most frequently from Jews.

However, their creators resolutely turned their backs on the old principles concerning the conditions on which loans were granted, which, with a few exceptions, were made subject to heavy liabilities—i.e., payment of interest. 'And let no one dare say', wrote Jacopo della Marca, 'that it is usury, for I, brother Jacopo, and many other worthy men who have carefully studied the matter, would never have allowed it.'[15] It was truly a revolutionary decision, in tune with the rest of the Franciscans' economic liberalism already mentioned, and which also implied a justification in principle of the Jews' practices. Of course, the interest demanded—usually 6 per cent, 10 per cent sometimes—was much below the rate the *banchieri* had charged. But also on many other points, the first Monti di Pietà imitated their predecessors' techniques and organisational methods.

In this context, it is important to understand that, having arisen as a result of the onslaught of the Franciscans' preaching, they slipped out of their hands and into the administration, direct or indirect, of the municipal councils, which were under the supervision of the ecclesiastical hierarchy. Like the Jewish banks, in fact, they had to secure papal approval, since in both cases the doubtful domain of the money trade was involved. To this, the Monti di Pietà added the supplementary title of charitable institutions; a juxtaposition which tells its own story about their 'hybrid' character.

Information is particularly plentiful concerning the Monti di Pietà at Perugia (the earliest, 1462) and in Macerata, respectively the subjects of studies by Giuseppe Mira and Lodovico Zdekauer.[16] The latter pointed out many analogies between the internal organisation and book-keeping of the Monti di Pietà and the private banks. But contemporaries had already noticed this: the Dominican Nicolaus Barianus, for example, in the pamphlet *De monte impietatis*, criticised them for imitating the Jews, even in externals. Mira, in his first-rate essay on the Monte di Pietà of Perugia, describes how tickets and receipts were drawn up: it is approximately the same as the method used by the Jewish banks. He also states that interest (10 per cent annually, lowered to 6 per cent in 1468) was calculated, as the Jews did, by the 'rounding off to the whole month' process and that the Monte di Pietà *depositario* or manager, in addition to his salary, collected one-eighth of the

interest levied, as well as a share of the gifts and legacies made to
the institution—which could not have failed to arouse his
enthusiasm.[17] It must be assumed that the men who formulated
the statutes of the 'primogenito Monte di Pietà' were experienced
merchants, and one might perhaps be forgiven for thinking that
they sought advice from the local *banchiere*.

Although, in this way and right from the start, the new credit
establishments at least seemed to comply with the principles of a
healthy financial policy, the capital, we know, was collected by
appealing to the charity of fellow-citizens, by the processions and
spectacular events typical of the time. But it would seem that the
funds thus raised, probably inflated by the chroniclers' imagina-
tion, would usually have been quite inadequate. Another source
of finance consisted of interest-free deposits (on this point, the
canonical prohibition remained fully in force) which were
provided by individuals attracted by the promise of reward in
the next world. Most frequently, this was not enough, so an
appeal for capital then would go out to the Jewish *banchieri*, as
occurred at Perugia, where the Monte di Pietà was able to get
going only as a result of a loan of 1,200 florins (in all probability
free) granted by local Jews who, in their turn, borrowed it from
co-religionists at Florence. In return, they were authorised to
continue to practise their profession. The founders of the Monte
di Pietà at Gubbio (chronologically the second, in 1463) also
planned to turn to the Jews (it is not known if this loan was
actually contracted). In Macerata, there is evidence of an interest-
free loan of 200 ducats. A significant detail here is that the
*condotta* of the Jews was at the same time incorporated as article
XVIII in the statute of the Monte di Pietà. We lack information
on the origin of the capital in most other places, but research has
been carried out into the origins of the Monti di Pietà at Piacenza
(1489) and Reggio Emilia (1493) sufficiently to conclude that the
first working capital was almost certainly drawn from solely
Christian sources. In larger, more commercial towns where, as
a general rule, Monti di Pietà were slower to appear, their
founders resorted to Jewish money; Lucca in 1493, Pisa in 1496.
Finally, the Monte di Pietà at Florence, also created in 1496, did

not get off the ground until 1498 when the Republic allocated it a sum of nearly 6,000 lire paid out of funds confiscated from the Pisan rebels. But at the same time, and despite the resolutions passed, the Jews were authorised to stay in the town and lent far larger sums to the Republic. Could nothing in fact have been involved here but meaningless documents?

The financial links between the Jews and the Monti di Pietà were certainly not limited to the contribution, forced or voluntary, of the first working capital. The *banchieri* subsequently stepped in and 'subsidised' those Monti which were in jeopardy by providing funds for new buildings or even, in some small towns where probably they still had the freest hand, accepting all the goods pledged, as security for their loans, as in Macerata, at San Severino Marche, Urbino and Rovigo. Thus behind the smokescreen of Franciscan propaganda and in spite of pious declarations of principle, officials and managers of Monti di Pietà were handling various types of deals with Jewish *banchieri*, and one may assume that the Jews did not always lose thereby. At Cherso in Istria, the Monte even cleared the way for a Jewish lender.[18] In every case, the help given to the Monte di Pietà could only have made it easier for the bankers to obtain an extension of their *condotte*—all the more so as their socio-economic usefulness was not belied, despite the apparent competition of the Monti.

In fact, nearly a century passed before the Monti di Pietà were able to secure stable and firm financial bases. Some disappeared rapidly; others gradually atrophied or functioned only intermittently. With the exception of the Monte at Florence, none seems to have adequately and regularly satisfied the needs of the population it served. The more or less rapid exhaustion of the treasury seems to have been an endemic phenomenon. In addition, if customers all too often found the doors closed, it was not solely because of lack of funds. It could also have been deliberate policy on the part of the manager or camerlengo, as described in the following discussion in the general council of Siena in 1492:[19]

Many of the camerlenghi of the Monte di Pietà hand over thousands and thousands of lire of Sienese money to the camerlengo who succeeds them at the end of their period of office, as their own records reveal. It is widely known that they do this so as to keep their hands on and to be able to use these funds; and thus they help and oblige each other, while the deposits remain 'frozen'. This is contrary to the wishes of all the citizens, because needy people, who come to borrow and become tired of waiting over and over again for someone to attend to them, are finally obliged to go to the Jew.

While the Jews were thus launching out into hazardous transactions for fear of leaving their money idle, the directors of the Siena Monte di Pietà tended to practise the opposite policy: a contrast between private and 'state controlled' capital. It is not venturing too far to suppose that managers of other Monti acted in the same way; that is, that they worried more about the abundance of hard cash in the till than the needs of the poor who could, after all, go to the Jew.

Just as natural seems the tendency of managers, particularly when capital was scarce, to give priority to the needs of their friends and relations. Zdekauer quotes the case of an influential person in the town, *Messere Amico*, *legum doctor*, who distributed letters of recommendation which granted recipients the privilege of borrowing without leaving securities as guarantee. Eventually, in 1478, legal proceedings against this imprudent official were opened, but the sums so lent were never recovered.[20]

Another example of corruption which probably occurred frequently was the proliferation of useless officials who lived off the Monti di Pietà. Mira cites a 1466 brief of Paul II, which mentions 'the multitude of unnecessary officials' (over forty in 1572) connected with that at Perugia—which still seems to have been one of the most prosperous and best administered, since it opened a second branch in the town in 1471, and a third in 1475. Mira underlines the varied privileges reserved to them by statute, and says that their extent could have caused serious financial damage to the Monte itself.[21]

Not surprisingly in these circumstances, the first Monti di Pietà went through frequent crises, or purely and simply disappeared. A brief of Leo X relating to the re-establishment of that at Piacenza in 1515 says that it had been administered without diligence and without honesty. It is not known to what irregularities the pope was referring. But misappropriations and financial scandals, 'holes in the till', recur with such regularity and to such a degree in the history of the Monti that they deserve attention.

The cases of the Monti di Pietà are not isolated. They can first be compared with the swindles of the managers of Jewish *banchi* thought worthy of a whole chapter in *The Book of the Lender and the Borrower*. Public office must have given all types of swindlers even better possibilities to exercise their talents than private enterprise. Generally speaking, breaches of trust and maladministration seem to have been infinitely more frequent than now. Apparently there was no Monte at that time without an example of one or more financial scandals.

At Perugia, for example, as early as 1481, there was a deficit attributed to badly-kept books; in 1503 it was explicitly ascribed to frauds committed by officials.[22] In Macerata in 1510, following an embezzlement, Antonius Ser Andrea the cashier repaid 47 florins and pledged himself to repay 300 more in several instalments.[23] The San Severino Marche Monte was founded in 1470 but disappeared as early as 1473, following an 'enormous theft'. The closing of that at Cherso in 1576, according to Antonio Cella, was due to lack of capital, bad administration and, above all, breaches of trust by employees. The local historian of Ascoli Piceno, Giuseppe Fabiani,[24] whose harshness concerning the Jews was only equalled by his enthusiasm for the Monte di Pietà, speaks of its 'inglorious end' in 1542 because of 'governors with elastic consciences; and bad administrators into the bargain' embarking on disastrous transactions. Garrani, another ardent champion of the Monti di Pietà, sums up the general development as follows:[25]

> For a whole collection of reasons—among which we must recall misappropriations committed by disloyal employees, the sacking of towns by invading armies, the greed of numerous princes, loans to insolvent communes, to say nothing of minor causes—patrimonial funds were diverted [from their destination] and, in certain cases, directly wiped out.

Such practices often overshadowed the life of the Monti di Pietà in the main Italian towns, even when some of them subsequently grew into great banks, to be counted among the most important in the country.

Historians of the Siena Monte describe no less than a dozen successive financial scandals of this type;[26] this total can, I think, be attributed to the meticulousness and attention to detail of Narciso Mengozzi and Niccolò Piccolomini rather than to some unfortunate peculiarity of Sienese practice. To finish the list, there is also the case at Ferrara.[27] Is it necessary to add that the Monti di Pietà customers, in the same boat as the Jews on this count, also indulged in every variety of fraud: pledging false jewellery, falsifying receipts, robberies, etc.—Piccolomini gives many examples.

These practices, the result of the morals and the harshness of the times as well as of the imperfections in the internal organisation of an institution which had always laid itself open to fraud, slowed down the development of the Monti di Pietà. They contributed to their dubious reputation just as much, perhaps, as the ferocious attacks and accusations of usury hurled by their opponents on grounds of principle. But, in my opinion, one must look elsewhere for the main reasons why, over a number of generations, very many of the customers continued to prefer the Jews, so that, in certain regions, Jews were able to engage in pawnbroking until the beginning of the nineteenth century.

First of all, as a general rule, the first Monti di Pietà fixed a statutory limit to the total amount of sums lent, which could not exceed a ceiling varying from 2 to 20 florins according to the individual transaction. Even supposing that these provisions had been strictly observed (and, from what we have seen, this would often not have been so), a small proportion of borrowers would have found themselves thrown back on the Jews as a result. Yet the Jews must have had some customers who came from choice.

Another equally common provision must have had more significance: the fixing of a relationship between the value of the security and the amount of the loan granted on it. These were generally the same proportions, half or two-thirds of the value of the security, prescribed for *banchieri* in *The Book of the Lender and the Borrower*. But one may well think that the Jews, whose profits were proportional to the sum lent, proved more accommodating than the official estimators when valuing the security, and that they had a more practised, more reliable eye. Given the possible state of mind of people harassed by need, this is a first significant reason for many a hard-pressed client to go to the Jews. In addition, the *banco* was open at any hour of the day, the Monte di Pietà only at certain hours or certain days (two days a week at Rome, in the sixteenth century, for example; at Milan, three days a week). To the advantage of speed was added, of course, that of greater simplicity, of formalities reduced to a minimum, of the absence of embarrassing and, above all, humiliating supervision.

From this last point of view, the charitable character of the first Monti di Pietà was reflected in statutory provisions that clients had to declare, on oath and on pain of imprisonment, that they were borrowing only for their personal needs and those of their family, and not for business; or worse, to satisfy their appetite for luxury, vanity or some other carnal greed or vice. In other words, the borrower—who nevertheless did not come empty-handed to the door of the Monte, as the deposit of the security constituted a bilateral contract in law—was in fact treated like the pauper aided by a charitable institution, which tended to set itself up as a judge of the morals and private life of its beneficiaries.

In the style of other charitable organisations pleasing to God, and in accordance with current aesthetics, Monti di Pietà were normally set up with a certain amount of splendour, often in sumptuous palaces, decorated with valuable statues and pictures. Descriptions of them are in marked contrast to the recommendations in *The Book of the Lender and the Borrower* on the siting of the Jewish *banco*. One certainly did not find there a curtain to shield the borrowers from the sight of passers-by. Perhaps the contrast between the condescending or arrogant manners of their officials and the professional humility of the Jews was equally important. 'To give charity is to play at being God', a man with a keen understanding of human nature has remarked.[28] Charity was at all times a slippery slope for those who administered it. It is a fact that for Italians of the past, particularly when they were people of some quality, recourse to the Monte di Pietà seems to have been a discreditable or at the least a compromising move.

Of course there were various ways of avoiding the humiliating publicity following a personal appearance at its door. Masters pawned valuable objects through their servants. It was also possible to use a figurehead. That was how the activities of the *rigattieri* subsequently grew up after the abolition of the Jewish banks. The *rigattieri*, according to Moroni's *Dictionary*, 'have always existed for the convenience of the public, because of the shame and the resistance that many people have to displaying their economic embarrassment publicly, which discourages them from appearing at the Monte, where such publicity is inevitable'. It will be seen in chapter XIII how this sort of conventional reason, that is to say the unseemliness, for people of quality to resort to Monti di Pietà was invoked by the champions of the Jews when the withdrawal of their licences was discussed at Rome. We now come to one of the most typical aspects of the problem. The same types of attitudes which had formerly contributed to the eviction of the Lombards by the Jews were to enable the latter to maintain their banks side by side with the Monti for generations on end. These attitudes were primarily held by the rich; but Zdekauer is probably not wrong when he envisages legions of poor devils at the other end of the social scale staying loyal to the *banchi* because the Monti undervalued or simply refused their possessions. Cardinal da Luca did not fail to turn this into an argument in favour of the Jewish banks which accepted woollen clothing or other articles as security, subject to deterioration.[29]

In short, to the extent that the increase in number of the Monti injured the Jews' business, the difficulties were primarily social and political. When Manuele and Isaac Vita, bankers at Reggio Emilia, asked for a reduction in taxes in 1498, as their trade, they said, had become 'abnormal and, for them, impossible', they did not mention competition from the recently established Monte di Pietà, but the 'harsh beatings' inflicted on them.[30] And although descriptions of assaults and pogroms in all sorts of Jewish sources increased from the end of the fourteenth century, recriminations against the Monti cannot be found. Everything seems to indicate, therefore, that the agitation aroused by their establishment represented only a new and more serious form of the Franciscan campaigns of the first half of the century. The economic suppression did not come until later.

## THE EXPULSIONS FROM NAPLES AND THE DUCHY OF MILAN

The Franciscan campaigns so far described were especially directed against the Jewish money trade, but inevitably they went further and challenged the Children of Israel as such. The obscure origins of the Franciscans' anti-semitic tradition, going back perhaps to distant heresies, have already been mentioned, and it is important to say a few words now about the forms and effects of their appeals to intolerance.

A fairly broad collection for use by popular preachers, the *Rosarium sermonum praedicabilium* by the Franciscan Bernardino di Busti dating from 1400, includes a *Consilium contra Judeos* written and signed by half a dozen members of the order. There is scarcely a mention of usury in it; the major accusations against the Jews are of systematically blaspheming Christ in their books and in their synagogues, and—according to an idea which was very widespread in the middle ages—of refusing to believe in the evidence of the Christian faith out of insincerity and sheer malice. Consequently, they had to be punished—as had in fact already happened in England and France—by their expulsion from Christian lands. One of the advisers even thought this punishment too mild and advocated classing them with heretics and treating them as such.

A glance at Sanuto's *Diarii* reveals these themes in the passages where the Venetian chronicler notes how the Franciscan preachers stirred up the people against the Jews, stating 'that it was permitted to strip them of their money and not to let them live', and how the Jews appealed to the authorities to put a stop to the disorders. But, as the *Diarii* show all too well, the disorders were renewed, year after year, in the Easter season, as we know.

Not that all Franciscans advocated the expulsion of the Jews. Nothing like this is to be found, for example, in the *Summa angelica* by Angelus de Clavasio (or Chivasso), vicar-general of the order. De Clavasio limited his demands to observance of the canonical legislation regarding the Jews and advising prohibition of their usury. In this latter context, he used a new argument which again shows how the relaxation of the canonical prohibition on lending at interest, under the influence of growing social pressures, was giving a fillip to polemics against the Jewish *banchieri*. The Christian usurer, said de Clavasio, although he sins more gravely than the Jewish usurer, is nevertheless to be preferred to him in one sense, because he quite often makes restitution; while the Jews, who over and above usury, bear hatred for the 'Christians', frequently strain their ingenuity to expatriate their profits 'to the lands of the Infidels' after they have grown rich[31] —which incidentally seems to confirm Milano's assumption of a voluntary emigration of Italian Jews eastwards, from the second half of the fifteenth century.[32] In another article, '*Judaeus*', de Clavasio takes care to make a distinction between Jew and heretic, and gives the following informative definition in the process: 'To be a Jew is an offence, not, however, one punishable by a Christian, unlike a heretic.'

None the less, although the Franciscans' propaganda resulted in many vicissitudes for the Jews in the course of the fourteenth century, it did not have any crucial consequences for their business dealings. In the following century, however, it combined with much more consequential events for Jews throughout the West, whose collective offence of 'being Jews' henceforth became a punishable crime. The word 'events' is used deliberately in the last sentence. Jewish historiography, even current Jewish historiography, has the habit of talking about 'good' or 'bad' princes and popes when discussing the vicissitudes of the dispersed people, and thus places the emphasis on the moral or temperamental qualities it attributes to those in power; the emphasis is thus on whims, infatuations, passions and other human caprices. In the last analysis, does not such a tendency express the truly specific nature of Jewish history, as the unique history of a people separated from its land for two thousand years, and thereby governed to a lesser degree than other national or collective histories by geo-historic determinism? Does not the survival of the Jews form an antithesis to the continued existence of nations preserved by the land to which they are attached? The geographic, economic and cultural entity of Italy during the 'long' sixteenth century enables such an assumption to be tested; in other words, it makes possible an examination of the interaction of the economic, social and purely emotional factors by virtue of which Jewish history takes its course or is rudely interrupted, in one country or one region of the world.

The facts are extremely simple. Between 1492 and 1597, step by step, the Jews were expelled from all the territories of the peninsula under Spanish control, whereas they were not expelled from any other part of Italy. How did this happen?

In 1492, immediately after the conquest of Granada, the Catholic kings decreed the expulsion of the Jews from a Spain exalted by the mystique of its Crusade, and effected it with an absolute rigour arising from the great upsurge of collective feeling. In the same year, the edict was extended to the Italian islands belonging to the crown of Aragon. The Jews of Malta, Sardinia and Sicily—some 40,000 of the latter—were expelled, despite the protests of the population, in even harsher circumstances than their Spanish brethren.[33] These variations in treatment may be related to the difference in socio-economic structure, since these Jews were craftsmen or small merchants who by no means occupied key positions in the money trade or tax-farming.

The kingdom of Naples was conquered by Ferdinand of Aragon in 1495; in 1496 edicts for the expulsion of the Jews were published but not enforced, and marrano Jews fleeing from Portugal were welcomed in the following year as 'subjects, friends and confederates'. Was the crusading spirit already beginning to flag? But during the ensuing years, threats hung over the heads of the Jews and finally, at the end of 1510, a new

161

expulsion, involving at least some tens of thousands, was decreed and this time was carried out. Unlike the expulsions of 1492, however, a big exception was made in favour of 200 rich Jewish families, who pledged themselves to pay an annual tax of 3,000 ducats. Here it was probably a case of protecting economic and financial interests to which rigid principles were momentarily sacrificed. (A curious document mentions that a certain 'magister Moyses' made approaches to the Holy See at that time to facilitate the arrangement and paid out 600 ducats to this end, which the Apostolic Chamber ordered to be returned.[34]) It should be added that in 1515 the Portuguese marranos, who had until then lived there quite freely, were also expelled from the kingdom of Naples.

The '200 rich families', who were joined by others in 1520, kept lending-banks and carried on various other financial and commercial business. It is estimated that there were over 600 of them in about 1530.

In 1533 their expulsion was decreed by an edict which His Imperial Majesty justified by his disappointment that the Jews' sojourn in his Italian lands had not opened their eyes to the evidence of the Christian faith. The deputies of the town of Naples protested, claiming that the expulsion would result in general ruin. Then discussion and delay followed, this time on the grounds of financial needs; *inter alia*, the necessity to equip a fleet to fight the Turks. The Jews were granted a new decennial *condotta* in November 1535 on payment of 10,000 ducats, but this agreement was not observed. In 1541, on the orders of Charles V, they too were forced to take the road into exile. The Jews' departure coincided with the establishment of a Monte di Pietà at Naples. Discussing its origins, Riccardo Filangieri, the scholarly historian of the Bank of Naples, came to the following conclusion:[35]

> From what we have just said, it is clear that the two facts, the expulsion of the Jews and the birth of the Monte di Pietà, are closely linked as both cause and effect. But it was not the establishment of the Monte which led to the expulsion of the Jews; it was the expulsion which made people realise the need for the charitable institution.

Other authors have formulated slightly different hypotheses. All do agree that the Monti di Pietà did not make their real advance as deposit and lending banks until after the Jews' departure, and that they were therefore expelled before they could become useless and even before they could provide serious competition. From this it can be seen that although the anti-Jewish tradition of the Spanish empire gradually relaxed in the course of the generations, it continued to disturb and speed up the slow organic development which was continuing in independent or semi-independent countries which will be examined later.

That the momentum of the Spanish crusade, with a mystique that demanded total dejudaisation, still retained a certain force of inertia at Madrid until the end of the century, can be seen from events in the duchy of Milan, which became Spanish in 1535.

The 'Constitutiones Mediolanenses' promulgated by Charles V in 1541 contained a chapter on the legal position of the Jews. The governor of Milan next year granted them a new *condotta* to replace that previously concluded with Francesco Sforza.[36] This situation remained unchanged for some twenty years. Then, in 1565, Philip II decreed the expulsion of the Jews, although they did not in fact leave the duchy until thirty-two years later, and even managed meanwhile to consolidate their position in the town of Milan more firmly than before.

What were the reasons behind these delays? According to a contemporary Jewish chronicler, the Jews sent an emissary to Madrid to remind Philip II that 'his servants . . . had given assistance to him and his father at times of difficulty, and that they were still ready, there and then, to make him, as well as the poor and needy, the same advances and more if need be; and they would gladly supply guarantees for the execution of this promise.'[37] Modern scholars, on the whole, merely confirm this naïve account when they state that while a heavy debt owing to the Jews remained unpaid by the court of Madrid, their expulsion was delayed. Carlo Invernizzi estimated this debt at 32,000 ducats, but Mario Bendiscioli has recently put it at the much more striking figure of 153,288 ducats.[38] But it can be assumed that the existence of the debt, whatever its real amount, was not the whole story.

In a memorandum submitted to the governor of Milan in 1570, the Jews of Pavia attributed the intrigues directed against them in the name of the vow in memory of Bernardino da Feltre (see p. 62), to 'someone in this town himself keen to practise the function of the Jews'. What did this function exactly comprise? In the first place, of course, it involved classic short-term loans; in addition, I think, discreet public credit transactions were concerned, advances to municipalities, and strangely enough to the municipality of Milan, which enabled them to meet the demands of the imperial Exchequer. The circumstances in which the Jews were actually driven out of the duchy in 1597 makes such an assumption probable.

This expulsion, in fact, coincided with the creation of the San Ambrogio Bank and at the same time fits into the background of prosperity and rising population which characterised the region at the end of the sixteenth century. The Spanish government decreed expulsion in 1591 justifying it by the unseemliness of tolerating false belief any longer in a Catholic state. Perhaps it is not irrelevant to note that Antonio Zerbi, the bank's founder, happened to be in Madrid just then.[39] At the insistence of the governor of Milan, the Jews were initially granted a further period of respite. In Milan, however, one Doctor Bartolomeo Carranza, 'representing the interests of the industrial bourgeoisie who were tired of usury, undertook to fight the last battle, making a great to-do around him, and backing Zerbi's suggestion to the king for the establishment of San Ambrogio.'[40] This was authorised in May 1593, but at first only to provide the *Cartulario*, or free deposits. It seems that its success with the public then was only mediocre.

In March 1597 the San Ambrogio Bank was authorised to issue credits (*luoghi*): in other words, to pay indirectly for the money it was trying to attract into its coffers—and which immediately flowed in abundantly. As a result, it was able to grant advances to the town of Milan, as well as other Lombard communities. A few weeks or a few months later, the Jews, numbering about a thousand, were finally forced to go. According to the Jewish narrator quoted above, the confessor of Philip II added his own request to those of the representatives of the Lombard towns to obtain this expulsion. If the anecdote is true, it is easy to imagine that the financiers' arguments carried more weight than the confessor's, the main factor being that Christian banking circles thenceforth had liquid assets or possibilities at their disposal which enabled the Spanish government to dispense with the Jews' services. This government also insisted that the towns bear the 'loss of earnings' it would suffer following the Jews' departure; which it calculated to be 32,000 ducats.[41]

It thus seems very likely that at the end of a financial and political struggle in which the Jews were, as usual, both the actors and the stake, it was Madrid's anti-Jewish tradition which was expressed in the theoretical decision of 1565 and which allowed the Jews' enemies or competitors to triumph in 1597. But on this particular occasion, all the evidence indicates that they wanted to be sure that the substitute institution worked well before they deprived themselves of the Jews' services. One great privileged family, though, the Sacerdoti of Alessandria, was allowed to stay and safe-conducts continued to be granted to distinguished financiers even after 1597. It was probably convenient to surround such exceptions with some discretion, as is shown by the scandal that Count Duke Gaspar de Guzmán Olivarès' plan to negotiate a loan with Jews in Salonika or Amsterdam aroused in Spain itself in about 1640. In the metropolis, the anti-Jewish tradition continued unabated.[42] It must also be added that the question of re-admitting the Jews, in order 'to allow the duchy to be able to avail itself of some relevant sum of money every year',[43] was raised in Milan in 1633. The project had no sequel. It was perhaps a reflection of the growing difficulties of the San Ambrogio Bank at a time of general economic crisis. Elsewhere, great epidemics (Lombardy had just been ravaged by the plague of 1630) were often followed by such invitations to the Jews.

# CHAPTER X

# *The Jews and the Development of Financial Techniques (Florence)*

We should now discuss the independent Italian states. In that their governments did not expel the Jews, they demonstrated a more realistic attitude. But they did take preventive measures with regard to them, for which the sovereign pontiffs both set the example and gave the signal. The condition of the Jews worsened everywhere, as the power of Jewish banking declined: the phenomena are certainly connected, but not through any simple direct relationship. In view of the magnitude of the subject, it seems best to consider only the three great centres of Florence, Rome and Venice, in that order. Each provided a different solution to the social problem of pawnbroking. A comparison of these solutions discloses the manifold and often changeable factors which governed the fate of the dispersed people.

Florence, as has been said, was the first large town to benefit from a well-organised and stable Monte di Pietà. The decision to set it up was first taken in 1473. One of its promoters, the Franciscan Fortunato Coppoli, took the opportunity to formulate a subtle and complicated theory to dispel the doubts and dismiss the objections of rigid moralists. Within pawnbroking, he distinguished four separate contracts (*mutuum* free of charge, deposit of security, hiring of labour and promise to pay), none of which constituted usury. His stratagem was approved by forty-eight theologians and scholars in Florence. The council voted a grant of 6,000 ducats and Lorenzo the Magnificent promised to put his name down for 500 ducats, but things went no further because of the commune's financial difficulties and the local people's lack of enthusiasm. It was necessary to wait for a change of régime with the advent of Savonarola before the plan could be put into effect in 1496. The Monte di Pietà was able to go into business thanks to nearly 6,000 lire paid out of property confiscated from the Pisan rebels, and to over 3,000 lire in deposits and gifts. This last sum included 200 lire bequeathed by the Jewish banker Manuele da Camerino, which makes it legitimate to assume, since this was a *post mortem* donation, that relations between the *banchieri* and the Monte were not as bad as persistent tradition would have us believe.[1] After its establishment, the *banchieri*'s concessions at Florence itself were revoked (see p. 107), but those in towns in Florentine territory remained in force. This makes it easier to understand how the Jews were able to go on living in Florence, to advance 16,000 florins to the Republic, and probably to make themselves useful if not indispensable in many other ways.

The Monte, which lent at 6 per cent, seems to have expanded steadily and quite rapidly. Shortly after the restoration of the Medici in 1512, Pope Leo X, advising his young nephew Lorenzo on matters of state, described it as 'the heart of the town', and recommended that men of ability be put in charge of its administration; that rich men be chosen at times when it was able to lend, and shrewd and devoted men when it was not in a position to do so[2]—so that one may conclude that even this exceptional Monte functioned by fits and starts. The da Pisa, in conjunction with the Rieti, had even been authorised in 1514 to re-open their lending bank in Florence, but it was closed down under the last Republic of 1527–30—once again, the Jews remained in the town.

The decisive blow to Jewish banking in Tuscany was dealt after the fall of the Republic, but it was not until some forty years later that the full effects were felt. In 1533 the Senate reported that the Monte di Pietà, which had been lending at 10 per cent since the previous year, was out of funds and consequently the Jews remained indispensable. In order 'to remove from the Hebrews any hope they might have of lending more', it proposed to subsidise the charitable establishment and make money flow into its coffers by promising customers interest of 5 per cent.[3]

What can this mean, except that the Jews could be eliminated only by a transformation of the charitable organisation into a commercial deposit bank? Unfortunately there is no information on whether the *banchieri* were still making the Florentine reservoir of loans yield a profit, as they had done fifty years earlier. But it is known that this reservoir, which included an 'immense number' of large fortunes, was often reduced to idleness in the years around 1530 as the result of a slack period in trade,[4] and that later on, particularly in the second half of the century, it was swollen by repatriated capital. One wonders whether many of the well-to-do henceforth sought greater profit by depositing their money in the Monte di Pietà, which in addition offered a mortgage on all the commune's income as guarantee. Besides, it still had to put itself right with the Church, and obtain its sanction for the principle of paid or passive interest, in the wake of charged or active interest definitively legitimised at the Lateran Council of 1516 by the *Inter multiplices* bull. The way in which the Holy See authorised the Florence Monte di Pietà to round this 'most difficult cape' (as an account dated 1600 puts it) is not known, nor even if authorisation was requested. But from 1542 the sovereign pontiffs began to issue briefs to Italian Monti di Pietà which authorised them to pay interest to depositors (usually 5 per cent) for reasons of *lucrum cessans*, and the Council of Trent consented to the practice on condition that these depositors were motivated by charitable, not lucrative, intentions.

This, in my opinion, was a very far-reaching reform which throws a sharp light on the development of attitudes and on the slow, difficult germination of the capitalist spirit. Certainly, the innovation did not come into effect at one go, nor without conflict. Pius V (1566-72), who imposed severe regulations on the *cambi*, for his part refused to grant such licences, 'liable to lead men into sin', and they were condemned by the 1569 Council of Milan. At Florence itself, the archbishop threatened the Monte di Pietà with ecclesiastical censure in 1574. Intervention by Gregory XIII smoothed the incident over, but the Monte was reformed in 1616 by issuing *luoghi* (credits) so as to camouflage the interest that three generations of depositors had until then openly collected. Moreover, the very nature of the privileges granted by the Roman Church to the Monti di Pietà shows how far Catholic attitudes to the problem of 'usury' remained indecisive at the beginning of the modern period.[5] In fact, a veil or pretext was still necessary. Clearly, the substitution of the Monti for the Jews meant that some sort of religious intrusion or participation still remained indispensable in this sphere. But all the evidence indicates that the religious element was becoming weaker, since the Christian bourgeoisie had renounced and rejected heterodox management in order to handle these delicate matters itself and to its own advantage, under the guise of a charitable organisation.

It is easy to understand that once the Monti di Pietà had guaranteed interest to depositors, they had no alternative but to invest their capital appropriately, so that their transformation into merchant banks became inevitable. Although the Florence Monte is exceptional because of its inordinate activity, it is still typical of the spirit in which this transformation took place. During the second half of the sixteenth century, it expanded rapidly—'as if infinite', wrote Father Buoninsegni in 1588. This rise reflected a general phenomenon, since private banks were failing throughout Italy and were losing ground to public banks. All the same, it would be unwise perhaps to make too sharp a distinction between the two categories. The Florence Monte in any case seems to have belonged to both: while it was the principal bank of the Tuscan state, it also became a tool of the grand dukes—their private bank. Typically, Ferdinand I in 1588 forbade the Siena Monte to pay interest to its depositors, thus strengthening the monopoly of the Florentine establishment. Loans to the poor moved into the background and continued to exist only as a pretext; it was to emperors and kings that loans were thenceforth made. Father Buoninsegni even denied the establishment's right to the name: 'Having made itself into a depository and a business, and being usurious, it can no longer be called a Monte di Pietà . . . it seems rather to have become a secure communal savings fund and a great heap of deniers which are received on payment to the usurers and are likewise devoted to usury . . . and this Monte seems to be infinite in its growth'.[6]

The rise of the Monte enabled the grand dukes to become the bankers of Europe. Around 1580-5, the old Florentine savings were used to advance hundreds of thousands of ducats to the king of Spain, who converted the debt into bonds on the black slave trade with the Indies in 1598. Its debtors also included the emperors of Germany, Matthias and Ferdinand II (60,000 ducats in 1618), while Duke Ludwig of Bavaria (15,000 scudi), and Queen Marie de Medici who used 'la Galigaï' as a figurehead (200,000 scudi), were numbered among its depositors and creditors. Needless to say, the Monte di Pietà—that is, the grand duke— also handled a vast amount of business with less highly placed personages: 'There was no mercantile enterprise in which he was not involved', wrote Jacopo Galluzzi.[7] But he was probably twice as interested in the deals he negotiated with crowned heads, since they enabled him, the leader of a small state, to negotiate as an equal with the most powerful monarchs in Europe.

Contemporaries complained that profitable investment in the Monte di Pietà diverted Florentine capital from industrial and commercial enterprises. Father Buoninsegni spoke of 'great damage, in that, tempted by this certain profit, a number of people are abandoning commerce and the industries of trade, not without damage and financial embarrassment to the town and provinces, accustomed to live by this commerce and these industries'. These were the same grievances that the Florentine authorities had expressed in the previous century about investment with the Jews. According to Galluzzi, 'the prosperity of the first successes prompted all the merchants to gather beneath the banner of the Monte to seek profit with greater security'. This suggests that the expression 'monopoly', often used about the Monte, is no exaggeration. A commission established by the grand duke in 1630 to remedy damage caused in Tuscany by the plague (but probably involving more deep-seated ills connected with the downward trend in preceding years and the inflation of credit) proposed to restore freedom to trade, to put an end to the financial monopoly of the Monte di Pietà, and to make it revert 'to its original foundation to administer on behalf of widows and those in its care'. However, it retained its role as a great merchant bank throughout all the crises of the seventeenth and eighteenth centuries, funding its debts, which merged with the public debt of Tuscany. In 1774 the economist F. M. Gianni, who was instructed to review it, passed extremely harsh judgment on the Monti di Pietà in general:[8]

Experience has taught those who have had the opportunity to study in depth the intrinsic behaviour and transactions of the Monti di Pietà that these institutions, sanctified by the name they have been given, in no way differ from other establishments whose object is to provide, with the help of a public title, for the specific needs of individuals.

Because of this, in the administration of the Monti, thieves and swindlers behaved like irresponsible custodians towards this sort of sacred patrimony and on many occasions robbed and pillaged it, as might justifiably have been feared with more secular organisations.

As with secular enterprises, the economic disasters of the Monti have sometimes made it impossible for them to satisfy their creditors or, at least, payment has been greatly delayed.

Neither is there any lack of examples which lead to the conclusion that the increase in the patrimony or revenues of the Monti endangered the patrimony of other communities, religious places or other public administrations.

Yet such governmental practices, which otherwise—lacking the title of charitable institution—might have been regarded as irregularities or an unjustifiable use of other people's property, have deserved to be ranked as holy works, because the holy name of Monte di Pietà has been conferred on them . . .

Gianni then criticised the utilisation of the capital of the Monti for very different purposes from those for which they had been established. He suggested listing how many times 'the devout veneration of the Monti di Pietà that one wanted to exact from the public had been betrayed', and how many times their capital, 'instead of being used as envisaged for helping the poor, has, notwithstanding its religious character, been used for numerous secular grants, for excessive luxury, for the dissipation of the property of the wealthy, who are reduced to need through the extravagances of pernicious ostentation and conceited indolence'.

In conclusion, Gianni recommended the abolition of the Monti di Pietà, 'leaving to the public the money trade which is at present carried on in the Monti under the auspices of their sacred name; in many cases in circumstances which are harsher for debtors than those commonly practised by the greediest of traders.'

All in all, the judgment this enlightened economist passed on the Monti di Pietà was almost as hostile as that once pronounced by the Franciscan pioneers of the Monti on the Jewish *banchieri*.

To return to the *banchieri*: their leaders, the da Pisa, disappeared (fairly abruptly, it would seem) from the Florentine scene in 1570, after the closure of their provincial banks. It is not impossible that the excessive fine with which they were threatened on this occasion was due to their manoeuvres or intrigues to avoid internment in a ghetto. In any case, there is certainly some connection between the abolition of the bank and the creation of the ghetto at Florence in 1570.[9] On the other hand, the immediate cause of the creation of the ghetto was Cosimo I's desire to please Pope Pius V in order to obtain the grant of the title of grand duke from him, and therefore seems to belong merely to the sphere of 'minor history'.[10] This shows how far the power of Jewish banking had declined at that time. Why the Counter-Reformation papers thought it important to segregate and debase the Jews will be seen later.

In 1570 and 1571 respectively, ghettos walled off from the world outside were set up at Florence and Siena at great expense, and the Jews of Tuscany had the choice between segregation and exile: most chose the ghetto. Thenceforth, these Italian Jews of old stock or old style seem to contribute but very little to the economic history of Tuscany or any other part of Italy. None the less, a new type of Jew was coming forward to take over from them.

In Tuscany itself at the end of the century, the grand dukes created the free port of Leghorn. The 'Hebrew nation', protected by the broad immunities granted to the Portuguese marranos, became its most valuable jewel. They were the richest nation in the town, carrying on 'almost all the trade with the Levant',[11] and not afraid to display their wealth, since, as the saying had it, in Leghorn it was less dangerous to beat up the grand duke than to beat up a Jew.[12]

There are no studies in depth of the Leghorn Jews, although there is no shortage of archival material on the subject, even in Paris. Of course, their history remains outside the scope of this book, but it is quite clear that, again, Judaism was asserting itself and prospering in Christian lands, because the Children of Israel excelled at fulfilling tasks for which Christians were less well equipped. Once more the tragedy of the dispersion, the socio-political weakness, was proving rich in economic possibilities.

In fact, from the second half of the sixteenth century, the ex-marranos of the Iberian peninsula became a powerful commercial consortium with a network stretching from Turkey to Great Britain, from the Indies to Brazil, which was at the same time a semi-secret society whose members had undergone initiation by successfully thwarting the designs of the Spanish Inquisition. They thus maintained solidarity and close contacts among themselves. Scattered in all the ports of the world by the hazard of their escapes and wanderings, they were admirably placed to hasten the pace of all types of trade and thus contribute to making the modern world what it is today. One of their principal trump cards was the permanent state of peace they preserved with the various powers, Christian or Moslem, Protestant or Catholic. As a result of their trade, they had an intelligence service every-where—from their unsurpassed informers the governments of the great powers sought, even begged, information, no matter whether intrigues or wars with the Levant or the affairs of America were involved.[13] As diplomatic agents, they negotiated peace treaties; as adventurers working on their own account, they instigated reversals of alliances.[14] Their great maritime trade was a family affair. Look at the Franco clan operating from Leghorn, for example, around 1740–5: two brothers settled there, two more at London, and a fifth at Amsterdam, as well as a brother-in-law; there were cousins by marriage at Bayonne, at the gateway to Spain; nephews were in charge of running the Smyrna branch. What resources they must have possessed to be able to load iron and cattle on to two English vessels at St Petersburg for sale in Smyrna, or to load a rich cargo of 320 pieces of serge, 2,562 skins, 280 barrels of tin on to a Dunkirk vessel at London, under a false Dutch bill of lading (for fear of Spanish pirates); or to arm the privateer Le Diamant at Algiers (or at Leghorn itself?) in the name of Messrs Godfrey and Chamberlain, English merchants!

But although we have histories of the prestigious Sephardim—those at London, Amsterdam and Hamburg, and those at Venice described in masterly style by Gino Luzzato[15]—we know nothing about those of the trading centre of Leghorn—'the largest, as well as the most commercial, town of the states of Italy', to quote a French account of 1773, from which Venice tried to steal the Jews in 1732 to revive its own 'exhausted trade'.

# CHAPTER XI

# The Jews and the Evolution of Christian Attitudes (Rome)

One ghetto of Jews proves the truth of the religion of Jesus Christ better than a whole school of theologians—Gianbattista Roberti, *Del legger libri di metafisica e di divertimento* . . . , Rome, 1773, p. 20

## UNDER THE LAST RENAISSANCE POPES

Jewish historians are almost unanimous in describing the first half of the sixteenth century as the happiest period in the history of the Jews in the Papal State. The appeal by the humanist Johannes Reuchlin to Bonnetto de Lattès, Leo X's doctor, requesting him to intervene in his conflict with the Dominicans, is a good illustration of the influence of certain Jews at the papal court at that time. Other examples can be found in the adventures of David Reubeni who in 1524 came to offer Clement VII an alliance with a mythical Jewish realm in Arabia, to fight the Turkish Empire with him. Most of the Jews who frequented the corridors of the Curia believed his statements, and the pope followed their advice. He furnished the adventurer with letters of recommendation to the king of Portugal and other monarchs, and encouraged his activities over several years. The affair can be properly understood only against the background of the restlessness and dreams of the Portuguese New Christians. Objects of cupidity and an apple of discord between the powers, they were an active and industrious population, 'thanks to whom trade, industry and public revenue are growing daily', to quote their king, John III of Portugal. The last Renaissance popes treated the New Christians very liberally. At Rome, the main theatre of their struggle against the Portuguese Inquisition, they maintained a sort of permanent 'pressure group' charged with obtaining the favours and indulgences of the Holy See. Clement VII and Paul III welcomed them into the Papal State with open arms—and the latter was sharply criticised for so doing by the Portuguese delegate to the Council of Trent. Paul, according to a lampoon, was 'as pleasant to the marranos, who denied the divinity of Christ, as he was harsh towards the Protestants, who denied the divinity of the pope.'

Mention has already been made of the interaction between the rise of large-scale maritime and colonial trade in the sixteenth century and the persecution of the New Christians; the arrangement of channels for the flight of men and capital or, put another way, how religious fanaticism can spur on commercial transactions in certain circumstances. So far, this fascinating topic of economic history has primarily been tackled in studies of religious history.[1]

It is of interest here only insofar as the existence of the marranos inevitably had certain repercussions on the money trade of the Italian Jews, in the unexplored territory of attitudes and beliefs. Some of the accounts circulating about the sack of Rome in 1527 stated that the Spanish troops consisted of marranos or even that they included thousands of Jews, thus reflecting the common conviction that the Spaniards' faith was tainted with Judaism. From this, it can be assumed that the reason why the refugees from the Iberian peninsula, though less numerous than indigenous Jews or those originating elsewhere, seemed to predominate was perhaps not so much their wealth as a sort of ubiquity which they acquired in the eyes of Christians. However, while hatred of them grew, the Holy See worked out a policy towards them which foreshadowed that of the mercantilist princes of following centuries. After the annexation of Ancona (1532), Paul III attracted marranos to the free port he created there and granted them a broad range of privileges. Their influx seems to have ensured the prosperity of port and town; in 1549 they were granted the concession of the local lending bank. The two most striking points in their *condotta* were the interest rate, which at 15 per cent was unusually low for the period, and a special clause whereby these ex-marranos were under the sole jurisdiction of His Holiness, and protected from that of the Inquisition. In 1553 Pope Julius III again renewed the privileges of the Portuguese of Ancona, on condition that an annual tax of 1,000 *scudi* was paid.

At Rome, however, many signs foreshadowed the drama to come. If the setting up of a Monte di Pietà in 1539 did not have serious repercussions on the money trade of the Jews there until the following century, the missionary activity which Ignatius Loyola embarked on in 1540 fairly quickly degenerated into systematic harassment. Above all, the creation of the Roman Inquisition in 1542 threatened almost immediate consequences for all the Jews of Italy, from the beginning of the following decade. In 1553, in fact, a squabble took place between two patrician Christian printers at Venice, Giustiniani and Bragadini, who printed rival editions of the Talmud and other Hebrew works (or were acting as figureheads for Jewish entrepreneurs?). It was followed by accusations and counter-accusations of blasphemy contained in the competing versions, and resulted in a condemnation by the Inquisitor-General, Giovanni Pietro Caraffa, of all versions of the sacred book on the grounds that it contained a number of blasphemies against the laws of both Christ and Moses. Copies of the Talmud, together with other Hebrew books, were confiscated and burned throughout Italy. The operation was repeated later to such good effect that in the following century Leon da Modena could write: 'The Talmud remains particularly forbidden in Italy, where it is neither read nor to be seen.' The rabbis immediately gathered for an inter-community conference at Ferrara (1554), and instituted their own preventive censorship in an effort to save what could be saved of the repositories of their traditions. The vast wave of emotion which swept through the Jews of Italy was also perhaps caused by a presentiment born of ancestral experience that the burning of their books ran a great risk of being followed by the burning of their people.

## FROM PAUL IV TO PIUS V

In May 1555 Cardinal Caraffa ascended the throne of St Peter under the name of Paul IV. 'This Paul', wrote the chronicler Joseph Ha-Cohen, 'was, for our many sins, a passionate, quick-tempered man, who invented all manner of decrees against the Jews ... He also did a great deal of harm to the Catholics and his greed was the cause of a violent war among them ... All the thoughts of Paul, this perverse Theatine, in respect of the Jews were aimed only at causing them ill, never good ... Like crimes had never before been committed in Italy'.[2]

Such tones recur when nineteenth- and even twentieth-century classic Jewish historians mention Caraffa. Their tendency to 'moralise' history by setting the sufferings of the Children of Israel against the cruelty of their persecutors, thus giving priority to the role of individuals in historical development, has already been noted. The worsening of the Jews' lot under Paul IV was truly spectacular. The terror which crashed down on the marranos of Ancona and the flames of the stakes which put a temporary end to the prosperity of the port are hard to explain simply as a coincidence. On the other hand, they did augur an upheaval in Church structure concerning the relationship between the Holy See and the Jews, which led to a completely new integration of the Jews into the world of Catholicism. The turning-point in this change was the *Cum nimis absurdum* bull in which Paul IV decreed a series of measures relating to the Jews, designed to reduce to a minimum their contact with the Christian population. The most radical of these measures was the creation of a Jewish *vicus* or *seraglio* (the word 'ghetto' was used only later), set up on the banks of the Tiber in the most ill-famed district of Rome. Such ghettos were also set up in provincial towns and larger villages in the Papal State. Jews were also forbidden to engage in different types of business, with the exception of pawnbroking and rag-picking. Other provisions refer to the liquidation of landed property and the annulment of dispensations from wearing the distinctive badge. The pope tried to get the other Italian states to adopt these decrees but, despite his remonstrances, marranos in Venice were not harassed, and the duke of Tuscany refused to force his Jewish subjects to wear a yellow beret. 'There can be no question of making the Jews wear a yellow beret, the thing is absurd', was the opinion of Lelio Torelli, one of the duke's counsellors. None the less, the near future was going to show that the time for such measures was ripe.

At first, the Jews of Rome seem to have thought that the *Cum nimis absurdum* bull was only a means of bringing financial pressure to bear, but it was really something quite different. The new pope, who had once exclaimed: 'It is a miracle that this Holy See has been able to keep going, since our predecessors did everything to destroy it', behaved like a convinced and sincere man. An offer of 40,000 *scudi* did not move him. As a gesture of silent protest, many Jews then threatened to clothe themselves in yellow from head to toe 'in order to be even more reformed'. Others fled from a rule which had become inhospitable. The anti-Jewish ardour of Paul IV might be compared with his animosity towards the Spaniards, 'those God-damned heretics, the seed of Jews and marranos'. By including the refugees from Spain and, by extension, all Jews within the same hatred, he was only following a recurrent line of thought.[3] But whatever the personal motives behind his actions and decrees, this reformer was first and foremost behaving like a child of his generation and his day.

The century of the Reformation did in fact see a deterioration in the condition of the Jews throughout the West under both Catholic and Protestant princes, and doctrine and revealed Scriptures were cited to justify the measures taken against them. In this sense, Paul IV did not introduce any innovations. All he did was to reiterate the provisions contained in the *Corpus juris canonici* (in the chapter 'De Judaeis') and in his predecessors' bulls. What was new was the strict application, the final shot, fired at the practice of every sort of toleration and indulgence which the aforesaid predecessors had liberally dispensed to the Jews; in other words, at dealings permanently tainted with simony. By taking the struggle against such abuses seriously, Caraffa was proving faithful to the spirit of the Catholic Reformation and the Council of Trent. It is true that the morals of the Curia could be effectively reformed only in spheres where the interests challenged were not too enormous; it is remarkable to realise that the pope reorganised the régime of the Jewish *banchi* only on points of secondary importance, although the money trade practised by the Jews was equally only by toleration, according to doctrine. But the weakness of the commercial bourgeoisie of Rome, the financial 'squeeze' and the non-existence of a local monied aristocracy apparently excluded a vigorous expansion of the Monte di Pietà which would have made it possible to dispense with the Jews' services, as at Florence. In this context, the question of 'Jewish usury' was not even raised at the Council of Trent.

It was not, therefore, as usurers that the Jews of the Papal State were first penalised, but as infidels *condemned by God to eternal slavery because of their transgression,* who, none the less, abusing the charitable toleration of the Christians, *have risen to such a degree of effrontery that they not only make so bold as to live amidst the Christians, but also in the vicinity of their churches, with no distinguishing dress, renting palaces and buying and owning land in the main streets and squares* . . . (Introduction to the *Cum nimis absurdum* bull).

The most original provision in the bull (since this point had only been sketched out in previous papal decrees) was the collective segregation that its first article laid down. Jews in all the various countries of the Diaspora had always had a habit of clustering together in their own district, sometimes protected by gates and inside padlocks; in other words, they themselves chose if they wanted to live inside or outside the Jewry. In future this choice would no longer be theirs for their district was to be bolted from without. The *banchieri*, and others enjoying the privileges of wealth, who, despite age-old restrictions, had acquired residences in the best neighbourhoods of the Eternal City and lived among Christians, had to sell their houses or cancel their leases and move into the ghetto. These enforced liquidations caused them heavy losses, and generally, moreover, their wealth could no longer compensate for or mask their inferior status which the bull was trying to emphasise in various ways, and the resulting debasement and discredit could have only unfavourable repercussions on their business.

Jewish trade and banking declined as a new Christian bourgeoisie arose—this point has already been sufficiently stressed. But it is also important not to become hypnotised by too narrow formulae. Not only must this sort of competitive pressure be taken into account; the part played by the general evolution of attitudes, the new imperatives of the Counter-Reformation, and also the stress laid on external appearance, on conduct outwardly better ordered, cannot be ignored. This last factor applied particularly at Rome itself, where Tiepolo, the Venetian ambassador, noted in 1569 that men, if they were not, at least appeared to be, better. In the light of these improved morals, which were not achieved without recourse to severe administrative measures —the establishment of the ghetto takes on the utmost significance. The powerful personality of a pope may lie at its origin, but its success, its quite rapid spread to other Italian and foreign states, clearly show that it corresponded to the spirit of the times, to the new moral demands which characterised the second half of the sixteenth century.

The pope who succeeded Paul IV, Pius IV (1559–65), a Medici, considerably relaxed, though he did not abolish, the ghetto régime, and repealed some of the other provisions of the *Cum nimis absurdum* bull. This 'last of the Renaissance popes' saw no absurdity in collecting fines for not wearing the yellow beret and other transgressions, and this income was allocated to the restoration of San Giovanni, the Lateran basilica. On the other hand, he made the Jewish *banchi* lower the interest rate, with which his predecessor had not interfered, from 30 to 24 per cent. One might conclude from this that, unlike Paul IV, he was concerned with the earthly well-being of his subjects, whether Christian or Jewish. With Pius V (1566–72), another Inquisitor-General, another indomitable old man, mounted the throne of St Peter. He immediately restored the provisions of Paul IV to all their early rigour and, with greater success than the latter, succeeded in imposing them on other Italian states. Going further and citing the Jews' pernicious influence, he decreed general banishment in February 1569, though he made an exception in the case of the two ghettos at Rome and Ancona. The inhabitants of the rest of the ghettos in the Papal State, numbering some thousands, had to take the road into exile or else crowd into the two Jewries which were allowed to survive. When commenting on his decision, Pius V referred back to the example of the Catholic kings and other Christian princes. But, unlike them, he retained two important ghettos in his state: was this through missionary zeal, in accordance with the great tradition of the Holy See, or through fear of socio-economic repercussions? Was it, in a phrase, so as to convert the Jews better or to tax them better? Perhaps both considerations were involved. However, there is scarcely any mention of missionary projects or charity in the scant documentation which make it possible to glimpse the pope's real purpose.[4] In the decree of banishment, the exception made for the Jews of Rome and Ancona is justified by their economic importance. In the instructions the pope sent to the prelates of the Comtat Venaissin, the importance of the witness they bore for Christ figures as a subsidiary motive, but the merchants he allowed to remain seemed to him sufficient for that purpose.

From the first months of the papacy of Pius V, people at Rome seemed to have been expecting a general expulsion of the Jews, particularly after the early measures taken against prostitutes. A curious anonymous petition in August 1566 entreated the pope to *tolerate* both categories in his city, following the example set by Christ, 'who tolerated in the world Hebrews, adulterers and prostitutes'. By breaking with this tradition of charity, the unknown writer insinuated, did not His vicar fear to draw the wrath of God upon himself? In short, the old Roman realism must, I think, be taken into consideration, and it is particularly evident in the case of the Jews of Ancona, who were excepted from banishment by the terms of the bull because their presence facilitated trade with the Levant and because the pope could keep a closer eye on them.

According to Clemens Bauer, the historian of papal finances,

Pius V was 'the incarnation of the spirituality of the Counter-Reformation', and he estimates that 'the attempt to put the Christian idea into practice was matched by taking the opposite line on smaller points.'[5] It is perhaps worth remembering that Pius V is still the only pope between 1300 and 1900 to have been canonised. 'As he was the torment of the Jews, he was raised to the first rank,' wrote Joseph Ha-Cohen ironically on the subject of his election. Contemporaries criticised this saint for his moral severity; it was said that he wanted to make Rome the world's cloisters. He did in fact show extreme intolerance towards dubious faith or morals, vice and idleness: he hunted down prostitutes, expelled them from Rome and attempted to shut them too up in a ghetto: he expelled vagabonds; he wanted to create separate districts for beggars and the poor. He was particularly harsh on the gypsies, whom he sent to the galleys, and he threatened adulterers with the death penalty. In the eyes of history, he remains the pope who best symbolises the Catholic Reformation. But the two basic related ideas of *harshness* and *intolerance* deserve a moment's attention.

It is difficult to deny that Christian intolerance was accentuated as a result of the great increase in population during the sixteenth century. That principles, at least, if not morals, became harsher at the same period contains a warning against the temptation of direct interpretations or causalities. Harsher applications of ecclesiastical concepts and constitutions probably became inevitable, insofar as the reforms expressed the aspirations of a literate bourgeoisie to a religion which was integrated and internally logical; to a Church which would no longer hold up its own precepts to ridicule by the practice of indulgences, toleration and other licences. It can also be assumed that the regard for propriety and intellectual honesty, the hunger for a law which would not remain a dead letter—which would, on the contrary, become universally valid—were not alien to the germination of the Western scientific spirit, a distant corollary perhaps of the evangelical intuitions of clarity: 'Let your yea be yea; and your nay, nay'. But this harshness, ordained by or resulting from the struggle against the intellectual incoherence and naïve hypocrisy of the

183

middle ages, was going to lead to the subtler and far crueller hypocrisy of modern times. Caught in its own moral trap, the new order, rationalist, bourgeois and Christian, by virtue of the inflexibility of its structures, could do no more than deny or suppress by violence anything that challenged its achievement or ethical perfection. It put this denial into practice by driving everything that shocked or challenged it out of sight, relegated to the shadows of ghettos and prisons. This, I think, in the last analysis, is the deep-seated explanation of the creation of the ghettos, which was a prelude to other 'great confinements' on a much wider scale: imprisonment of beggars, vagabonds, the unemployed, the mad, freethinkers, mingled with criminals—some aspect of the Jews seemed to place them in each of these categories. It was also a prelude to the brutal events of colonial conquest and of exploitation, to innumerable persecutions carried out in a thousand different ways, but provided by the new harshness of principles with suitable ideological justifications, particularly imperative in the case of the Jews.

Thus one point in the 'Moral Reformation' which Christianity so ardently desired was carried out, starting with Rome, at the expense of the Children of Israel, whose delicate position emerges as being one of the lines of least resistance of the old order. Toleration of them was reduced to its simplest expression, as will be seen. Their crime of being Jews became punishable by a life sentence of collective relegation in the same way as the Christian bourgeois order tended to regard indigence, maladjustment, colour or madness as offences in other men and other groups. If the sad privilege of being the first to suffer this sum of suffering and injustice fell to the Jews, it was also perhaps that they, unlike their motley companions in misfortune, most frequently illiterate and unpolished, were not ordinary subjects of history.

## THE GHETTO PERIOD

*The Vale of Tears* described Gregory XIII (1572–85) as an 'educated and good man', and it is true that under his papacy some relaxations were granted to the Jews. He allowed them to carry on different types of trade and to travel to provincial fairs without the yellow beret. At the same time, the legal interest rate was lowered again, from 24 to 18 per cent. This must first of all be seen as the result of a general fall in the price of money, but the *banchieri* probably were also easier to persuade when the man in power was showing them some benevolence. Sixtus V (1585-90), the great reorganiser of the Papal State, was still more favourably disposed towards them, and even promised them that he would transfer the ghetto bodily to the outskirts of the city; the plan was not carried out. This pope deliberately surrounded himself with Jews: two of his doctors were Jewish, as was his financial adviser, Giovanni Lopez. Jean Delumeau has revealed the role of this marrano in the reorganisation of the papal finances and the expansion in the sale of positions.[6] Clement VIII (1592-1605), on the other hand, expelled those Jews whom Sixtus V had admitted into the provinces of the Papal State, and unleashed new persecutions of the Talmud.

Such variations from papacy to papacy never went so far as to challenge the principle of a closed ghetto, which was thenceforth respected by all the popes. The idea of the isolation of the Jews became rooted in custom so that other Italian governments were obliged to follow suit, though sometimes with considerable time-lags—some of these ghettos were created only in the eighteenth century. At the same time, the Holy See was concerned with evangelising its own ghetto. Another papal provision, three centuries old but hitherto entirely neglected, was put into practice in 1584. It obliged the Jews to go to church collectively and at regular intervals to be present at special sermons. Moreover, the custom of forcing unbelievers to listen to this type of preaching seems to have been fairly widespread in the sixteenth century. The stubborn flock were spared no invective.[7] The following sample gives some idea of the tenor of sermons which threw both the priest and his captive audience in Rome into a passion:[8]

> Compare, O Jews, the hatred you have for us with that we have for you, and the reasons we have, with those you allege. We are the

masters and you the slaves. We tolerate you in our country, we allow you to have dealings with us, we make use of you in many ways and, if you behave well, we give you privileges, favours and caresses. Knowing that your religion is erroneous, we tell you so with charity, we preach to you and publish books to make you see what everyone sees. We do not punish you with prison, exile and death except when we are provoked by your misdeeds; and yet we know that you have killed our leader, the Lord of the universe, that you have wanted to persecute and exterminate us . . .

Not surprisingly, the Jews did their utmost and employed all means to escape from the obligatory sermons: by paying someone to 'replace' them, by making a noise, or by stuffing their ears with wax, despite the presence in the church of guards ordered to watch them and to cane the trouble-makers. Otherwise, the wind of the spirit blows where it will, and perhaps one must believe the evidence which shows that conversions did take place as a result of these sermons.

Blows of fate and expulsions had better powers of persuasion. There were many baptisms of Jews under Paul IV and Pius V, particularly in 1569 at the time of the expulsions. The missionary zeal of priests or ordinary worshippers egged on the doctrine of free consent in this matter, particularly in the case of very young children, to produce other contingents of neophytes who were instructed in the Casa dei Catecumeni (Home for Converted Jews) founded by Ignatius Loyola with the help of gifts he had collected. Its maintenance was then made the responsibility of the Jewish community, which was consequently forced to nurse its own apostates. What categories of Jews could have let themselves be converted most easily? According to the Holy See, it was the poorest; according to the community, the richest. Perhaps neophytes were in fact primarily recruited from both extremities of the social scale, even though here and there the argument was advanced that financial considerations were involved.[9] It would be interesting to know more about this conversion movement which is of such real relevance to the study of both Christian and Jewish attitudes and which, besides, certainly had an effect on the size of the ghetto population, but we have no relevant statistics with any degree of reliability. A very questionable document mentions 2,432 baptisms in Rome between 1636 and 1790. T. K. Hoffmann refers to some forty conversions annually in the sixteenth century and a dozen or so after that, but not all the converts passed through the Casa dei Catecumeni. It might be added in this context that rich Jews on the point of conversion deliberately came to be baptised in the Eternal City, where the sovereign pontiff himself sometimes acted as godfather.[10] The sources contain information on a handful of personal conflicts and dramas resulting from conversions but, because of their small numbers, the absorption of the converts into the Italian population did not pose social problems such as those which faced the New Christians in the Iberian peninsula. It is also known that the Holy See granted the poorest of these Roman neophytes the licence to manufacture sulphur matches, which had been withdrawn from the Jews at the end of the seventeenth century. Others, even poorer, were reduced to beggary which, it can be assumed, preceded and did not follow a baptism requested with an issue of alms in mind. Rabbinic culture enabled other converts to devote themselves to peaceful scholarly works within the bosom of the church, unless they spent their time evangelising their ex-co-religionists, to the understandable fury of the latter. Still others excelled in commercial activities, sometimes continuing to trade with the ghetto.

To return to the ghetto: in order to isolate it better, to reduce contacts between Christians and Jews to the minimum, the papal administration formulated involved legislation. That it was imperfectly observed is shown by the frequent renewal of the prohibitions, which went as far as to forbid Christian barbers to shave Jews. It is best summed up in the synthesis which the Roman Inquisition made of it in 1829, when this legislation was still in force, moving from the nourishment of the body to that of the mind:

> We command that no one dare to transgress the decrees, constitutions and papal bulls which forbid individual relationships between Jews and Christians, such as those of sleeping, eating, playing or dancing together, and taking coffee, in the same way as Christians are forbidden to attend, and Jews to admit them, to their Hebraic

ceremonies, synagogues, sermons, marriages, circumcisions and festivals; it is besides forbidden to the one to visit the houses or schools of the other in order to learn or teach reading, writing, singing, dancing, or to render other services, or to nurse or educate the children, or to do anything else . . .

Spontaneous and generous relationships, through which people love their neighbours, were therefore prohibited. By trying in this way to limit contacts with the Jews, solely to commercial or financial relationships, in which the bargainers arranged things reciprocally, the Holy See paved the way for tension and hatred,[11] and accentuated the Jews' 'otherness', as well as the 'obduracy' and 'Christophobia' with which it ceaselessly reproached them. Such was the vicious circle of segregation and persecution but, at the same time, the Church was working objectively for the preservation of Judaism. A psychohistoric dialectic of this type, however sound, does not easily lend itself to documentary proof. Among other illustrations is a linguistic phenomenon: namely, the formation of a Roman-Jewish dialect, closely related to sixteenth-century Roman speech, of which some traces still remain. The tangible wall of the ghetto and the living conditions within this artificial isolation provide other touchstones regarding the alienation of its inhabitants.

To begin with some demographic data: the ghetto was established in the former Jewish quarter of S. Angelo, the most cramped district in the city. In 1527 it accommodated two-thirds of the Jewish population of Rome, according to the *Descriptio Urbis*, who lived intermingled with Christians. Between the first and the third quarters of the sixteenth century, this population as a whole had approximately doubled, so that its density tripled as a result. In addition, the removal into the ghetto of rich Jews whose money enabled them to procure extra space there resulted in increased crowding of those less well endowed. After its creation by Paul IV, the ghetto was slightly enlarged on two occasions, under Pius V and Sixtus V. The definitive area, calculated by Attilio Milano to be slightly under three hectares,[12] contained over a hundred houses (134 in 1676) containing between 3,500 and 4,500 inhabitants (4,500 in 1668): a density it would be hard to find equalled, and higher even than in the worst shanty-towns today. This was the cause of the animation and activity which probably increased the picturesque nature of the ghetto in the eyes of tourists; in any case, it featured among the curiosities to be visited in the Eternal City. Numerous descriptions are available: Charles de Brosses, President of the Dijon parliament, for example, summed it up in a single word, *'arch-filthiness'*, not the least evocative comment; another French traveller, François Deseine, went into more detail:[13]

> What they call *il ghetto* is the Jewish quarter, which is surrounded by walls and closed by doors, so that this perfidious nation shall have no communication with Christians at night; as they are not able to live elsewhere or enlarge their district, which is bordered on one side by the Tiber and on the other by the street of the Fish-Market, and because there are a very large number of them, this riff-raff multiplied extremely, this is why several families live in the same room, so that the whole quarter stinks, continually and intolerably.

According to current general opinion, this stench was constitutionally inherent in the Jews. 'It is wrong', wrote a great Italian doctor, Bernardino Ramazzini (1633–1714), 'to regard this stench as natural and endemic to them; that exuded by the lower classes among them is caused by the cramped conditions of their houses.'[14] An emotive sense *par excellence*, the sense of smell served to express the public's repugnance for the people of the ghetto. The papacy, for its part, appealed to the sense of sight, demonstrating its contempt by appropriate ritual ceremonies and acts[15] in accordance with contemporary taste for ostentation and displays. It is not possible to linger over the fascinating problems of collective psychology posed by the way in which the Jews, confident of the truth of their religion, resigned themselves to these humiliations, continued to revere their derided law, blessed the God of Israel for the compensations (sometimes substantial) of their trade, and even drew from their downfall the wherewithal to fortify ancestral pride or vainglory.

In the ghetto, which became the principal bazaar of Rome, one of its manufactories and its great centre for credit sales, the houses still legally remained in the hands of their former Christian

G*

owners, since Jews were forbidden to own landed property. To prevent speculation in rents, Pius IV included among the favours he did the Jews in 1562 an order that the amount charged should be controlled 'at a fair price', while the rabbis put into operation a Talmudic rule designed to forestall the eviction of a Jew to the advantage of a co-religionist who offered more. These were the two foundations of the *jus gazaga* of the ghetto which ensured that the Jews would permanently occupy their dwellings at extremely low rents. 'The ghetto is always growing in people, but never in rents', noted a Roman pamphleteer around 1665.[16] But the *jus gazaga* was a law of leasehold only, and rents did rise accordingly. There is a similarity here with the situation which grew up in Paris [and London] after 1945, when the rights of sitting tenants and the housing shortage resulted in the well-known emergence of 'key-money'. The statutory ghetto leases became one of the main factors in the wealth of its inhabitants, for the rich could speculate and invest their capital.

Contracts executed and authenticated by a lawyer tell, for example, of the transfer in 1619 of the *jus gazaga* on part of a house—three rooms and a staircase, described in minute detail and reminiscent of a labyrinthine pigeonhouse—for 1,050 *scudi*. The annual rent for the whole house, which belonged to the duke of Poli, was 53 *scudi*. Needless to say, Christians had no incentive to build in the ghetto in these circumstances, while Jews, who did not have the right to do so, were at the most content to make repairs at their own expense.

The lack of space, the co-habitation of several tenants, or even families, in every room led to the creation of rights of way over entrances and corridors (such as those existing over footpaths and tracks in the countryside through land which has been divided up). The congestion of the ghetto, the three-dimensional space transformed into a commodity as necessary as it was rare, which was cornered by the rich at the expense of the poor, is sufficient to explain the staggering key-money of the *jus gazaga*. Thus there must have been a good deal of money about.

The principal capitalists of the ghetto continued to be the *banchieri*. Their number had been fixed by statute at forty in the time of Gregory XIII, but was raised to seventy by the device of concessions granted 'supernumerally' at the end of the sixteenth century, to fall to twenty in the second half of the seventeenth. The author of a small book, *Il vero stato degli Hebrei di Roma*, who probably belonged to Apostolic Chamber circles and was remarkably well informed on ghetto affairs, estimated the capital of the *banchieri* in 1668, at six-sevenths of the Chamber's fortune, to be about 800,000 *scudi*—of which only 150,000 were invested with moneylenders. At the same period, the Rome Monte di Pietà was lending 400,000–500,000 *scudi* a year on security. It can be assumed that in the sixteenth century, when the Monte, according to the picturesque expression of *Il vero stato*, 'was only an atom', the capital of all the *banchieri* taken together was higher, and exceeded a million *scudi*. An order of magnitude can be obtained by remembering that the capital of one of the richest Christian businessmen in Rome (Giuseppe Giustiniani) was 500,000 *scudi* at this time, and that the fortunes of certain cardinals seem to have been higher still.

The positions or offices of the Jewish *banchieri* were in the gift of the cardinal camerlengo, who, at least before 1607, disposed of them at his will, via his chief auditor as intermediary. In the case of a vacancy, these offices reverted to him. It was certainly in the self-interest of these two prelates not to leave positions unfilled (a concession granted in 1575 expressly states this, speaking of the losses and harm suffered by the camerlengo because of a vacancy),[17] and it must be presumed that it was the stake they had in increasing their number which led them to create 'super-numary' positions. Responsum no. 38 by Leon da Modena says firmly that at Rome and Ancona their number grew 'daily'. This unusual feature must in my opinion be attributed to the fact that the camerlengo and his chief auditor also purchased their own offices and that these were the most expensive of all the great positions at the Curia.

Among the numerous offices which the camerlengo had at his disposal and in which he in turn traded, those at the Jewish banks must have played a part in fixing the high price of his own. This probably explains the proliferation of *banchieri* at Rome and

Ancona and the creation of supernumary positions. Another distinctive feature of these Roman concessions, which those of Ancona did not share,[18] was that they did not carry specifications as to duration, contrary to the *condotte* of other Italian states. This would seem to imply that they were granted for life.

In any case, it can be seen that it was through the expedient of the venality of offices that the Jewish *banchieri* were grafted on to the very individual financial structures of the Holy See. The time was past when Jews dealt directly with sovereign pontiffs. Interposed between the two, the camerlengo recouped from the one side part of his payment to the other; but the principle of 'give and take' continued. Not surprisingly Sixtus V, who considerably extended the sale of offices, was also concerned with expanding and reorganising the system of papal licences. It must be remembered too that the sale of positions and privileges granted to Jews posed problems of a moral order, similar to the difficulties which St Thomas Aquinas discussed in the advice he gave to the Duchess of Brabant. But it would be easier for the Holy See to suppress the Jewish banks, in view of the relatively modest revenue the Curia drew from them, than to put an end to the venality of offices, as will be seen.

Individual *banchi* certainly varied in importance, and it would seem that some were dormant, reduced to the simple possession of a personal *jus foenerandi* licence. In 1599 Sabbato Angelo da Serre, in a deed signed in the presence of a lawyer, sold the *jus foenerandi* which he himself had acquired from a neophyte to Prospero da Capua for 250 *scudi* cash down, all other goods and rights reserved. In another sale which took place in 1601, because the heiress, a widow, was unable to practise as a *banchiere*, the price was 1,078 *scudi*, and the document mentions the transfer of all property and securities. (These, as we shall see, had a much higher value in other cases.) It can therefore be assumed that 250 *scudi* represented the current value of the *jus foenerandi* licence alone; when he set up, the new holder also had to deposit 25 *scudi* with the corporation of Jewish *banchieri* of Rome. This gave the corporation as a whole a value in the sixteenth century varying between 10,000 and 18,000 *scudi*, according to the year. This is relatively little in comparison with the office of cardinal camerlengo which was sold for 50,000 to 60,000 *scudi*, but the Jewish *banchieri* of Rome were not his only source of income, and this chief official of the Papal State probably had ways, other than the purely statutory, of levying a tithe on Jewish business. The financial relationship between the ghetto and the papal administration—of the utmost complexity—will be discussed further at the end of this book.

The camerlengo and his circle, however, obviously had nothing to gain by encouraging the Monte di Pietà at the expense of Jewish banking. Neither would this have been to the advantage of rich Romans, already guaranteed regular yields of 10 or 12 per cent from papal loans. Consequently, despite effective reforms made under Gregory XIII, it was not until the middle of the seventeenth century that the Rome Monte di Pietà really sprang into action and became one of the principal tools of the financial policy of the Holy See.[19] In the interim, the Jews strained their ingenuity to utilise the competing establishment to their advantage by various stratagems, about which we have some vivid information, notably:

pawning or re-pawning by Jews at the Monte di Pietà in order to procure ready cash;

agreements at auction sales to lower prices;

a Monte di Pietà regulation of 1605 forbade bidders 'to insult, defy, glare at, harm, cut off a finger or in any way to threaten or mock those who bid at such auctions . . . or in any way whatever to shout at, defy, insult or mock our officials, by deed or by word'; and, if a 1680 report is to be believed, secret agreements between *banchieri*, and Monte employees who would deliberately put low valuations on objects offered as security in order to prompt borrowers to turn to the *banchieri* (Congregatio de Usuris, I, 6).

Part Two of this book gave examples of the classic credit transactions carried out by the *banchieri* in the richest and most extravagant town in Europe. It happened at Rome, as elsewhere, that rich Christians associated with Jewish lenders: in 1627, for example, Father Ottavio Costa went half shares with the banker Lazzaro Viterbo to advance 10,000 *scudi* to Duke Conti Sforza.

One of the richest ghetto families, the Toscano, who Attilio Milano thinks came to settle at Rome after the closure of the Jewish banks in Tuscany in 1570, seems to have been particularly well in with the Holy See. In 1623 one of its members, Salomone, became official valuer of 'ecclesiastical spoils'; i.e. the property of deceased prelates which reverted to the Holy See. The same year, Gregory XV gave proof of his favour by allowing him, on payment of a dispensation, to marry a second wife during the lifetime of the first: a curious survival of elastic medieval toleration into the seventeenth century.[20] One might say that the Jews' proverbial commercial acumen and flexibility increased as their humiliations grew and their fate became more uncertain: such a doom, only to be averted by the peaceful paths of trade, sharpens awareness of the desires and plans of others, makes it easier to distinguish their strength from their weakness, and teaches the art of turning them to profit. Nothing is more typical from this point of view than the skill of the ghetto people at making trade out of nothing, at exploiting the superstitions of the Romans— particularly the Roman women, by telling their fortunes, selling them magic philtres and, if the expulsion decree of Pius V is to be believed, confusing their faith in various other ways.

But to return to the main trade of the ghetto. Inventories taken after the deaths of *banchieri* describe accumulations of every type of article—often valuable ones. For example, the possessions of Alessandro Viterbo listed in 1688—therefore, note, after the disappearance of the Jewish *banchi*—consisted of piles of bric-à-brac, interminably described in no fewer than forty-three pages of the register executed and authenticated by a lawyer. The inventory for Giuseppe da Velletri in 1653 comprises various property to a total value of 9,407 *scudi*. The miscellaneous articles which filled the ghetto did not remain confined there. Stock was put into circulation in Christian Rome and constantly renewed by the rag-and-bone men, scrap-merchants and brokers of the ghetto, who scoured the town from morning till night, crying 'Aeio!', pushing small handcarts laden with goods, buying, selling and trading. No monopoly was involved, and the guilds of 'second-hand-dealers' and scrap merchants remained Christian guilds.

But it can be assumed that Jews predominated in them from the fact that these were the only two Roman guilds to admit Jews; a Jew could even become an official negotiator with the rag-and-bone men.

Jewish wholesalers also sold new goods and even raw materials, primarily skins from the Levant which they supplied to Christian merchants.

But the great speciality of the ghetto remained secondhand goods, in which, earlier, trade had become widespread. It is most interesting, besides, to note this trade beginning to be converted into *credit sales to individuals*, probably as a growing proportion of borrowers adopted the habit of turning to the Monte di Pietà at the expense of the *banchieri*.

The Jews' skill at this type of trade has attracted the attention of many historians and economists. Over sixty years ago, Werner Sombart thought that he could attribute it to a 'racial aptitude' *sui generis*. Henri Sée and Riccardo Bachi,[21] with a better historical sense, placed the emphasis on the adaptability of a minority group which, in order to survive, had to be satisfied with infinitesimal profits, 'undercutting prices', and some of this second explanation must be considered valid, although the documents suggest that the actuality was simpler. The profession of pawnbroking involved the practice of giving credit; it provided the savoir-faire and the necessary means for the recovery of debts; above all, it poured personal wealth from a variety of sources increasingly into the hands of the lenders. What would be more natural than to recirculate it among Christians by giving credit to the customer? The sale of a cloak of Perpignan wool to Bernardina da Orvieto in December 1598 by Moïse Antonio, a Jew, but not referred to as a banker, for 9 *scudi* payable at a rate of 5 *giulii* a week (four months' credit) is typical. It is interesting to note that in a good half of this type of transaction the purchasers were women; and that sales increased on the eve of the great festivals in April and December—a distant foretaste of today's 'great seasonal sales'.

It was, I think, the prospect of the profits that such dealings could bring in (which, of course, were handled in cash without anything being written down) which sometimes caused the *banchieri* to buy the securities of defaulting debtors, rather than leave them to be sold by auction. In such cases, the document simply said that the debtor who had pledged a certain object for a certain sum with the Jew, sold it, giving up all rights in it, to him for the same sum. According to *Il vero stato*, another practice was to replace the security on the eve of the auction by sending to the auctioneer an article conforming with its description, but of less value. In both cases, the practised eye of the Jew was a trump card of the highest importance.

Polemicising against Jewish grievances, *Il vero stato* paints the economic life of the ghetto in fairly rosy colours, one important statement being that, apart from 20 families of bankers, its inhabitants included 180 families of 'comfortably-off merchants'. Did this designation embrace the troop of traders, intermediaries and brokers, the lowest rung of businessmen who went into partnership or competed to buy and re-sell one lot of furniture or a modest family jewel? This sort of transaction, involving only a few *scudi*, also entailed drawing up complicated contracts, sometimes followed by interminable litigation.

The best streets of the ghetto served as a permanent market, 'the meeting-place', said a traveller, 'of the secondhand goods of the world; there, before every door, in every room, one sees indescribable piles of heaps of fabrics of every shape, every colour, every age; enough to make a coat of many colours large enough to envelop the globe.'[22] This imaginary patchwork coat was pieced together out of Roman cast-offs which the ghetto had laboriously salvaged. The hard-working lowest class of the ghetto who, according to *Il vero stato*, made up three-quarters of the inhabitants, now enter into the picture.

There is usually no documentary evidence about this category of people, who carried out the principal occupations of Jewish artisans: renovation and finishing of secondhand goods, sewing, glove-making and button-making. Ramazzini has left a striking description of their daily round and physiology:[23]

> Nearly all the Jews, and particularly of the lower classes who make up the greater number, practise occupations which require them to be seated. They are for the most part engaged in sewing and making

over old clothes. Their wives and daughters earn their living by their needle; they do not know how to spin, how to card, how to make fabrics or any art of Minerva other than sewing. In this they are so practised and so expert that they mend clothing of wool, silk and other materials so skilfully that the repairs cannot be seen; in Rome, this is termed *rinacchiare*. They make coats for young people out of several pieces sewn together, and live by this expedient.

Such work compels them to apply their eyes closely. All the Jewish women, moreover, keep at their sewing throughout the day and far into the night, using a small lamp and a thin wick. Hence they incur all the ailments consequent upon a sedentary life and in addition suffer in the end from serious shortsightedness; and by the time they are forty they are blind in one eye or else very weak of vision. In addition in almost every town, the Jews are housed or rather enclosed in narrow streets; the women, in all seasons, work by their open windows to be able to see more clearly, so that it is easy to identify the cause of the diseases of the head from which they suffer such as headaches, tooth- and earaches, hoarseness, and the bad state of their eyes; many of them thus become deaf and runny-eyed, as happens to tailors. As for the men, they sit all day in their booths, stitching clothes or stand looking for customers to whom they can sell old rags. Hence they are mostly wasted away, melancholic, hideous to look upon, and often suffering from the itch . . .

After describing other specific ghetto trades, such as the renovation of mattresses, Ramazzini concluded: 'I have known many of these workmen to be almost destroyed by this work and reduced to a state of incurable consumption, who are aware of the origin of their disease, and loathe their trade as the cause of their death'.

The Jews of Rome also practised other humble trades. A report submitted to the Apostolic Chamber by their community at the end of the seventeenth century listed trades from which they had been successively expelled there: the manufacture of gloves and buttons, which each brought in 14,000 *scudi* annually to the ghetto in the past and were henceforth allocated to 'convents, homes and pious establishments for young girls'; the manufacture of sulphur matches, which formerly allowed fifty Jewish families to live, granted to converts. At the same period, a papal adviser suggested the following remedy for the poverty of the Roman ghetto: 'Let them rather be permitted to practise those other arts and trades allowed to them at Florence and elsewhere, and which are prohibited to them here by human laws: these can be changed, for they are voluntary, unlike divine law on usury, which is essential'.

A very active solidarity and a network of charitable works, which increased from eight to thirty in the course of the seventeenth century, helped the lowest classes of the ghetto to bear their poverty. Over and above material assistance, there were brotherhoods created solely to offer consolation and moral comfort to co-religionists. Probably Milano was not wrong to glimpse in this solidarity 'the key to the steadfast resistance of the ghetto'.[24]

# CHAPTER XII

# *The Strange Case of Venice*

Errors and fallacies are the usual satellites of generalisations; truth
always accompanies and is the outcome of details and distinctions—
Simone Luzzatto, *Discorso circa il stato degli hebrei*, Venice, 1638, p. 28a

Like the other great Italian commercial centres, Venice held the
Jews at arm's length for a long time, and the fiscal and moral
advantages that Jewish banking offered did not overcome its
leaders' mistrust and fear of competition until the Republic
reached the summit of its power. When Mestre was acquired in
1336, local Jewish lenders were allowed to live there; in 1366, a
*condotta* was granted to *banchieri* of German origin which allowed
them to operate in Venice itself, but on condition that they
continued to live at Mestre, on the mainland. It can thus be seen
that their insular position enabled the Jews to be set apart in
accordance with canonic doctrine right from the start. Venetian
originality was expressed in other ways in the organisation of
lending banks; in particular, the Serenissima would never allow
any interference whatever in these matters by the Holy See, so
that the system of papal licences was not introduced there.

As Father Pietro Pirri has recalled, 'Venice was one of the first
European powers which arrogated to itself the right to legislate
on ecclesiastical and inter-religious matters independently of
Rome',[1] and it seems legitimate to add that the republic demon-

strated a much stricter regard for principles than the other Italian states (notably the Holy See), on the questions both of usury and of the Jews. As far as the Jews are concerned, I am not going into the minor incidents which marked the renewal of the *condotte* throughout the fifteenth century, but want to deal with debates and conflicts which arose over the lending banks at the beginning of the following century.

At the time of the wars of the League of Cambrai, the Jews of Mestre and the *terra ferma* sought refuge in Venice, as their *condotta* permitted in case of disturbances. This occasioned a renewed outburst of Franciscan agitation and increased propaganda in favour of setting up a Monte di Pietà. As the wars dragged on, the Senate took the decision in 1516 to isolate the Jews within the town itself, by transferring them to a small island in the parish of San Girolamo on the site of a disused cannon foundry ('geto' from *getare*—to cast metal—this could be one origin of the word 'ghetto'). Then in 1519, when the *condotta* expired, extensive discussions began in the Senate about future arrangements for the Jews. Many details of this are known from the diaries of Marino Sanuto, who had himself been a member of the Senate the year before.

The debate was opened on 9 November 1519 by Tomaso Mocenigo, who proposed renewing the *condotta* on payment of 6,000 ducats, but lowering the interest rate from 20 to 15 per cent. Antonio Condulmieri opposed the renewal. He invoked the holy canons to demand the Jews' departure, warned against divine wrath and held up the Kingdoms of France and Spain, where prosperity had followed the expulsion of the Children of Israel, as examples. Gabriele Moro went even further, recalling the recent misfortunes of princes at Naples and Milan who protected them. On the other hand, other speakers pointed out that the Turks had acquired a great deal of wealth as a result of their presence. Still in their favour, the old Senator Antonio Grimani argued on the basis of the needs of the poor, and Francesco Bragadini referred both to the absence of a Monte di Pietà in Venice and the toleration Rome was exercising towards the Jews.

The debate ended without a decision. In Sanuto's opinion, no one had spoken sincerely,

> so that the council was very much in two minds, some for and others against; but no one dared speak out [frankly] in favour of the *condotta*, lest it should be said that the Jews had bribed him in their favour . . . others did not want to allow the Jews to stay in this land on any account, *some out of pious righteousness and others because they themselves wanted to lend at interest, not at 20 per cent, but at 40, 50 or more, as goes on at the Rialto.*

There could be no clearer summary of the contrasting motives which have stimulated anti-Jewish campaigns in Christian lands throughout history. Sanuto concludes:

> And if I, Marino Sanuto, had belonged to the 'Pregadi', as last year, I would have taken the floor not to talk about the Jews and the swindles they perpetrate by lending at interest, but to talk about their *condotta*, to have it readjusted, and to prove that the Jews are at least as necessary to a country as its bakers, and above all to this one, for the general well-being; I would have quoted the laws, and the actions of our elders who have always advised keeping the Jews for lending at interest; this is what I would have talked about. This state has no need for such stupidities as driving out the Jews in the absence of a Monte di Pietà. The Monte Vecchio and Novo [banks] do not pay, and the Monte Novissimo only with great difficulty; trade is bad; shops are complaining that they are not selling their goods; how can people not be allowed to resort to the Jews at 15 per cent in order to keep alive and support their families . . .?

The debate was resumed in February and March 1520 and this time, Sanuto notes, several speakers proposed that a Monte di Pietà be set up at Venice. Others disagreed, since the state coffers were empty. Finally, the Jews' *condotta* was renewed for five years on payment of 10,000 ducats (4,000 in advance) and the lowering of the interest rate to 15 per cent.

When its expiry date drew nigh in 1524, the Monte di Pietà *condotta* was again put on the agenda, this time in a more concrete fashion. At the beginning of April the bursars to the Hospital for Incurables submitted a plan to the Senate whereby the Monte would function under their own aegis. Thirteen of them, from great Venetian families, pledged themselves to subscribe 1,000 ducats each. But ten days later the distrustful Council of Ten vetoed it and forbade Senate members 'on pain of death', to debate plans of this type. The prohibition was repeated ten years later, and not lifted by the Council of Ten until 1734. This governmental measure was justified by the prohibition on usury, 'so contrary to the Gospel', and it can be assumed that those in authority, traditionally touchy on this subject, did not give great credit to the recent *Inter multiplices* bull which authorised Monti di Pietà to charge interest. But it was probably a typically Venetian political precaution that was being taken in this particular instance, under cover of the anti-usury struggle. Might not the sort of Monte that the promoters envisaged in 1524 have threatened to become an autonomous financial power capable of influencing the conduct of public affairs? It was precisely in 1524 that control of banking transactions at Venice had been strengthened by the establishment of the *Provveditori sopra banchi*.[2]

Inoffensive from the political point of view, the Jews were more easily controllable. On this point, the sixteenth- and seventeenth-century pro-Jewish apologists can be believed. For example, in about 1550 the Dominican Sisto da Siena wrote: 'It is because the Hebrews are outlaws, serfs, timorous and unfavoured that the custom has been established in Christian countries of making them practise usury.' Rabbi Simone Luzzatto formulated the idea more clearly in the following century: 'the government of the Republic . . . has never wanted to allow the function of helping the needy financially to be practised by anyone but the weak and submissive Nation, who are absolutely remote from all seditious and ambitious thoughts.' The Dominicans and the rabbi emphasised, on the other hand, the better facilities and guarantees that the Jews offered for the control and moderation of usury, and it can in fact be assumed that Venetian prudence in the case in point was inspired not only by fear of a plutocratic hegemony, as at Genoa, but also by the traditional desire for public peace and well-being in a town where 'the people are less unfortunate than at Genoa, less profligate, and where there are fewer extremes of wealth', according to Braudel.

'Venice is unique': the originality of the Venetian solution therefore lay in adapting the Jewish *banchi* to the circumstances of the day, instead of transferring the institution into Christian hands. But this sort of policy, even if it corresponded to the well-understood interests of the needy classes, contained elements which could offend people in the days of bourgeois Christian order. An investigator, sent from Paris under the Regency with instructions to study the functioning of Italian Monti di Pietà, used kid gloves to describe the one at Venice:[3]

> I have great reason to fear that I will first impart a righteous disgust for this memorandum by explaining a strange feature which cannot, however, be concealed. The Republic of Venice, like the other sovereign states of Italy, has understood that it would be very useful to the poor to find a place where they can receive on their personal belongings the wherewithal to relieve their pressing poverty, but it has made strange use of this reflection and I believe it is only at Venice that the Monte di Pietà is run by Jews . . .

The transformation of the Jewish banks into Monti di Pietà or 'Banchi dei Poveri' dates from the second half of the sixteenth century. There were then three communities of Jews at Venice: the 'Levantini' or oriental Jews; the 'Ponentini' or ex-marranos (these two categories soon merged into one); and the community of Italian or Italo-German stock who were still designated as 'Tedeschi'. The Levantines and Ponentines, who were primarily engaged in international trade, ruled the roost as they did at Leghorn, and enjoyed privileges denied to the 'Tedeschi', who held the pawnbroking monopoly and carried on the usual allied professions such as secondhand dealing—in the eighteenth century, as at Leghorn, these distinctions disappeared. The statutory interest rate was successively lowered from 15 to 12 per cent, and in 1566 to 10 per cent. Then in December 1571, at the time of the anti-Jewish campaigns unleashed by Pius V, the Senate decided to celebrate the victory of Lepanto by decreeing the expulsion of the Jews, in order to 'manifest some gratitude to His Divine Majesty'. From this it can be seen that the Children of Israel could suffer not only because of the misfortunes and defeats of Christianity but also because of its victories. However, this decision was cancelled eighteen months later, against a background of political reversals. The following years saw the transformation of the lending banks into Banchi dei Poveri modelled on the Monti di Pietà set up in most of the other Italian towns to combat Jewish usury. The statutory interest rate was lowered to 5 per cent, an upper ceiling of 3 ducats was fixed for loans and, finally, the management and financing of the *banchi*, till then administered by individuals, was made the responsibility of the 'Tedeschi' community, as a *quid pro quo* for its toleration. This last reform is easily explained by the drastic lowering of the interest rate: 5 per cent could hold no attraction for private bankers. Later, probably at the beginning of the seventeenth century, the other communities were also associated with 'responsibility for the banks'.

In fact, as has already been sufficiently stressed, the main historical basis for the toleration of the Jews in Italian lands had always been their financial and political utility. It has also been seen that their transactions were by no means confined to pawn-broking, their most visible activity. Yet the financial relations between the communities and their leaders, the men with the money, were so close that it is difficult to draw a demarcation line between reciprocal interests. As statutory pawnbroking had become a form of servitude at Venice, where were the Venetian Jews to find profitable business in future?

In the first place, the managers of the *banchi*, and other Jews as well, certainly carried out lending operations which were outside the statutory specifications. The French investigator mentioned earlier pointed out that 'on their own authority and on sufferance, the same Jews, and each individually on his own behalf, lend larger sums on more valuable securities, when the borrower and the lender make their own conditions, whereby the borrower always comes off worst'. There follows a description of the ghetto, where 'one is assailed by that rabble, who outdo each other in asking if one wants to borrow; they promise good conditions so as to attract custom'. (Comment by the investigator: 'But in the discussion, the Jew is always a Jew.') On the other hand, the Jews profited from the right to arrange life annuities:

The Jews also arrange annuities, but life policies only, for different categories of interests according to age; the oldest get up to 9 per cent and the youngest 7 to 8 per cent, but as a general rule it is necessary to be at least fifty years old to be accepted for a life policy, on which the interest has so far been paid punctually; however, in a few privileged or special cases, the Jews arrange life annuities at sight for those under fifty, but the interest is in proportion to the age.

The functioning of the three Banchi dei Poveri which were distinguished by the colours 'red', 'black' and 'green', has already been described, notably by Cecil Roth and Attilio Milano. The following unpublished account provides details about them:

The establishment of a Monte di Pietà, as it exists at present, is as old as the settlement of the Jews; when that nation asked to be admitted to Venice, they were received there on condition that they ran the Monte di Pietà on behalf of the poor, which condition was laid down in the decree that was drawn up for their settlement.

The Monte is divided into three offices, each of which has its own colour; i.e. the tickets, which will be mentioned later, are printed in black, red [or] green. This is the sole distinction between the three offices, which otherwise function the same way.

The three houses in which the pawnshops are run are the property of individuals who rent them to the people who have undertaken the administration of the offices. These three houses are situated in the same rather gloomy square in the centre of the Jewish district. The administration of each of the three offices is made the responsibility of one specified Jew, who is obliged to provide an initial investment to serve as surety for what the community provides for the upkeep of the Monte. This individual is paid interest on his investment at 5 per cent and, in addition, enjoys the right to a certain percentage of the total of the money lent, out of which he must bear all the expenses of the office.

The office is on the ground floor of each of the houses which serve this purpose; these offices could be called shops, above which are the employees who keep the registers and value and receive the securities; there, too, is the safe where gold and silver securities are shut away. Next to these shops, and on the upper floors, are stores fitted with shelves not only along the walls but also filling the rooms, so that in the gap between two rows of shelves there is scarcely room for a person to pass. The securities are arranged on these shelves in very good order, so that a security reclaimed by its number is found instantly, but otherwise these stores have nothing to recommend them. No loans are made on mattresses and wooden or other too cumbersome furniture. After a security has been valued, a loan of about one-third is made, but never above 3 ducats, however valuable the security . . . The securities have increased immeasurably and in the last years as much as 300,000 ducats has been lent. This sum might give grounds for thinking that 100,000 people have borrowed on security: but the inference is not correct because the same person, who can borrow only 7.10 livres on one security, gives several securities on which he borrows a much larger sum, bit by bit.

Loans are made for one year, and one month's grace is given at the end of the year, before the security is sold . . .

About 60,000 securities are currently brought to the Monti di Pietà during the course of a year and only 1,500 are left to be sold; there is no cause for surprise that so many of them are redeemed, when the highest loan is only 3 ducats.

The auction where the securities are sold is held at the Rialto. Scarcely a day goes by without an auction of some sort; the sale is made in the presence of a gentleman and a public notary who makes the report of the sale, then the owner states his accounts. If a security is sold for less than the sum lent, the loss falls on the manager of the office.

The Republic derive no benefit from the Monti di Pietà other than the relief of the poor.

The Jews have more to lose than to gain by running the Monti di Pietà; the 5 per cent they derive from the poor cannot suffice to pay the interest on the funds they are obliged to hold for the maintenance of the Monti and the salaries of all the people employed in the business; the Republic well realised that it was imposing a burden on the Jews when it entrusted them with the Monti di Pietà.

The account also indicates the annual salaries of the employees of the 'offices': 150 ducats for the cashier and valuer, 120 for the book-keeper, 100 for the man responsible for guarding the gold and silver securities, and 60 for the warehousemen, of which there were five.

The manager himself annually collected 250 ducats in interest on his guarantee deposit of 5,000 ducats. To this was added an unknown percentage on the 5 per cent statutory interest (the rate was raised to $5\frac{1}{2}$ per cent from 1721) collected on the loans. In addition, there were probably various illicit profits realised by underhand means similar to those currently practised in Christian Monti di Pietà. But there is little information on this subject and the above account, however hostile on the subject of Jews, does not mention it. When the former prohibition by the Council of

Ten on public debate about the establishment of a Christian Monte di Pietà was lifted in the middle of the eighteenth century, the promoters of such a plan criticised the managers of the Banchi dei Poveri for undervaluing securities, muddling documents, and above all granting small commercial loans (which were strictly forbidden), especially to Jewish secondhand dealers, with consequent frequent shortages of money designed solely for the relief of the Christian poor. In any case, the administration of the Banchi dei Poveri, traditionally entrusted to certain ghetto families, should not have been a bad thing for them.

It certainly was a bad thing for the Jewish community of Venice, which was responsible for supplying the working capital, and, as a result, the conflict reappears between managers and sleeping partners which *The Book of the Lender and the Borrower* emphasises so strongly. The statutory capital of each bank was 50,000 ducats at the end of the sixteenth century, 100,000 in the seventeenth century and 160,000 after 1721. The community at first obtained these funds by loans from its members or from Christian financiers and then, in the eighteenth century, by turning to the Jewish communities of London, Amsterdam and Hamburg. In the opinion of certain Venetian rabbis, the interest on such loans—$3\frac{1}{2}$ to $4\frac{1}{2}$ per cent—was not 'usury', and the rabbinate of Venice received confirmation of this in 1706 from a high foreign authority, Rabbi David Oppenheim of Prague. The community therefore ran into debt, and in 1737 was declared insolvent: out of a total debt of 926,000 ducats, 596,000 ducats constituted the liabilities attributable to the *banchi*. Perhaps the important Jewish businessmen who were the major support of the community found advantages in an insolvency which affected them not at all or only indirectly.

Social assistance, through the maintenance of the Banchi dei Poveri, had, as the years went by, become a minor element in the burdens weighing on the Jews of Venice. The government was levying far larger sums on them directly in the form of taxes, extraordinary impositions and forced loans. In 1686, for example, at the time of the Second Turkish War, it forced the Jews to make a loan of 200,000 ducats at $3\frac{1}{2}$ per cent,[4] apart from various loans to Christian organisations. In the opinion of the French consul, this money could not have been found on the spot at less than 4½ per cent. The average annual revenue that Venice drew from its Jews at this period was estimated to come to 250,000 ducats.

Their wealth thenceforth came primarily from maritime trade, which expanded similarly and in analogous conditions to that carried on by the Leghorn Jews, while the Venetian nobility became increasingly idle and weak. In 1732, when a rumour was rife that Tuscany was about to fall to the crown of Spain, the *Savi alla Mercanzia* proposed that the Senate should take advantage of the panic which was seizing the 'Hebrew nation' of Leghorn in order to attract it to Venice, 'to revive our exhausted trade'. But though guarantees were given to the Jews by the government of the grand duchy, the plan went no further.[5]

We have valuable information on the gradually increasing part the Jews played in Venetian trade and shipping from the sixteenth century on from Gino Luzzatto, in two relatively unknown essays.[6] In particular, he quotes an account dating from 1760 which specifies that the sole motive for the toleration of the Jews at the beginning of the sixteenth century was the possibility of organising pawnbroking at a reasonable rate through their offices, but that from the middle of the century the Turkish wars and the dislocation of trade with the Levant began to provide an additional reason. A Senate debate in 1541, also quoted by Luzzatto, noted: 'The major part of the merchandise which comes from upper and lower Romania is brought by, and found in, the hands of itinerant Levantine Jews'.

For the period 1592–1609, some idea of the Jewish share in Venetian maritime trade can be gathered from data published by Alberto Tenenti.[7] In the northern Adriatic, 'this trade is to a great extent in the hands of Jews', but they took a more modest part in trading further afield. However, the Republic granted Jewish businessmen more and more extensive privileges. In 1689, according to Luzzatto, one Aron Oxid, owner of a Portuguese boat, was authorised to sail it under the banner of St Mark. At the beginning of the following century, out of sixty-nine Venetian ships, twelve were owned by Jews; at the end, several dozen Jews were part-owners of vessels. Jews also took a growing part in Venetian industry: the cloth-mills of Anselmo Gentili alone employed over a thousand Jewish workers in 1763. When an extraordinary tax was imposed on Venetian merchants and ship-owners by the French military authorities in 1797, Jewish firms had to bear over one-quarter of the total of 867,900 ducats.

Foreign observers also remarked on and, as is traditional, over-estimated the prosperity of the Jews. According to the French investigator already quoted, these 'people, solely employed in trade, carry on a principal part of that of Venice'. Cecil Roth quotes an English traveller at the end of the eighteenth century who said that almost all Venetian trade was concentrated in their hands. To the ex-Jesuit Gianbattista Roberti, who perceived the best proof of the truth of Christianity to be the poverty of the ghetto,[8] the Venetian writer Alberto Fortis replied that such an argument ran the risk of defeating itself and of having its credibility challenged, in view of the flourishing Jewries of Venice, Leghorn or the Low Countries. 'If the Jews of a country were generally rich, and the Christians wretched, would our protagonist convert to Judaism?'[9]

In his *History of the Jews in Venice*, Cecil Roth notes that the social and worldly life of the rich, their snobbery *sui generis*, showed a remarkable 'modernity', anticipating Judeo–Christian relations in western countries in the nineteenth century. It is impossible to resist the pleasure of concluding with one or two glimpses on this subject provided by French ambassadors at Venice at the end of the reign of Louis XIV. The shipowner Salomone Levi del Banco, 'a gentleman, although Jewish', served as their banker. Here is M. Arnauld de Pomponne's description of the wedding of this Jew's daughter in August 1690:

The aforenamed Levi del Banco, of whom Your Highness will have heard, married off one of his daughters a few days ago. There was a great gathering there, including some foreign ministers. A certain nobleman of the Miani family had undiplomatically sat down in front of Monsieur the Ambassador of the Emperor, and either because of an armchair, which I could not well know, or because of some impertinent words, the Ambassador manhandled him and gave him a kick in the arse. The nobleman disappeared without further ado. The Inquisitors, informed of the event, took the aforesaid Jew and the said nobleman off to their dungeons. This would be like beating the saddle when one cannot beat the horse I know that the Jew regained his freedom, but I think the nobleman is still in prison . .

# CHAPTER XIII

# The End of the System of Papal Licences

In 1682 Innocent XI decided to abolish the old system of papal licences and to close the Jewish lending banks at Rome. The circumstances in which this decision was taken must now be examined, but a glance at the financial situation of the Jewish community of Rome is an essential preliminary.

In order to meet the expenses which weighed down upon it, this community began contracting loans at the beginning of the seventeenth century, principally with monasteries and Christian charitable institutions. The debt, which amounted to 166,000 *scudi* in 1647, was then funded as a result of intervention by the Apostolic Chamber, which allowed Jews to participate in the 'second established Monte Annona' by the issue of 1,660 credits secured by the taxes paid by the ghetto which, therefore, from the financial point of view, tended to become nothing but a cog in the papal administration. The interest charges and its other expenses forced the community to contract new debts in the course of the following years. In 1668 a sort of concordat was concluded—again under the aegis of the Apostolic Chamber—between the representatives of the Christian 'Montisti' and the *fattori* of the community.

According to this concordat, the community's debt amounted to 259,000 *scudi*, comprising 237,000 to the 'Montisti' and 22,000 to Jewish creditors. The interest, to which certain other fixed charges were added, amounted to 14,560 *scudi* annually; apart from this, besides, was 9,770 *scudi* in annual contributions levied by the communal *buon governo* (welfare charities and social assistance). The total property of the ghetto was valued at 400,000 *scudi*; finally, it was specified that the Jews were to hold 150,000 *scudi* ready in their lending banks.[1]

Also in 1668 a special congregation, the Congregatio de Usuris, was called in order to examine the state of the ghetto's finances and the problem of Jewish usury. There was certainly a connection between the creation of this congregation and the publication in the same year of the tract *Il vero stato degli Hebrei di Roma* which has been mentioned before; the closure of the lending banks was probably envisaged as early as this period, if not before (it is not known at what point the Jews asked Cardinal da Luca for a *Consilium* in favour of the banks, which he published in his *Theatrum veritatis* . . . in 1669).

In 1670 Clement X reformed the organisation of the *banchi* in three respects: the interest rate was lowered from 18 to 12 per cent; the rounding off to a full fortnight in the calculation of interest was forbidden; and finally, the traditional pawnbrokers' privilege in cases involving the pledging of stolen goods was abolished. The same pope, however, in 1674, decided to revert to the former procedure as far as the second and third points were concerned, alleging that these experimental innovations hurt Christians more than they benefited them.

From the moment Innocent XI (1676–89) was elected, the debates on the Jewish banks resumed with renewed vigour. There can be little question that this pope, renowned for the strictness of his principles and the strength of his character, was personally hostile to a practice which had always been in doubt. But the rapid growth of the Roman Monte di Pietà during the second half of the seventeenth century is a prime consideration: its turnover, according to calculations by Donato Tamilia, rose from 373,000 *scudi* in 1639 to 480,000 in 1669, to 867,000 in 1680 and, after the closure of the Jewish banks, to 1,030,000 *scudi* in 1683.[2]

The records of the Congregatio de Usuris show that the opponents of these banks based their arguments for their abolition, in the first place, on the growth of the Monte di Pietà. As an unsigned *Consilium* phrased it, 'today, when a Monte exists, the reason for the authorisation has disappeared, and the authorisation granted has become illegal, because the need can no longer be invoked.' In these circumstances, the problem became simpler, and the theologians could excuse themselves from examining the thorny question of the basis of the toleration granted to the Jews with respect to usury. It sufficed to state that this toleration no longer had a *raison d'être*. As the Oratorian Mariano Soccino put it, in one instance only could the prince permit and tolerate moderate and not excessive usury: when such toleration was totally necessary to avoid a greater public ill which could not be avoided by any other means. But now such a means would exist, since a flourishing Monte di Pietà was functioning in Rome. Soccino added that if the Jewish bankers granted loans more quickly and readily than the Monte, from the point of view of the public benefit, this was an evil rather than a good, since this convenience was such as would foster dissipation and debauchery. The purely moral arguments follow on from this. The *Consilia* give a great deal of interesting information on this type of argument which continued to be put forward in favour of the Jewish banks. 'Arguments citing shame and convenience are too frivolous and are no authority to violate the law of God!', exclaimed the anonymous adviser quoted above. Another, also anonymous, expressed the problem in these terms:

> Rome is a city of foreigners, with crowds of lay and ecclesiastical personages of every rank and every condition who are ashamed to go to the Monte di Pietà; therefore the usury of the ghetto is necessary. *Reply:* the Monte di Pietà contains securities deposited by cardinals, counts, marquises and princes; therefore the foreign personages' alleged embarrassment is merely a veneer to prettify the authorisation of Jewish usury and to make it seem licit when it is illicit . . .

The writers of *Consilia* were also concerned with the reputation of the Catholic Church: but judging by the arguments, the Holy See risked suffering just as much criticism by maintaining as by abolishing the *banchi*. According to the first anonymous adviser,

213

H

'heretics and the ungodly will say that the Roman Church is preaching one thing and doing another', while the second tried to parry the argument whereby the abolition of the Jewish banks would be an implicit censure of the popes who had tolerated and protected them in past centuries—which gives a glimpse of one of the sources of strength of tradition at Rome. He placed the emphasis on the change in circumstances: 'He who thinks that a woollen coat is unsuitable wear for August does not think it unsuitable for January.'

Finally, the first anonymous author recalled the reputation of the Eternal City, which he compared with the holy place mentioned by the prophet Daniel, where abomination prevailed: 'All states have replaced usury by bills of exchange [cambii] at 5 or 6 per cent at the most: and Rome, which is a holy city because it is a priestly city governed by the vicar of Christ, maintains the abomination.' He also put forward some practical arguments, suggesting that the Jews be allowed to practise other trades: 'Let them rather be permitted to practise those other arts and trades allowed to them at Florence and elsewhere, and which are prohibited to them here by human laws: these can be changed, for they are voluntary, unlike the divine law on usury, which is essential'.

This leads to the economic situation. Here, the information supplied by the advisers is only very meagre. None the less, it does emerge that the opponents of Jewish usury were trying to find an answer to two problems which were obviously worrying the papal administration: the fate of the ghetto and its financial situation, and the fate of its Christian creditors. The first problem was bluntly stated as follows by the first anonymous author: 'If usury is abolished, all the Jews will find themselves reduced to such poverty that they will be forced to flee: Rome will therefore lose 5,000 inhabitants to the great privation of the public, as trade will decline, and to the detriment of individuals, who will lose rents from the ghetto.' Their reply to this was that it could only be to the advantage of the population of Rome to be rid of 5,000 thieves: 'The disappearance of a robber who steals a baker's money so that he can buy bread from him with this money is no loss, but a gain, for the baker.' Another argument claimed that the Jews exaggerated their poverty: witness the valuable ornaments in their synagogues, which were said to be worth 15,000 *scudi*. Consequently, according to the opponents of Jewish usury, it should not be impossible to force the ghetto to repay its Christian creditors, while making the latter return the dues and profits they had collected, described as usurious gains.

Two of the four memoranda submitted to the Congregatio de Usuris in favour of the Jews were presented officially in the name of the community by the two lawyers, di Lancetta and Clarusio. As far as the economic aspect of the questions was concerned, they took their stand on the *Consilium* of da Luca, whose theological arguments in favour of Jewish usury we saw at the end of chapter II. The cardinal said in effect that toleration of the Jews had a threefold utility from the practical point of view: the presence in Rome of an industrious population of producers in the service of Christians, their value as consumers, and the revenue the Treasury collected from them. He also mentioned that the expenses weighing on the Jewish community had led it into debt, on which most of the interest was borne by the *banchieri*. Finally he listed the advantages of the *banchi* as compared with the Monte di Pietà: that they accepted cumbersome securities, or securities that required particular safe-keeping, which the Monte did not take; the speed and ease of transactions; and their discretion, which was appropriate to the respect due to people of quality.

As for the theological aspect, it is interesting to note that the last champions of Jewish usury were no longer trying to justify it in the traditional way, as da Luca was still doing: that is to say, by invoking the Jews' lack of hope of salvation. The old privilege of the unbeliever was thus ended, and in this sense, concerning lending at interest, it is possible to talk of the movement of the Holy See at the end of the seventeenth century towards modern ethics, which does not distinguish between businessmen on the basis of religion.[3] The main point of the proof of the Jews' advocates tended to justify the interest they collected by arguing from current prevailing views on Christians' financial transactions. In reply to Soccino, a certain Marcus Battaglinus, after

THE DECLINE OF THE JEWISH MONEY TRADE

examining eight cases in which the collection of interest was regarded as permissible, likened the profits of the Jewish *banchieri* to those drawn by the *foenus nauticum*. Clarusio, the official pleader for the Jews, referred to the *lucrum cessans*, since their money could have been invested in another way. Di Lancetta, also referring to the *lucrum cessans*, emphasised the expenses of the *banchieri*—those which encumbered the functioning of the banks as well as those which devolved on them as the principal taxpayers of the community—and set out to demonstrate that the interest they collected was as legitimate as that demanded by the Monti di Pietà.

A pro-Jewish anonymous note invoking political and moral arguments is also worth quoting. It recalled that numerous princes, notably those of Savoy, were continuing to protect Jewish banks licensed by the Holy See: if the licences were abolished, these banks would continue to function notwithstanding, and a scandal would result both for the Catholic subjects of these princes and for heretics in neighbouring countries. These heretics would then be able to gloat and cry shame because the Holy See would have had to eat its own words. On the other hand, the old tradition of Jewish banking had not been questioned either at the Lateran Council of 1516 or at the Council of Trent. Finally, the note emphasised the various inconveniences of the Monte di Pietà and the 'way its employees victimise the poor, even today.'

An undated document reports a last meeting, when questions of a practical nature were examined. Was it necessary to reduce the interest rate again, to 8 per cent this time, in which case it would be justified by the *lucrum cessans*, or was it right purely and simply to close the *banchi*? And did one or other of these measures risk disorganising the life of the Jewish community? The Congregatio was of the opinion that there was no fear of this, since in each of these contingencies the Jews would be able to invest their money commercially at 10 per cent. To this end it proposed that they be allowed to start up trade in fabrics outside the ghetto in the area bordering on the Piazza Giudea. In addition, to overcome the disadvantages of the Monte di Pietà, it suggested 'setting up another pawnbroking establishment in the same building, where anyone might come freely, without having to enter the Monte di Pietà, and pledge his goods discreetly; and to reduce even further any embarrassment these people might feel, two fathers of the Chiesa Nuova, or other monks in whom people could have full confidence, might perhaps be present at these transactions'. Thus the trust placed in a priest was suggested as compensation for the professional discretion of the Jew.

As the Congregatio de Usuris had foreseen, the closure of the lending banks did not have serious repercussions on Roman economic life and did not lead to serious 'disorders' in the ghetto, at least in the immediate future. But the community certainly was affected financially, so that in 1698 it was officially placed under the trusteeship of the Apostolic Chamber and was officially declared bankrupt in 1755. Attilio Milano, who studied these questions in minute detail, quotes figures to illustrate this progressive insolvency: for example, the community's debts of 261,063 *scudi* in 1682 rose to 307,048 *scudi* in 1702, and to 414,723 in 1717; its receipts dropped from 13,768 *scudi* in 1696 to 10,768 in 1721; in 1801, they were no more than 6,090 *scudi*. The rich ghetto families became impoverished to the same degree, as emerges from their tax statements, which Milano also published. In his *Storia degli Ebrei in Italia*, he rightly emphasises the contrast between Venice, where the great Jewish businessmen prospered while the community was declared bankrupt, and Rome, where, as a result of the strict control exerted by the Holy See, Jewish private and public finance overlapped so closely that they could only follow the same downward curve.[4]

It is well known that the Rome ghetto lasted as long as papal theocracy. One might even say that it survived it—and for quite a long time: even today a Jewish district, the only one of this type in Europe,[5] exists on the site of the former Jewish *seraglio*, and the people of Rome continue to call it the 'ghetto'. (The majority of the Jews of Rome, who live in other districts, are hardly enamoured of this designation.[6]) Its population has preserved many of its original and unique features. As an investigation undertaken some years ago by the American scholars L C. and S. P. Dunn has shown,[7] objective criteria, social, and even biological (which are available from the study of blood groups), make it possible to distinguish it from both the surrounding Roman population and other Italian Jews. In other words, in the eyes of the anthropologist, it is characterised by the beginnings of genetic individualisation which is like the first step in the establishment of a race. Small-scale trading and peddling predominate among its activities. The women are still renowned for their skill as dressmakers and invisible menders. As demographic statistics show, since the beginning of the nineteenth century this population has served as the last reservoir of original Italian-Jewish stock in process of assimilation. In an excellent piece of research published in 1938, the demographer Roberto Bachi pointed to the contrast between 'the rapid decline of the old communities in the north and centre of Italy' and 'the remarkable residual vitality of the small Roman group'.[8] It seems obvious that this vitality was related to the system of special legislation and segregation dating from the Counter-Reformation, and even that it resulted directly from it. It is worthy of note that the Holy See, which made such tenacious efforts to convert the Jews, served in a way to preserve Judaism. Certainly, a similar vitality can or could be found in Jewries in many other regions in the old continent, insofar as they remain or remained apart from the economic, social and cultural transformations characteristic of our time— in Eastern Europe, North Africa, the Middle East. Czechoslovakia between the World Wars is a particularly good example: the Jewish population there decreased in Bohemia, remained almost stationary in Slovakia and was in process of rapid increase at the eastern end of the country, in Ruthenia (Subcarpathian Ukraine). In the West proper, the Roman phenomenon remains unique of its kind.

# Conclusion

... a good strong base, the land which bore them and fed them. Without a geographic base, the people, the historic actor, seem to be walking in the air as in certain Chinese paintings where the ground is missing—Michelet, *Preface*, 1869

Discussions of the social and economic factors which led the Jews of medieval Europe to specialise in lending at interest place the emphasis on either their exclusion from other occupations during the economic upsurge which followed the Crusades, or the Church's anti-usury struggle which secured them an unquestionable advantage in this sphere. Both these factors must have played a part, varying according to time and place: in the case of Italy, the predominant influence of the second factor has been seen at the basis of the system of *condotte*, which were preferably (and, in the last resort, solely) granted to Jewish lenders. I have even suggested that this specialisation contributed to the preservation of Judaism, and in this context I have picked out the Jews of southern Italy who, to a large extent, practised manual trades and were not able to hold out against the forced conversion campaigns. This suggests the idea of a sort of professional selection at the root of the survival of medieval Judaism, at least of certain Jewries, in certain socio-historical situations. Yet I do not think this idea can be regarded as really new, for it seems to be implicit in many works by Jewish historians. They did not specifically state it—either for apologetic reasons, or simply because of the caution required by a delicate subject which easily lent itself to the most distorted caricatures, as in writings of Karl Marx and Werner Sombart, not to mention their followers.

Leaving all this aside, the old and sempiternal problem must be dealt with: the relationship between beliefs and socio-economic factors. No serious contemporary author dealing with economic history would uphold the Marxist theses about 'money, the jealous God of Israel'—a god Sombart replaced by a 'racial characteristic'. Yet how can the problem be avoided? How can it not be seen that in the present case a relationship does exist between beliefs and economic factors which, without much fuller information, cannot simply be reduced to the Jews' adaptation to a hostile environment, and to the subsequent rabbinic interpretation of the commandments of the Torah and Talmudic precepts? (Note the Talmudic texts and rabbinic exegeses quoted in chapter II.) Any research, however superficial, into a permanent general relationship between the teaching of the Talmud and the activities of the Jews reaches an impasse when the fact emerges that the Talmud teachings were formulated in the midst of a Jewish population primarily engaged in agriculture and manual labour. It therefore seems to me that the best way to express the present problem would be to establish the relationship between Judaism in medieval Europe and the beliefs which surrounded it; for an uprooted minority, the closeness of this link leaps to the eye. The task, in other words, is to search within Christian thought and religious awareness for the secret of the economic and social behaviour of European Jews.

Once again the question arises whether this is not a truism, since this sort of relationship has been either implicitly postulated or even clearly formulated by generations of Jewish historians in the course of discussions, most frequently apologetic, about Jewish usurers. They have not, however, set out to study it in depth and in particular they have not concerned themselves, as it were, with the doctrinal position of the Church on the question of Jewish usury, or with the social consequences, by means of slow and devious by-ways, of this position for medieval society. It may not be out of place, therefore, to make up for their reluctance to embark on matters of Christian theology. It was a non-Jewish historian, Jean Stengers, who pointed out that the doctrinal position of the Church vis-à-vis Jewish usury 'is—extraordinarily enough—an almost untouched subject. Jewish historians generally barely skim the surface of it.'[1] Let it be added that this is equally applicable to Church historians.

But should not one attempt to set the problem, by way of introduction, within a wider context: to discuss Jewish usury— or heterodox usury—as it existed in certain other societies, in the Far East, for example? As far as the West is concerned, it is necessary in this context to refer to the astonishing 'Exception of St Ambrose' of Christian theology, which, under cover of Deuteronomy 23:20, permitted interest to be collected from unbelievers (and *vice versa*). Unfortunately for the present investigation, the origins and method of application of this 'Exception'—which was, however, included in the *Corpus juris canonici*—are still not known. Its first mention goes back to the sixth century; would it have helped at this period or even earlier to make it easier for Christians to do business with unbelievers? Was it later invoked in the agrarian society of the early middle ages to justify the privileges of Jews and Syrians? Nothing is known at present. The 'Exception of St Ambrose' is known only through canon law and from the discussions which took place among scholars in the twelfth and thirteenth centuries. How it was introduced into the real life of the first millennium of Christianity, we have no idea whatever. There are grounds for thinking that it reflects a moral philosophy, probably going back to very remote times (a moral philosophy of 'tribal brotherhood', according to Benjamin Nelson's terminology[2]), which was still the ethical code of a society with a primitive economy which was inclined to abandon business, and particularly money-lending, to aliens and 'outsiders' (who 'foris sunt'). It has also been seen that the Jews brought in Christian intermediaries in money dealings among themselves. This similarity between the practices of the Christian macrocosm and those of the Jewish microcosm suggests that a general framework of medieval ethics and attitudes is involved.

In the Islamic Empire at the same period, Christians and Jews practised all the occupations connected with the circulation of money in apparently exactly the same way. This is additional proof, if proof need be, that taken by itself and other things being equal besides, the relationship between the doctrines of the Talmud and the activities of its followers is as undefined as that between the occupations of the Christian flock and the patristic doctrines. There were also, in a more recent period, the Moriscos of Spain, 'condemned to be rich', to use Fernand Braudel's strong phrase. Here is material which, if it does not support Max Weber's theses on the economic functions of 'pariah peoples', at least (and specialists in Far Eastern civilisations might be able to supply other examples) gives food for thought about a possible consequence of the disparity of religions which directs followers of the subject religion, insofar as they are subjugated and politically powerless, into commercial activities, and helps them to prosper.

To return to Christian Europe: however it may have happened —and this is still a mystery—the Jews are seen to emerge there in the early middle ages as the only officially tolerated infidels and, after the disappearance of the Syrians, as the only professional merchants. As Europe sprang into life in the twelfth to thirteenth centuries, their niche in the structure of medieval life shrank, and lending at interest became their main function. This they practised officially and under papal protection in Italy; more irregularly, and sometimes semi-secretly, on the other side of the Alps. In Eastern Europe during the same period, on the contrary, their occupations became more diverse, and they formed a significant proportion—in some places, the largest part—of the urban population. This is a reminder that living history is always richer than the cause-and-effect explanations in which people try to squeeze it. Italy, though, from where all Europe borrowed techniques and ideas, does seem to be more important than other countries. The Italian cities in granting *de facto* toleration to the Jews who practised a reviled but useful trade, took their stand on the old theological concept of toleration of the 'witness people', so that this trade appears to become the pledge for the survival of this people, and 'religious' toleration and 'economic' toleration seem to amalgamate. We have also seen that, at the beginning, it was a process which occurred spontaneously against the background of economic differentiation, anti-usury campaigns and a sophistication of attitudes. It was only at a later stage that Italian canonists adjusted doctrine accordingly and clarified those points which had hitherto been vague. After this, the Holy See sanctioned the practice, tailored it and turned it to its advantage. In the same chronological order, in modern times, when the Monti di Pietà were transformed into lending and deposit banks as channels for bourgeois savings, this practice was abandoned and fell into oblivion.

The correlation—the adaptation of doctrines to the social situation—also took place with regard to the Jews. As it happened, this situation was primarily a function of the surrounding attitudes, of a collective psyche. Perhaps it would be appropriate to ask how they shaped the psyche or, if one prefers, the 'collective soul', of the Jews in the course of the generations?

This is a question, I believe, of prime importance. It is a question which is implicit throughout this book.

As ever, the origins are still a mystery. At the start, there is the paradox of a dispersion, a historical fact which, instead of obliterating a collective identity, becomes the symbol of this identity. Separated from their native land, the Jews preserved their identity: it is important to see first and foremost that as a human group or people,[3] they are no longer under the 'influences' of (or, to adopt the terminology of Lucien Febvre, connected with) the geographic environment created by other peoples which, in its turn, fashions and identifies them. The Jewish people have connections with this environment only through the intermediary of the indigenous population, and these connections are all the looser or more casual in that through their wanderings, the Jews' setting completely changes from one period to another. But there is one environment or tract of soil to which the Jews remain closely linked and which they regard as their own, although this land is a dreamland which eludes their actual clutches and acts on them only as a myth. This is the land of Canaan, flowing with milk and honey: a land whose hills and plains they invoke incessantly during their daily prayers and their festivals, and from which they believe only their sins keep them away. 'Next year in Jerusalem!' The importance and uniqueness of such a phenomenon cannot be sufficiently emphasised. Moreover, its many-sided implications have been the subject of innumerable literary and philosophical variations on the theme of 'Jewish rootlessness' over the generations.

But the present state of the human sciences makes it possible to go slightly more closely into these questions.

Take the great actor in human geography, 'man, moulded by the environment that his ancestors created' (Pierre George's phrase), and consider what is the environment and who the ancestors when that man is a Jew. A strange paradox immediately appears. In a given area (the Middle East, North Africa, Europe), the Jews' genetic ancestors, we now know, came basically from the same stock as the surrounding population,[4] although the tradition of the Jews enjoins them to disclaim both these ancestors and this environment. The local population, especially when Christian, shares the belief that the Children of Israel are descended from the 'patriarchal race'. Thus one can immediately recognise the intrusion of a collective outlook which forms a barrier between the Jews and the natural setting. Certainly, in all human groups, a 'human environment' comes between the individual and this setting, but in the case of the Jews, the *de facto* barrier erected by man's social nature is reinforced by a theoretical psycho-religious barrier raised by the particular nature attributed to the Jews, since it is their lack of identity with or religious separation from the 'indigenous' human environment which identifies them as what they are. As a result, their natural setting, from the psychological point of view, is *twofold*.

The very real and very tangible setting in which they live they tend to be the first to regard as a land of exile, a place of punishment, not as a protective foster-homeland. The host people, for its part, excludes them and, particularly in Christian Europe, goes so far as to forbid them to own landed property, to take possession of the soil. The other setting which, however incompletely, spiritually fulfils this maternal role for them, is but a memory, but one they cultivate with obsessive fervour and all the hypnotic power inherent in the ritual and observances of Judaism. It even seems that this fervour and power increased over the centuries since the legendary separation.[5] However, the fact that the word for *a man* in ancient Hebrew is *adam*, and the word for land *adama*, is an indication of the emotional—almost erotic—nature of roots sunk in a native soil.[6] One could consider, besides, whether Jewish tradition would have been enough to preserve Jewish identity, to prevent the fusion of the Jews with the host peoples, in the melting-pots of the Christian West, had it not been for the excellent reputation which the tradition, and consequently the identity, enjoyed with these nations.

As a result of this twofold character, the Jews' civilisation is, as has been seen, a dual civilisation: they have two sets of first names (i.e. two forms of identification); they follow two different calendars simultaneously. They write from left to right in Latin characters when they are addressing Christians, and from right to left when they correspond with one another in Hebrew (while introducing a smattering of words borrowed from the local language). Among themselves, they speak the language of the country they inhabit (but stuffed with Hebrew words).

They are permanently tempted to lay down roots wholly in the host country (where they had more often than not settled before the establishment of an 'aboriginal' people). The fourteenth-century Italian Jews we have studied are typical from this point of view. When Ismaël Laudadio da Rieti told the messianic agitator David Reubeni that Jerusalem held no attraction for him because he felt that he could not be better off than in Siena, it would be wrong to interpret this solely as a banker's *ubi bene, ibi patria*. It has been said, and it may be true, that the Jew's attachment to the country he lives in can reach unparalleled intensity precisely because possession is incomplete: possession is, in fact, challenged by both Jewish tradition and Christian attitudes, which concur on this point.

Confining discussion to the Jews settled in the West where, as I have tried to show in the first two volumes of *The History of Anti-Semitism*, certain articles of the Christian faith in a strange way helped them to keep their sense of identity, it can be noted that, depending on the country and the situation, it was sometimes the relationship with the host country, and sometimes that with the promised land which was in the foreground of their collective consciousness. But neither relationship was ever completely dominant. This resulted in their secular split into two 'basic personalities' (in cultural anthropological terms) or the conflict (in psychoanalytical terms) between two 'mother figures'. This split, this constant tossing between two settings or sets of emotional ties—and in the last analysis between two identities—may be thought to lie at the root of the proverbial 'Jewish restlessness'. While no attempt to express this very vague and quasi-metaphysical idea in precise terms will be made here, the relationship between such an unusual intrusion into the existing order and all the Jews' emotional and intellectual characteristics should be pointed out. In the first place, therefore, it is to such a conflict situation[7] that both the economic vitality and the cultural fertility they have demonstrated during the Dispersion should be attributed. Of course, over-determination, which plays a part in a variety of ways, must also be taken into account: 'restlessness' grows in proportion to persecutions which are necessarily traumatic; the culture was historically bolstered up by the compulsory religious instruction to which the 'sages of the Talmud' were already subjecting their flock.

Thus quasi-physical roots in a country are, for the Jews, replaced by a complex body of ideas, a doctrine whereby taking root becomes an eschatological event, which it is incumbent on the Chosen People to hasten. It is not surprising that Jewish historians almost always postulate, if only implicitly, an *idée-force* as fundamental to the preservation of Judaism, and that their philosophy of history is, explicitly or not, a voluntarist philosophy, and that in a variety of ways, as I have frequently demonstrated, it takes so much account of man's possibility of choosing between good and evil—i.e. of free will (for non-Jews just as for Jews), giving its full weight as a factor in history.[8]

Jewish historiography has no other option: it might even be said that, in terms of strictly economic and social method, Jewish history does not exist as an autonomous subject of historical research.[9]

Here, therefore, is a whole range of unique characteristics which have marked out the Jews—some from the distant past, others since the first millennium of the present era—and from which, in various ways, probably originated the hatred and persecutions to which they were exposed. The psychoanalytical school has clearly emphasised the manifold and powerful symbolisms of the Jew, who at different levels is said to be deicidal, or God the repressive Father, or a bastard without heart or home[10] (cf. the wandering Jew). Since his exile was a punishment imposed by the Almighty, such an admission of auto-culpability was probably the stimulus for the indictments of the surrounding world.

To what extent did such distinctive characteristics actually predispose the Jews towards commercial rather than other activities? We are aware, at least, of how far the comparative method bristles with difficulties and, in the last resort, is quite inadequate. At the extreme, was not the Jews' 'heterodox usury', in itself and for itself, 'Jewish usury'?

The great historical phenomenon which sheds light on ideas in this field is indisputable: the general urbanisation of the Jews of the Islamic Empire in the twelfth to the thirteenth centuries. The author who has studied this most closely, S. D. Goitein, attributes it to the oppressive régime of the Moslem conquerors which led to the deterioration in the position of the rural populations, although this did not apply, or applied only very partially, to the Christian fellahin. One is therefore justified in connecting this urbanisation with a specific feature of Judaism. Was the idea of the exile translated into fact through the oppressive régime of Islam, which contributed to the abandonment of a land which was doubly harsh? Did the requirements of Israelite worship, in particular the indispensable daily quorum of the *minyan*, contribute, for their part, to the concentration of Jews in towns? Such assumptions, which come to mind naturally, are still unverifiable from present evidence. It is known that, in Europe, the Jews seem to have been town-dwellers from the start. However, a certain tendency to 'return to the land' and to agricultural activities seems to be apparent among them in the early middle ages. The manifold reasons which soon put an end to it are sufficiently well known.

What happens once the Children of Israel are physically 'detached from the land'? 'Among the Jews of the East, every man lives by the work of his hands,' said the polemicist Jacob ben Elijah; in fact, they were engaged in every urban occupation, as artisans as well as in trade. It is possible to speculate on the theory that the Jews, because of their culture, had a predisposition or were better equipped for trade: in fact, the present survival throughout the East of several Jewries consisting solely of artisans shows that education was only one of many factors involved in their specialisation in trade. It will also be noticed that trade in the East was carried on within a static or immobile economy, in which the capitalist chain reaction, which would have developed a corresponding state of mind amongst Jewish traders, had not been set off.

In Europe, on the contrary, a whole range of specific factors seems to have been at work. There was, on the one hand, the general upsurge in economic life as well as in urban culture, the progress in accountancy and business—in short, the necessary preliminaries to the capitalist mentality. From the particular viewpoint of the Jews, on the other hand, there was an increase in economic hazards and ills which secreted their own antidote, since medieval Christianity's growing 'self-awareness', though ill omened for the Children of Israel, at the same time threw usury into discredit and offered them a profitable living. The same beliefs and attitudes which, as they became established, led to the burnings and the massacres and laid the foundations for the economic position of the Jew, also, by degrading him, gave him the advantage of practising a profession which had become degrading. As the life of the sons of the 'deicidal race' became increasingly more insecure, money became the first and last basis of their security, 'their life, their strength, their power' (Jacob ben Elijah). Their money trade, whereby anticipated profit in the form of interest was calculated openly and precisely, in effect implied rational anticipation, when time was converted into money-value, when the Jewish businessman, detached from both production and from the land, juggled with figures and abstractions. Looking towards the future at the same time as he was exposed to specific vicissitudes and hazards, deprived of the elemental and static security which comes from the possession of roots, from stability and from the repetition of the known, the Jew took refuge in the dynamic security of acquiescence in change, confidence in the promise of new horizons or in plans to master an uncertain future. The relationship between existential predispositions such as these, and those displayed by a capitalist whose success depends on the acceptance of 'calculated risks', can be seen.

Many of the features of Werner Sombart's famous portrait of the Jewish entrepreneur can also be recognised here. But Sombart's theory, although acute in several details, is basically spoiled by an anthropological assumption which was fairly typical of Europe in his day: the attribution of differentiating, clearly defined and stable psychological characteristics to 'races'. In addition, he restricted his field of study to the continent of Europe, while we have seen how much light even a superficial look at the Jews in the Islamic Empire in comparison with the Christian world throws on the subject of 'the Jews and economic life'. Neglecting data on Eastern history already easily accessible during his lifetime, Sombart attributed to the Jews a semitic 'racial fixity' as well as an equally semitic 'desert nomadism'. This enabled him to connect the driving role in the development of capitalism that he ascribed to them with hypothetical 'racial properties' relayed through a religious tradition about which he understood very little. But Sombart's capital error lay in speculating on specific affinities between Jews and capitalism without observing that this was a question of only one particular aspect of a much wider relationship between the people detached from the land and the need for, or spirit of, innovation.

Jews probably contributed to the triumph of the new economic forms of organisation to the precise extent that this spirit of innovation haunts the birth and growth of the capitalist system. The final stage in the socio-economic process under review should now be clarified—when, on the threshold of modern times, Christian attitudes, and notably the doctrine on usury, changed in such a way as to make the Jews' old privilege disappear. The evolution then becomes extremely complex. The manifold factors which govern Jewish economic activities grow in number and act in diverse ways, primarily in accordance with a growing differentiation in European Judaism which reflects the great differentiations between nations. But the prime fact is the appearance in the sixteenth century of a completely new type of Diaspora: that of the marranos. Anyone reading Sombart carefully will see that his most convincing examples refer to the enterprises of this 'secret population and mutual aid society' which possessed associates and agents in every large international port at the period when the network of maritime trade was extending world wide. In such a situation, and above all enjoying the appreciable advantage of being Jews when it pleased them and Christians when it was convenient—i.e. being largely unencumbered by the shackles or bridles that medieval socio-religious traditions still placed on economic activities—they did in fact display a remarkable modernity in mentality and method. That they were deprived of the stabilising element which 'overt' Jews possessed in the institutional forms of their communities again suggests a relationship between rootlessness and economic and cultural dynamism in the case of these doubly-uprooted people with whom the inexorable conflict between two identities, breaking through to the surface, had become the very mode of their apperception and their definition as a human group.

In Italy, on the other hand, the new prevailing attitudes, which were expressed in moral and ecclesiastical reform rather than in the mystical dynamism of a crusade, led to a reverse evolution in the case of the Jews (but only according to a plan which does not apply in its entirety to other European Jewries). The downfall of the Italian Jews has been essentially explained by the loss of their privileges and by the rise of large banking establishments in the guise of Monti di Pietà, but it is significant that it was at Rome that this downfall reached its lowest point. Certainly at Rome too, and perhaps at Rome more than elsewhere, the Jews' social position seems to have been a function of their wealth: but, as chapter I sets out to show, if there is one field where such a simple relationship does not exhaust the problem, it is truly that of the relationship between the Jews and the Holy See. Moreover, the rise of administrative fanaticism in respect of the Jews under the Counter-Reformation popes and the edifying poverty of the ghetto of modern times can be interpreted as the expression of the local factor which governs even the economic history of the Jews and distinguishes it. This is the factor which, while very important as a buffer against the effects of circumstances, trends and cycles, also exposes it to the same extent to the influence of ideas, collective representations and religious or political passions: in short, to purely human arbitrariness.

The Jews, ousted from their position of strength by the Christian bourgeoisie and rendered useless from any but the theological point of view, were exposed to mistrust and popular hatred: chapter VIII attempted to bring out the various causes of their debasement. The essential factor is the relegation to the ghettos, the isolation of the Jews as a result of segregation imposed by the Church. Moreover, this isolation corresponds to the essential nature of the Jewish character, which becomes a reality expressed more or less clearly according to the conditions in which it exists. It is certainly a far cry from the days of the fourteenth century when *banchieri* consorted almost as equals with the upper classes and princes, and a pious rabbi would honour an important guest by taking him to visit the churches of his town. Behind the ghetto walls, the Jews retired within themselves, and their internal cohesion increased accordingly: it was those belonging to the Eternal City who finally demonstrated the greatest Jewish vitality. Between the two extremes of a Spanish-type persecution and an emancipating toleration, institutionalised oppression seems henceforth to provide in Europe the best conditions for the preservation of the 'Eternal People'. (Spinoza remarked at the time that 'the Jews are preserved by the hatred of the nations'.)

In any case, the foundations of this preservation are thereafter to be sought in socio-religious structures, and preferably in economic factors. From this economic point of view, as they were gradually ejected from pawnbroking, the Jews clung to the various ancillary trades which the Christian world left to them— not on the basis of some ethical prohibition but because it did not know how or scorned to profit from them. In the middle ages the status of 'Jew' conferred a special immunity for the money trade, while in modern times this status in many cases reduced him to a poverty which drove him to the baptismal font. Yet at the other end of the social scale among the rich merchants, ex-marranos and others, whose fortunes partly cancelled out the social infamy, worldly vanity and ambition to be noticed prepared the ground for other factors conducive to disintegration.

The emancipation of the Jews again upsets the data on the problem. 'All for the Jews as men, nothing as a nation!' But the abolition of discrimination and legal disabilities, plus the abolition of the Jewish communities' autonomy—the legal and religious controls they exercised over their members—created a situation not unlike that from which the marranos profited two or three centuries earlier. It is true that far from being forbidden, the Israelite religion was placed on an equal footing with the other religions, just as its worshippers were theoretically placed on an equal footing with other citizens. But persistent social pressure exercised a similar influence to the burnings of the Inquisitions, the difference being only in the distinction between *shame* and *fear*: penalties continued to exist outside all the machinery of repression. Another difference lay in the fact that the Jewish entrepreneur had no further need of a Christian mask to conduct his business. The logical result of this is the difficulty of recognising the Jewishness of this business or of that bank. In the 'get-rich-quick' century, a banker is a banker before he is a Jew, and perhaps that is all. In the eyes of a large number of Christians, however, the Jewish banker, in his role as banker, is a Jew who engages in banking, in his role as a Jew.

Consequently, the 'Jews' once again seem to dominate the financial scene at the time of the industrial revolution; the remarkable case of the Rothschilds, who did exercise an inter-national influence and have a policy of their own,[11] strengthens the misleading impression that the Children of Israel were the kings of the period. In reality, two sets of facts are henceforth involved. While the Jews in the nineteenth century, like the marranos before them, possess an impalpable but real advantage for success in their undertakings (although this was going to shrink fairly rapidly), within a European society for whom the term 'Jew' was charged with emotional secular undertones, a process of magnification, little short of a mirage, was going on. This society is uneasy. The deep socio-economic upheavals and all sorts of revolutions inflicted on the population psychological trials and tensions not unlike those the Jews endured during their exile. From the point of view of Jewish history, the salient feature was to be the West's growing fear in the face of its own destiny. The Jews, as precursors of this destiny, seem to thinkers of every shade of opinion as well as to the mass of the population to be the effective cause of this fear, with the well-known resultant consequences for their history.

# Appendix:
# The Epistle of Jacob ben Elijah

The polemical letter by Jacob ben Elijah, a thirteenth-century talmudist from Provence, was addressed to his cousin and former pupil Pablo Christiani, a convert, best known for the 'disputation' he had in 1263 with the famous rabbi Moses ben Nahman (Nahmanides) before the king of Aragon. This letter was published by J. Kobak in his review *Jeschurun* (6-7, Bamberg, 1868). The passage translated below shows the author's understanding of the significance of the money trade for the Jews. In other parts of his letter, Jacob ben Elijah comments on a few striking political events of his century, such as the defeat of the Almohades in Spain, or the collapse of the Latin Empire of Constantinople, in a favourable sense for the truth of Judaism. See Jacob Mann, 'Une source de l'histoire juive au XIIIe siècle', *Revue des études juives*, 82, 1926, pp. 363 ff.

You have also made us odious in the eyes of the masses by raising the question of money. But you know the people of Edom who have ever loved the red;* they run after gold and silver and their voracity is insatiable. How can one close the jaws of the bears and the lions if not by these two torches, which are a help in misfortune? These two great lights reign day and night, diverting evil blows and foiling plots, so that the cow and the bear can

* Edom—the 'descendants of Esau' designates the Romans in Jewish tradition and, by extension, the Christians. Edom also means 'red' in Hebrew. 'Have ever loved the red'—cf. Gen. 25:30: 'And Esau said to Jacob: "Let me swallow . . . some of this red, red [pottage]".' On the other hand, the colour of gold is a yellow which often verges towards red

234

browse together, and their young sleep side by side. King Solomon has already said that 'money answereth all things' (Eccl. 10:19), and how can the man who accumulates gold and silver increase them if not by lending at interest? It is true that among the Jews of the East, every man lives by the work of his hands, for the kings of Ishmael, however sinful and evil they are, have enough judgment to levy a fixed annual tax on them; from the rich according to his fortune, and from the poor according to his. It is different in our countries; for as far as our kings and princes are concerned, they have no thought but to harass us and to strip us entirely of our gold and silver.

And now look at and consider this court of Rome to which all Christians are subject, and which extends its dominion from one ocean to the other, 'And the Lord, whom ye seek, Will suddenly come to His temple' [i.e. the pope; Mal. 3:1]; everyone is greedy for profit, and sends out collectors to extort money from the people; 'Is not the gleaning of Ephraim better than the vintage of Abiezer?' (Judges 8:2). In truth, it is thus that they establish their pre-eminence, carry out their decisions, bring their projects to successful conclusions, fulfil their plans and foil those of their adversaries, ravage towns and erect fortresses! How do they gather armies for great massacres and vast attacks? How do they dethrone kings and set up others in their place? How do they contrive their alliances and unite dynasties? How do they arrange princely marriages? How do they humiliate their adversaries and reduce them to their will? How did they break the pride of the people of Ishmael who aroused the wrath of the Almighty? How did they overthrow the arrogance of the despicable Greek kingdom? How did they conquer the execrable heretics and their crowd of followers? How did they exterminate them, over-throwing their fortresses, laying waste their towns, burning them, themselves and their children?

Is not all this the work of the prelates who come from every country to hear the decrees [of the pope] and to bow down [before him]? Now, when they are short of money, when they can no longer offer gifts, what is left for them to do?

Certainly, the people of Tuscany are at the bottom of it all.

They are legion; some of them possess a hundred thousand or
fifty thousand [livres?], 'the smallest shall become a thousand'
(Isa. 60:22); their houses are filled with silver, gold and precious
stones. The unfortunates [prelates] are reduced to having recourse
to these usurers. With tears and supplications, they must borrow
the sums they need, 'so as not to appear empty-handed before the
lord' [i.e. the pope; cf. Talmud, Baba Metzia]. They promise
interest, a hundred on a thousand and a thousand on ten thousand;
they obtain postponements, but 'the new moon [shall] devour
them with their portions' (Hos. 5:7), for they must celebrate their
festivals, offer gifts to the lords and distribute alms to the poor.
If they do not keep their promise, they will be 'cursed with the
curse' [i.e. excommunication; Mal. 3:9]. Now, the latter [the
Christian usurers] behave so as to establish their pre-eminence and
to increase their prestige, they demand usury from their own
brothers, who yet worship the same God, observing the same
law, and follow the same faith . . .

As for us, what sort of a life have we, what is our strength and
our power? We must thank God for having multiplied our
wealth, because this enables us to protect our lives and those of
our children, and to halt the schemes of our persecutors.

What, then, is our crime and what do they want of us? . . .

# Notes

*Preface*

1 Ermanno Loevinson, 'La concession des banques de prêt aux Juifs par les papes des XVIe et XVIIe siècles', *Revue des études juives*, 92–5, 1932–3 (Regestes); Vittorio Colorni, *Legge ebraica e leggi locali*, Milan, 1945; Colorni, 'Prestito ebraico e comunità ebraiche nell'Italia centrale e settentrionale', *Rivista di storia del diritto italiano*, 8, 1935, pp. 408–58 (p. 422 n. 2)

2 The problem was touched on by Gabriel le Bras in his study of the canonical doctrine of usury which appeared in the *Dictionnaire de théologie catholique*, Paris, 1947, vol. 4, col. 2354. There are earlier glimpses in the great treatise by Wilhelm Endemann, *Studien in der romanisch-katholischen Wirtschafts- und Rechtslehre*, 2 vols, Berlin, 1874, 1883, and in the excellent study by Colorni mentioned above

3 Lucien Febvre, 'Les origines de la Réforme française et le problème des causes de la Réforme', in his *Au Coeur religieux du XVIe siècle*, Paris, 1957, p. 58

*Chapter I   The Basis of the Papal Protection of the Jews*

1 These legends have been published by A. Jellinek in *Beth Ha-Midrash*, 5, 1873, pp. 60–2 and 6, 1877, pp. 9–14, and retold in German in H. Vogelstein and P. Rieger, *Geschichte der Juden in Rom*, vol. 1, Berlin, 1895, pp. 165–9; Moritz Güdemann, *Geschichte des Erziehungswesens und der Kultur der abendländischen Juden . . .* , Vienna, 1880–8, vol. 2, pp. 44–6, 80–2. See also A. A. Neuman, 'A note on John the Baptist and Jesus in Josippon', *Hebrew Union College Annual*, 22 (2), 1950–1, pp. 137–50; J. H. Greenstone, 'Jewish legends about Simon-Peter', *Historia Judaica*, 12, 1950, pp. 89–104

2 *Discorso circa il stato degli hebrei*, Venice, 1638, Considerazione XII. 'They have been settled there for over eight hundred years'—writing in about

1630, Rabbi Luzzatto probably made the Jewish community of Rome go back to the time of Charlemagne. In fact, it was at least twice as old: it must be remembered that its establishment in Rome preceded that of a Christian community

3  This curious document published by C. Bernheimer in *Revue des études juives*, 65, 1913, pp. 224 ff. has been studied by Joshua Starr in *Romania, the Jewries of the Levant after the Fourth Crusade*, Paris, 1949, pp. 48–54

4  Renouard, *Les Relations des papes d'Avignon et des compagnies commerciales et bancaires de 1316 à 1378*, Paris, 1941, p. 125; The Diploma of Alexander IV, in *Monumenta Germaniae Historica*, Ep. Saec., vol. 13, p. 335

5  See Robert Davidsohn, *Geschichte von Florenz*, vol. 1, Berlin, 1896, p. 798

6  Renouard, op. cit., pp. 108–9. He states (p. 106 n. 58) that at the papal court at Avignon, too, the role of Jewish finance was insignificant

7  Moritz Stern, *Urkundliche Beiträge über die Stellung der Päpste zu den Juden*, Kiel, 1893, no. 44, pp. 48–50. The same comment occurs in the *Rechtsbuch* of Johannes Purgoldt compiled in about 1500 (see Guido Kisch, *The Jews in Medieval Germany*, Chicago, 1949, p. 58)

8  Raphael Straus, *Die Juden im Königreich Sizilien unter Normannen und Staufern*, Heidelberg, 1910; Attilio Milano, 'Vicende economiche degli Ebrei nell'Italia meridionale durante il Medioevo', *Rassegna mensile di Israel*, 20, March–October 1954

9  'The mass conversion of Jews in southern Italy', *Speculum*, 21, 1946, pp. 203ff.

10  See Solomon Grayzel, 'Reference to the Jews in the correspondence of John XXII', *Hebrew Union College Annual*, 22 (2), 1950–1, pp. 73–5, quoting a letter published by G. Mollat

11  See *The History of Anti-Semitism*, vol. 2, London, 1974

12  Among the different studies devoted to the episode of San Nicandro, mention should be made of the excellent work by Elena Cassin, *San Nicandro*, Paris, 1957; London, 1959. On the subject of crypto-Jews in the kingdom of Naples in the second half of the sixteenth century, see F. R. Martin, 'La expulsión de los Judios del reino de Napoles', *Hispania*, 35, 1947, pp. 105–8

13  I am thinking particularly of the following comments formulated by Herbert Lüthy in the introduction to his book *La Banque protestante en France*, Paris, 1959, vol. 1, p. 20 and p. 23: 'The Protestant religion disappeared from the countryside, apart from those regions in the Midi and the West where it had gained a strong popular hold; because outside the towns . . . the scattered minorities of peasants and poor rural inhabitants, materially and spiritually defenceless, without chapels, without pastors, without instruction, without books, and furthermore generally illiterate, were left with no means to keep going. The "people" of this period lived in such obscurity, ignorant and despised beasts of burden, that in many cases it is impossible to know when and how the spark went out'. On the subject of emigrants, on the other hand, having compared them with the 'ex-territorial people', the Jews, Lüthy writes: ' the religious motive is hard to separate from the economic motive. In every realm, persecution and insecurity of status made the French Protestants a particularly

"restless" minority and forced a mobility upon them which, though often cruel, was greatly to their advantage.'

## Chapter II  The Doctrine of Usury and the Jews

1   On the Christian *judaei* of Cremona, see Vittorio Colorni, 'Prestito ebraico e comunità ebraiche', *Rivista di storia del diritto italiano*, 8, 1935, pp. 445–7 (the long note 3). On 'Blancardo the Jew' see Benjamin Nelson, in *Studi in onore di Gino Luzzatto*, Milan, 1950, vol. 1, pp. 96–116

2   *Les Relations des papes d'Avignon et des compagnies commerciales et bancaires de 1316 à 1378*, Paris, 1941, p. 106 n. 58

3   On the early middle ages particularly: see the numerous examples supplied by Bernhard Blumenkranz in *Juifs et Chrétiens dans le monde occidental*, The Hague-Paris, 1960, pp. 59–64: 'The least divergence from strict orthodoxy, however far removed from any connection with Jews and Judaism, is accused of having a judaising tendency', which Blumenkranz defines as 'exorbitant extensions' of this criticism

4   *Sermones in cantica canticorum*, Sermo IX, 'De incredulitate Judaeorum', Migne, *Patrologia Latina*, vol. 183, coll. 1066–7.

5   *Enchiridion militis Christiani*, quoted by Lucien Febvre, *Au Coeur religieux du XVIe siècle*, Paris, 1957, p. 131

6   From *La Dépêche de Paris*, 2 June 1892, p. 1. I am quoting from the study by Edmund Silberner, 'French socialism and the Jewish question', *Historia Judaica*, 14 (1), 1954, pp. 3–38

7   Babylonian Talmud, Baba Metsia 70 b

8   Baba Metsia, 73 a; see also *Shulhan Arukh*, Yoreh Deah, 159[1]

9   See J. Rosenthal, 'Ribbith min ha-nokhri', *Talpiyyoth*, 5, 1952, p. 488. The comment was made by the rabbi of Barcelona, Solomon Ben Adreth (1235–1310)

10  See Siegfried Stein, 'The development of the Jewish law on interest', *Historia Judaica*, 17, April 1955, p. 32, quoting an unpublished manuscript by Gersonides

11  Stein, op. cit., p. 22, quoting a Responsum by Rashi

12  However, in places where Jews possessed other means of livelihood, certain rabbis protested violently against the money trade; as in Provence, for example, Rabbi Nissim of Marseilles in 1306: 'And our contemporaries today have acquired these perverse tendencies, namely, to lend at interest to non-Jews, tendencies which have become a firm habit with them.' Various passages on the same lines by Franco-German rabbis can be found in the famous *Sefer Hasidim* (*Book of the Pious*) by Judah the Pious (about 1200)

13  *Sefer Ha-Iggur*, New York, 1959, p. 64

14  These relaxations were suggested by Rabbenu Gershom (960–1028); see Jacob Katz, *Exclusiveness and Tolerance*, Oxford, 1961, p. 33

15  Ibid., pp. 34–6, *et passim*, where Katz shows with a great deal of subtlety that the Tosafists' arguments applied only in special cases; the general doctrinal principle, whereby Christians were not idolaters, did not appear until the fourteenth century

16  See Moses Hoffmann, *Der Geldhandel der deutschen Juden während des Mittelalters bis zum Jahre 1350*, Leipzig, 1910, p. 107, quoting several rabbinic Responsa. These made a distinction: if the object offered as a pledge could be used only for worship, it would be refused; if it were capable of other use (for example, clerical robes), it could be accepted
17  See Blumenkranz, op. cit., pp. 318–19
18  The transaction is explained more clearly by Yehiel Nissim da Pisa in *The Eternal Life* (see Gilbert S. Rosenthal, ed., *Banking and Finance among Jews in Renaissance Italy*, New York, 1962, pp. 96–7): 'If a Jew gave a pawn to a gentile in exchange for a usurious loan from another Jew, the lender is permitted to take interest from the gentile because the gentile acquired the pawn from the Jew (the borrower) by the act of taking possession and anything he pays to the lender is for him . . . According to the Rosh, of blessed memory, if the lender knows that the borrower was a Jew, it is surely prohibited. But if he does not know for sure, he will not believe the words of the borrower, for who can prove that this money which the gentile took was indeed for the use of a Jew? Perhaps he merely kept it for himself and gave the borrower some of his own money? If it was clearly known that it belonged to a Jew, for example it was the jewel or garment of a Jew, then it is surely prohibited to take interest . . .'
19  J. J. Rabinowitz, 'Some remarks on the evasion of the usury laws in the middle ages', *Harvard Theological Review*, 36, 1943, pp. 49–59. The English Jews' financial transactions were registered in a royal central office (the 'Exchequer of the Jews'); a large part of its archives is still in existence
20  As E. E. Hildesheimer (*Das jüdische Gesellschaftsrecht*, Leipzig, 1930, pp. 89–131, esp. 129–31) shows, the Talmudic contract called *iska* was adapted to the conditions of medieval Europe so that in its contents it did not differ appreciably from the *commenda*. As far as form was concerned, the *iska*, half deposit, half loan in classic Talmudic law, evolved in Europe towards a particular type of administrative contract in which the manager was excused from presenting his accounts to the owner or the moneylender on regular payment of an indemnity; this made it possible to circumvent the prohibition on lending at interest within certain limits
21  Giulio Morosini, *Via della fede, mostrata a' gli Ebrei*, Rome, 1683, pp. 1415 ff.
22  Shalom bar Isaac Sekel, quoted by Moritz Güdemann, *Geschichte des Erziehungswesens und der Kultur der abendländischen Juden*, Vienna, 1880–8, vol. 3, p. 183
23  Letter from Calvin to Pastor Morel, 10 January 1562, *Corpus reformatorum*, vol. 47 (*Calvini opera*, vol. 11), Brunswick, 1878, pp. 245–6
24  Examples: for England, article 17 of the Council of Worcester (1229); for France, article 4 of the Council of Melun (1226), article 1 of the Council of Rouen (1231) (texts in Solomon Grayzel, *The Church and the Jews in the XIIIth Century* . . . , Philadelphia, 1933). Innocent III seems to have been alluding to such a practice in his letter to the duc de Nevers in January 1208 (ibid.). For later periods: Brussels, 1369—two priests financed a Jewish lender (P. Lefèvre, 'A propos du trafic d'argent exercé par les Juifs de Bruxelles au XIVe siècle', *Revue belge de philosophie et d'histoire*, 1930; fifteenth-century Germany—synodal condemnation of

monks pursuing similar practices (Max Neumann, *Geschichte des Wuchers in Deutschland* . . . , Halle, 1865, p. 521 n. 4); fifteenth-century Provence— see the curious general admonition quoted by Roger Aubenas (*Cours d'histoire du droit privé*, Aix-en-Provence, 1958 (duplicated), vol. 6, p. 140): curés were instructed to harangue Jews in synagogues in order to make them reveal the names of the Christians who, afraid of practising the art of usury themselves, were lending their money at interest to Jews—'artem usurarium temere exercentes, ipsis judeis sub modo . . . fenoris seu usure eorum pecunias habent mutuare'. For Italy, see the remainder of this book

25 *Corpus juris canonici*, Decretals, V. 19. 12; V. 19. 18

26 For example, Max Neumann, op. cit., p. 222: 'Bei ihnen allein erkannte man den Wucher als erlaubt an . . . und zog ihm nur, aus Gründen der Billigkeit, eine bestimmte Grenze.' ['Only among them was the usurer acknowledged as permitted . . . and given certain limits on the grounds of economy.'] More recently Raymond de Roover (*Money, Banking and Credit in Mediaeval Bruges*, Cambridge, Mass., 1948, p. 157 n. 15) speaks of 'Jewish money-lenders to whom, because of their religion, the prohibition of usury did not apply'

27 Among authors who have come to the conclusion that St Thomas was unconditionally hostile to the Jews' money trade, it suffices to mention Henri Pirenne (see his study 'La duchesse Aleyde de Brabant et le *De regimine Judaeorum* de Saint Thomas d'Aquin', *Bulletin de l'Académie Royale de Belgique*, 1928, pp. 43–55). Much less dogmatic interpretations have been made by Wilhelm Endemann in his *Studien in der romanisch-katholischen Wirtschafts- und Rechtslehre*, vol. 2, Berlin, 1883, chap. 'Die Juden', and particularly by Amintore Fanfani, *Le origine dello spirito capitalistico in Italia*, Milan, 1933, pp. 19–20

28 In particular by Pirenne, op. cit.; the duchess asked St Thomas if she could raise taxes or levy fines on Jews and accept their offerings of money. The Angelic Doctor replied that she could so do (otherwise they would have enjoyed unlimited impunity!) but on condition she restored this money, if it was usurious in origin, to those from whom it had been extorted or, if they could not be identified, to offer it to charitable institutions. He also added the wish that the Jews earn their living by working with their hands, as they did in Italy. But he scarcely mentioned any express prohibition on the practice of lending at interest, as far as they were concerned

29 Definition of toleration, according to the *Summa juris publici ecclesiastici*, 1938 edition. A. Michel, from whom I am quoting, completes it as follows: 'Negative permission of a real or supposed evil' (*Dictionnaire de théologie catholique*, vol. 15, pt 1, col. 1208)

30 Pietro d'Ancarano, *Consilia sive iuris responsa Petri Ancharani iurisconsulti clarissimi* . . . , Venice, 1585, Consilium 243, fos 129a–129b

31 *Consilia*, Frankfurt, 1583, Consilium 397, fos 191b–192b; see also Consilium 293, fos 150a–151b

32 *Consiliorum seu responsorum Alexandri Tartagni Imolensis: Liber secundus. Casus consilii primi*, Venice, 1610

33 *Diarii*, 9 November 1519, on the subject of the discussions about the renewal of the *condotta* of the Jews in Venice

34 The *Consilia* of de Nevo were, if I am not mistaken, the first incunabula especially devoted to the 'Jewish question' in Christian lands. The first *Consilium* was written before 1442; the other three between 1445 and 1455. I have used the Nuremberg edition of 1479 (Bibliothèque nationale, Paris, Rés. F 1289)

35 *Summa theologica*, IIᵃ IIᵃᵉ, Quaest. 10, art. II

36 The cases in question are of course those in which, according to the canonists, usury was exceptionally permitted (five cases according to Innocent IV, seven according to Celestine V and Raymond de Peñaforte, twelve according to Panormita, thirteen according to Hostiensis (Cardinal Henricus Bartholomaeis); see G. Salvioli, 'La dottrina dell'usura secondo i canonisti e i civilisti italiani dei secoli XIII e XVI', in *Studi in onore di Carlo Fadda*, vol. 2, Naples, 1906, separate extract, pl. 19)

37 [The original text has the traditional pun on 'pécher' (to sin) and pêcher (to fish)]

38 Sisto da Siena, *De foenore Judaeorum* . . . , Venice, 1555, pp. 31b-32a. The idea that Jews are sinning against the articles of the Christian faith by remaining Jews seems to have been current. See for example *Super Clementinae* by Giovanni da Imola (Venice, 1486), p. 139b: 'iudei peccant in articulis fidei quia non credunt humanitatem Christi: hoc est certum, et Ecclesia hoc scit, et tamen tolerat et sustinet et non punit' [Jews sin against the articles of faith in that they do not believe in the humanity of Christ; this is certain and the Church knows it, and yet tolerates and sustains it and does not punish it]

39 Gia. Battista da Luca, *Il Dottor Volgare, ovvero il compendio di tutta la legge civile . . . moralizzato in lingua italiana*, Venice, 1740, vol. 2, chap. 17 ('Dell'usure delli Giudei'), pp. 431-2

40 Responsa of Leon da Modena (*Zikne Yehudah*), ed. S. Simonsohn, Jerusalem, 1956, no. 88, pp. 138-40

*Chapter III   The Jewish Money Trade in Italy*

1 'I primordi del prestito ebraico in Italia', *Rassegna mensile di Israel*, 19, 1953, p. 452

2 Robert Davidsohn, *Geschichte von Florenz*, vol. 4, pt 3, Berlin, 1927, p. 104

3 'I prestiti comunali e gli Ebrei a Matelica nel secolo XIII', *Le Marche*, 7, 1907, pp. 249-72

4 *I banchieri ebrei in Urbino nell'età ducale*, Padua, 1902, p. 10

5 Georges Bigwood, *Le Régime juridique et économique du commerce de l'argent dans la Belgique*, 2 vols, Brussels, 1921; Raymond de Roover, *Money, Banking and Credit in Mediaeval Bruges*, Cambridge, Mass., 1948

6 'Banquiers, commerçants, diplomates et voyageurs italiens à Fribourg (Suisse) avant 1500', *Zeitschrift für schweizerische Geschichte*, 7, 1927, pp. 1-59

7 Quoted in Davidsohn, op. cit., vol. 4, pt 2, 1925, p. 234

8 'Les Génois en Angleterre: la crise de 1458-1466', in *Studi in onore di*

*Armando Sapori*, Milan, 1957, vol. 2, pp. 816–17; also *Gênes au XVe siècle*, Paris, 1961, p. 257

9 *Les Juifs dans les Pays-Bas au Moyen Age*, Brussels, 1950, pp. 62–4 and n., 178–9

10 All the authors who have dealt with the decline and the expulsion of the Jews from England in the thirteenth century agree that the decisive factors were the increase in influence and the concurrence of the Cahorsins—see G. J. Meisel, *Jewish Moneylending in Angevin England*, London, 1933; P. Elman, 'The economic causes of the expulsion of the Jews in 1290', *Economic History Review*, 7, 1936–7, pp. 145–54; Cecil Roth, *The History of the Jews in England*, 2nd ed., Oxford, 1949; and more recently H. G. Richardson, *The English Jewry under Angevin Kings*, London, 1960. The Beraldi (or Béraud) were the oldest merchant dynasty of Cahors known—see Philippe Wolff, 'Le problème des Cahorsins', *Annales du Midi*, 62, 1950, pp. 229–38; E. Albe, 'Les marchands de Cahors à Londres au XIIIe siècle', *Bulletin de la Société des Études du Lot*, 1908, pp. 31 ff.

11 This time-lag in research is also to a large extent explained because the documentation is scattered (unlike England, with its archives of the 'Scaccarium Judaeorum')

12 'Die Stellung der Juden im Mittelalter . . .', *Zeitschrift für die gesamte Staatswissenschaft*, 31, 1875, pp. 503–26

13 *Economic and Social History of Medieval Europe*, London, 1936, p. 133

14 Davidsohn, op. cit., vol. 4, pt 3, p. 233

15 Ibid., pt 2, p. 139

16 Raymond de Roover, *The Medici Bank*, New York, 1948, pp. 55 ff.

17 'The usurer and the merchant prince: Italian businessmen and the ecclesiastical law of restitution', in *The Tasks of Economic History*, vol. 7, 1947, p. 118

18 Armando Sapori, 'La funzione economica della nobiltà', in *Studi di storia economica*, 2 vols, Florence, 1956, p. 717

19 *Le origine dello spirito capitalistico in Italia*, Milan, 1933, p. 131

20 Op. cit., p. 106

21 Gino Barbieri, 'L'usuraio Tomaso Grassi nel racconto bandelliano e nella documentazione storica', in *Studi in onore di Amintore Fanfani*, Milan, 1962, vol. 2, pp. 19–28. The memory of this very rich usurer has survived at Milan thanks to his acts of liberality and to the works he founded

22 From E. Caïs de Pierlas, *La ville de Nice pendant le premier siècle de la domination des princes de Savoie*, Turin, 1898, pp. 124, 265–6, 467

23 See Davidsohn, op. cit., vol. 4, pt 2, p. 147 ('Die Pfandleiher')

24 'Types économiques et sociaux du XVIe siècle: le marchand', *Revue des cours et conférences*, 1921, p. 63

25 The team in question was led by Dr Ernst Dichter, generally regarded as the creator of 'Motivation Research'. I would like to thank him for his kindness in letting me have the conclusions of his investigations: *A Psychological Research Study for the Personal Finance Company*

26 Numerous examples of the allegedly greater greed of Christian usurers have been collected by James Parkes, *The Jew in the Medieval Community*, London, 1938, pp. 336–8. For France, very informative is the *Chronique*

*rimée* of Geoffroi de Paris, talking of popular complaints after the expulsion of the Jews in 1306: 'For the Jews were much milder/In the conduct of their business/Than the Christians are now' (ll. 3122-4), and calling for the recall of the Jews

27 See G. Salvemini, 'Firenze ai tempi di Dante', in *Studi in onore di Armando Sapori*, vol. 1, p. 474

*Chapter IV   The Rise of Jewish Banking in Italy*

1 For Todi, see L. Leonij, 'Documenti tratti dall'archivio segreto di Todi', *Archivio storico italiano*, 3rd series, 22, 1875, pp. 182-90; for Matelica, see Gino Luzzatto, 'I prestiti comunali e gli Ebrei a Matelica nel secolo XIII', *Le Marche*, 7, 1907, pp. 247-72 (an offprint which the author was kind enough to send me); the contract for Ascoli has been published by Giuseppe Fabiani, *Gli Ebrei e il Monte di Pietà in Ascoli*, Ascoli Piceno, 1942, pp. 169-72.

   The presence of Jews in the same region at the end of the thirteenth century has been recorded at Recanati and Montegiorgio, but with no mention of the money trade; see Luzzatto, *I banchieri ebrei in Urbino* . . . , Padua, 1902, p. 14

2 Luigi Fumi, *Codice diplomatico della città d'Orvieto*, Florence, 1884, pp. 416-19

3 See the public chronological registers published by Robert Davidsohn, *Geschichte von Florenz*, vol. 2, Berlin, 1900, nos 2460-8. A contract discussed with the Jews of Siena in 1309—but we do not know if it was concluded—imposed a fine of 500 golden florins at San Gimignano, in case of infraction, *medietas cujus pene sit ecclesie Romana et alia medietas sit* . . . *de dictis judeis* (no. 2461)

4 At Pisa, the statute of 1286 forbade the practice of lending at interest, while that of 1313 controlled it. At Pistoia, prohibition was in 1296, and control in 1344. See Lodovico Zdekauer, 'L'interno d'un banco di pegno nel 1417', *Archivio storico italiano*, 5th series, 17, 1896, p. 76 n. 1. At Lucca, the statute of 1308 forbade the lodging of complaints of usury before ecclesiastical tribunals; see *Inventario del R. Archivio di Stato di Lucca*, ed. S. Bongi, Lucca, 1872, p. 211. On the subject of prosecutions for usury under ecclesiastical law, see also Armando Sapori, 'L'usura nel Dugento a Pistoia', in *Studi di storia economica*, Florence, 1956, pp. 182-9. At Lucca, where the proceeds of the *gabelle* (salt tax) paid by the pawnbrokers was farmed out, foreign lenders had to pay a higher tax and provide firmer guarantees in the middle of the fourteenth century; E. Lazzareschi, 'Il beato Bernardino da Feltre, gli Ebrei e il Monte di Pietà in Lucca', *Bollettino storico Lucchese*, 19 (1), 1941, pp. 12-31

5 See Attilio Milano, 'I primordi del prestito ebraico in Italia' ('Le tappe della marcia discendente degli Ebrei tedeschi'), *Rassegna mensile di Israel*, 19 (8), 1953, pp. 360-6. As far as Friuli is concerned, Federico Luzzatto casts doubt on the presence of Jewish lenders at the end of the thirteenth century; see his 'Ebrei in Aquileia', in *Scritti in onore di Riccardo Bachi*, Città di Castello, 1950, p. 143 n. 3. See also the inexhaustible Davidsohn, op. cit., vol. 4, pt 3, pp. 458-63

6   See Giovanni da Imola, *Clementinae Clementis Quinti Constitutiones . . . ,* Lyons, 1541, pp. 61b–62a

7   Several German towns recalled the Jews in the years following the Black Death: Nuremberg and Zürich in 1352, Vienna in 1353, Erfurt in 1354, Heilbronn in 1357, Basle before 1364. They were also recalled in France in 1360

8   According to Cecil Roth, there were no burnings of Jews except in Parma and Mantua in 1348–9; *The History of the Jews of Italy*, p. 142

9   A few typical surnames of Italian Jews whose ancestors had had to emigrate from Germany or France were: Luzzatto, Luzzatti (Lausitz), Ottolengo, Ottolenghi (Ettlingen), Morpurgo (Marburg), Basola (Basle), Tedesco; Marsella (Marseilles), Lattes (Lattès near Montpellier), Marli (Arles), Provenzali.

    'German' ritual had spread widely among Italian Jews at the end of the middle ages. As for 'French' ritual, extinct everywhere else since the fifteenth century, it was perpetuated in certain Jewish communities in Piedmont until the nineteenth century; D. Disegni, 'Il rito di Asti-Fossano-Moncalvo (APAM)', in *Scritti in memoria di Sally Mayer*, Jerusalem, 1956, pp. 78–81

10   S. Bongi, *Bandi Lucchesi del secolo decimoquarto*, Bologna, 1863, nos 290, 294, 296, 303, 304

11   On the Jews of Siena in relation to the money trade, see the thorough work by Niccolò Piccolomini and Narciso Mengozzi, *Il Monte dei Paschi di Siena*, vol. 1, Siena, 1891

12   See Nicola Ferorelli, *Gli Ebrei nell' Italia meridionale*, Turin, 1915, pp. 66–7, 71 ff.

13   Alfred Doren, *Italienische Wirtschaftsgeschichte des Mittelalters und der Renaissance*, Jena, 1934, vol. 1, p. 427

14   Giuliano Nannino de' Bardi; see Mario Ciardini, *I banchieri ebrei in Firenze*, Borgo San Lorenzo, 1907, p. 27

15   In his *Ricordi* (quoted by Umberto Cassuto, *Gli Ebrei a Firenze*, Florence, 1918, p. 16), the goldsmith Oderigo di Credi tells how he pledged a jacket in a public *presto* at Florence in 1412; when he took it out six months later, he had to pay 4 lire 13 *soldi* in interest for a loan of 20 lire, which corresponds to an annual rate of 45 per cent. Thus, contrary to what Sapori thinks (op. cit., p. 186), 40 per cent was not solely 'parto della fantasia del popolo'. It has been seen that the maximum authorised rate had been 40 per cent since 1372 at Lucca, and was 30 per cent at the end of the fourteenth century at Siena. The real rate was higher, on account of the method of deducting interest, which will be studied later, by the Jewish *banchieri* (rounding off a month which had already begun to a whole month, rounding off a sum to the nearest lira or using variations in the rate of the lira compared with the florin, etc.). The maximum rate allowed to Jews was almost always a few points below that of Christian lenders. It is tempting to say that before monopolising this field of activity, they first served as 'pilot lenders' in the same way as 'pilot shops' exist today to check rising prices. And this occurred against the background of the slow

I

NOTES TO PAGES 59-72

fall in the rates for lending money, as reflected in the fall in maximum rates between the fourteenth and the sixteenth century

16 The connection between the return of Cosimo de Medici and the appeal to the Jews has been brought out by F. R. Salter ('The Jews in fifteenth-century Florence and Savonarola's establishment of a Mons Pietatis', *Cambridge Historical Journal*, 2, 1936, pp. 193 ff.): 'May it not have been a part, even though only a small part of the Medicean policy to remove from his banking rivals, with papal assistance, some part of their potential (if not actual) business, that dealing with the smaller folk, and yet conciliate that smaller folk'. This is really the 'equalisation of economic sacrifice' mentioned by Sapori ('Cosimo Medici e un patto giurato a Firenze', in *Studi di storia economica*, p. 412). See also F. Schevill, *History of Florence*, 2nd ed., London, 1961, pp. 356-7, 364-5

17 Quoted by Carlo Invernizzi, 'Gli Ebrei a Pavia; contributo alla storia dell'ebraismo nel ducato di Milano', *Bollettino della Società Pavese di storia patria*, 5 (3), 1905, p. 292 n. 2

18 'Predicatori a Brescia nel Quattrocento', *Archivio storico Lombardo*, 15, 1908, pp. 83-144

19 Fabio Glissenti, *Gli Ebrei nel Bresciano* . . . (*Nuove ricerche e studi*), Brescia, 1891, p. 9

20 Op. cit., pp. 191-240

21 F. Bonfiglio, *Notizie storiche di Castelgoffredo*, Brescia, 1922, p. 135

22 Fabio Glissenti, *Gli Ebrei nel Bresciano al tempo della dominazione veneta*, Brescia, 1890, p. 20

23 See the study by G. B. Piccotti, 'D'una questione tra Pio II e Francesco Sforza per la ventisima sui beni degli Ebrei', *Archivio storico Lombardo*, 20, 1913, pp. 184-213

24 Piccolomini and Mengozzi, op. cit., vol. 1, p. 152

25 Ciardini, op. cit., appendix doc. VI and p. 68; Cassuto, op. cit., pp. 155-6

26 *Summa theologica*, II, pt 1, cap. 6, s. 2

27 The account which follows is based on the study by Piccotti quoted above and the documents he published

28 This list appears in a 'petition' by the traders of Florence to the grand duke to dissuade him from instituting the inspection of business records, which would run the risk of frightening such depositors away; Sapori, 'La registrazione dei libri di commercio in Toscana nell'anno 1666', in *Studi di storia economica*, p. 50

29 *The Medici Bank*, New York, 1948, p. 57. On the subject of similar camouflage in the books of a rich Genoese merchant, see Jacques Heers, *Le Livre de comptes de Giovanni Piccamiglio, homme d'affaires génois (1416-1459)*, Paris, 1959, p. 32.

30 *The Jewish Community*, Philadelphia, 1942, vol. 2, p. 270

*Chapter V    The Banchieri and the Holy See*

1 *Les Relations des papes d'Avignon et des compagnies commerciales et bancaires de 1316 à 1378*, Paris, 1941, esp. p. 106 n. 58

2  Archivio di Stato di Mantova, Arch. Gonzaga, S. 1°, busta 3389. It can probably be assumed that this absolution was preceded by the *Consilium* of Pietro d'Ancarano, which was studied in chapter II, while the *Consilium* of Tartagni (Alessandro da Imola) might have been requested on the occasion of a conflict which blew up in Mantua in 1462-4

3  See Moritz Stern, *Urkundliche Beiträge über die Stellung der Päpste zu den Juden*, Kiel, 1893, nos 3-7, 14, 15, 29; Félix Vernet, 'Le pape Martin V et les Juifs', *Revue des questions historiques*, 51, 1892, pp. 373-423, appendices nos 23, 31, 64

4  See L. Münster, 'Maestro Elia di Sabbato da Fermo, archiatra pontificio', in *Scritti in memoria di Sally Mayer*, Jerusalem, 1956, pp. 224-58; Stern, op. cit., no. 21 *in fine* (p. 36)

5  Stern, op. cit., no. 161, §41 (p. 179)

6  The text of these decisions has been published by S. Halberstam, *Heinrich Graetz Jubelschrift*, Breslau, 1887, Hebrew section, pp. 53-9

7  This bull was registered in the register of the Apostolic Chamber and not as normally in the register of bulls for, as a mention in the margin indicates, the *regestratores* had already left Mantua to go to Ferrara; P. M. Baumgarten, 'Miscellanea cameralia: II. Zur Register- und Bullentaxe', *Römische Quartalschrift*, 19, 1905, pp. 168-70

8  Bernardino Ghetti, 'Gli Ebrei e il Monte di Pietà in Recanati nei secoli XV e XVI', *Atti e memorie della Deputazione di storia patria per le Marche*, n.s. 4, 1907, pp. 11 ff., esp. pp. 17-25

9  Stern, op. cit., no. 20

10  Ibid., no. 24; Johannes Hofer, *Johannes von Capestrano, ein Leben in Kampf um die Reform der Kirche*, Innsbruck, 1936, p. 110, quoting a passage from his treatise *De conscientia serenada*

11  Hofer, op. cit., pp. 136 ff.; Joshua Starr, 'Johanna II and the Jews', *Jewish Quarterly Review*, 31, 1950, pp. 67-78; Giovanni Pansa, 'Gli Ebrei in Aquila nel secolo XV', *Bollettino della Società di storia patria A. L. Antinori negli Abruzzi*, 16, 1904, p. 203

12  Vernet, op. cit., appendix no. 63

13  This document found in a synagogue at Ferrara has been published by S. H. Margulies, 'Un congresso di notabili ebrei tenuto in Firenze nel 1428', *Rivista Israelitica*, 2 (5), September-October 1905, pp. 177-8

14  Vernet, op. cit., p. 386 and appendices nos 69 and 70. It might possibly be that this Salomone Bonaventura and the scholar Salomone di Ventura, the pope's protégé mentioned above, were one and the same person. It is not always easy to identify Italian Jews by their names. For a discussion of this problem, see Umberto Cassuto, *Gli Ebrei a Firenze*, Florence, 1918, pt 2, chap. 6, 'L'onomastica'

15  Cardinal Condulmieri being also bishop of Verona, the council of that town turned to him in 1441 to obtain the absolution necessary for the admission of Jewish *banchieri*. He replied: 'Quod materiam Judaeorum, pro quibus conducendis ad foenus exercendum licentiam petitis, hoc pro vestra prudentia scire debetis, non esse in potestate nostra, neque alterius viventis in ea re votis vestris satisfacere, obstante Dei et Domini nostri prohibitione qui ex necessitate salutis omnis anima veluti ejus sublimi

potestati subdita obedire tenetur.' ['As concerns the licence you seek to hire the Jews to practise usury, you ought to know out of your own experience that it is not in our power or in that of any other living person to satisfy your wishes in this matter since there stands against it the prohibition of our God and Lord, which every soul subject to His sublime power is bound to obey in the interests of his salvation.'] (Alessandro de Nevo, *Consilia contra Judaeos foenerantes*, Nuremberg, 1479, p. 446)

16 Gino Barbieri, 'L'usuraio Tomaso Grassi', in *Studi in onore di Amintore Fanfani*, vol. 2, Milan, 1962, pp. 19–88, n. 6

17 Vittorio Colorni, 'Prestito ebraico e comunità ebraiche nell'Italia centrale e settentrionale', *Rivista di storia del diritto italiano*, 8, 1935, pp. 408–58 (p. 422 n. 2)

18 In about 1445, when he was nearly forty years old, Pietro da Noxeto wrote to his friend, Aeneas Sylvius Piccolomini, the future Pius II, that he hesitated to get married because of his poverty. When, after the death of Nicholas V, he retired to his native town of Lucca, he was distinguished for his munificence, and acquired, among other possessions, the Guinigi palace; see his biography by C. Minutoli, 'Di alcune opere di belle arti della Metropolitana di Lucca', *Atti della R. Accademia Lucchese*, 21, 1882, pp. 7–30

19 Antonio Ciscato, *Gli Ebrei in Padova*, Padua, 1901, appendix, pp. 243–5, doc. VI. This discussion took place on 10 April 1455; Calixtus III was elected on 8 April

20 Documents published by Carlo Canetta, 'Gli Ebrei del ducato Milanese', *Archivio storico Lombardo*, 8, 1881, pp. 632–5

21 On the effectiveness of ecclesiastical censures in fifteenth-century Italy, see W. K. Gottwald, *Ecclesiastical censure at the end of the fifteenth century*, in *Johns Hopkins Studies*, Baltimore, 1927, in particular pp. 44 ff. (at Florence) and pp. 75 ff. (at Venice)

22 Two letters sent to Lorenzo the Magnificent by Pellegrino da Lucca on 18 February and 6 March 1478 have been published by Cassuto, op. cit., pp. 417–18, docs LXI, LXII. It was a question particularly of proving to the Medici that the other Italian princes were in agreement about levying the *vigesima*: 'et per questo mando a prefacta V.M. magistro Moyse hebreo et lactore presente, el quale più a pieno exponerà ad essa V.M. el bixogno; per parte mia prego quella a quello se degni dare piena fede come a mi proprio'. As has been seen, under Pius II it was the Jew Simone da Piacenza who took the Holy See's instructions to the Apostolic collectors of the duchy of Milan

23 See the patents published by Ermanno Loevinson, 'La concession des banques de prêt aux Juifs par les papes des XVIe et XVIIe siècles', *Revue des études juives*, 92, 1932, pp. 1–30; 93, 1932, pp. 27–52, 157–78; 94, 1933, pp. 57–72, 167–83; 95, 1933, pp. 23–40

24 Ed. S. Simonsohn, Jerusalem, 1956

25 Attilio Milano, 'Un azienda di banchieri e provveditori ebrei alla corte dei Gonzaga–Nevers nel Seicento', in *Scritti in memoria di Federico Luzzatto*, Rome, 1962, p. 190

*Chapter VI    The* Banchi

1    Fabio Glissenti, *Gli Ebrei nel Bresciano* . . . (*Nuove ricerche e studi*), Brescia, 1891, p. 21

2    A. Schulte, *Die Fugger in Rom*, Leipzig, 1904, pp. 237–8. These were precious stones which the German soldiers pillaged and sold to the Welser bank. The bank in its turn deposited them in the Fuggers' counting-house, which was under the special protection of the German troops

3    In 1680, on the eve of the abolition of the Jewish banks, the number of transactions at the Rome Monte di Pietà was 125,386. In 1766 it was 223,940 (Donato Tamilia, *Il sacro Monte di Pietà di Roma*, Rome, 1900, pp. 82, 85)

4    *Gli Ebrei e gli Estense*, Reggio di Emilia, 1930, pp. 32–5

5    Letter published by Cassuto, *Gli Ebrei a Firenze*, Florence, 1918, p. 407, doc. LI

6    'L'interno d'un banco di pegno nel 1417', *Archivio storico italiano*, 5th series, 17, 1896, p. 71

7    The choice of terms used in section IV, 8 of *The Book* shows the influence of Exod. 23 : 3. The scholarly author is amusing himself by recommending the Jewish lender to set an example to his Christian clients of the equity which is prescribed to the judge who is settling a dispute between plaintiffs

8    The Responsum of Leon da Modena (no. 106, early seventeenth century) concerns a *banco* manager who was charging interest above the statutory rate. Having caught him in the act, the owner wanted to share in the additional profit without, however, accepting responsibility for the fraud. The rabbi's verdict was that, in these circumstances, the owner could not claim the additional profit

9    Gia. Battista da Luca, *Theatrum veritatis et iustitiae* . . . *Liber Quintus*, Rome, 1669, disc. VI, pp. 24–9

10   Enrico Castelli, 'I banchi feneratizi ebraici nel Mantovano', *Accademia Virgiliana di Mantova, Atti e memorie*, 21, 1959, pl. 10, pp. 53, 60

11   Niccolò Piccolomini and Narciso Mengozzi, *Il Monte dei Paschi di Siena*, vol. 1, Siena, 1891, p. 151

12   Guido Pampaloni ('Cenni storici sul Monte di Pietà di Firenze', in *Archivi storici delle aziende di credito*, Rome, 1956, vol. 1, p. 531 n.1 7) mentions a few authors, ancient and modern, who have revived this legend for their own purposes. Cassuto, op. cit., writing some fifty-five years ago, thought it necessary to devote some six whole pages of his book to refute it (see pp. 68–73). It occurs again in Michel Bazire, *Les Institutions de prêt sur gages en Italie et en Allemagne*, Paris, 1939, p. 12: 'At Florence the annual tribute charged to the population by the Jews was estimated at 49 million *grossi*'. Actually, they were not *grossi* at all but florins (on the assumption of an initial investment of 100 florins); very precisely 49,722,556 florins, 7 *grossi* and 7 *piccoli*, according to Cassuto's calculations

13   *Money, Banking and Credit in Mediaeval Bruges*, Cambridge, Mass., 1948, pp. 127 ff.

14   Venice, 1519, no. 15

15   Cassuto, op. cit., pp. 136, 137 n. 1, 144

16  Piccolomini and Mengozzi, op. cit., pp. 97, 151, 195
17  Carlo Invernizzi, 'Gli Ebrei a Pavia', *Bollettino della Società Pavese di storia patria*, 5 (3), 1905, pp. 191–240, 281–319
18  Castelli, op. cit., pp. 62, 74–6
19  It was a question of the venality of the offices and the recovery of their price—a question which Pope Urban VIII, shortly before his death, had submitted for examination by a committee. Cardinal Lugo concluded: 'Videntur autem esse lucre libera, quia non tenetur gratis dare occasionem lucrandi, et quia poterat gratis dare—et quia est fructus industriae, quem non capit ab ecclesiae, sed ab officiali ex suis lucis, et *porque el mayordomo puede recibir dal carnizero por ir a él a comprar la carne*, dum it non praejudicat domino'. ['But they seem to be free of profit because although he is not bound to give free the opportunity to make money, he could give it free—and because it is the fruit of industry which he does not receive from the Church but from the official from his own grove, and *because the steward can receive from the butcher to go to him to buy meat*, so long as this does not compromise the lord'.] (J. Grisar, 'Päpstliche Finanzen, Nepotismus und Kirchenrecht unter Urban VIII', in *Miscellanea historiae pontifitiae*, vol. 7, pt 14, Rome, 1943, p. 298.) It is significant that in trying to illustrate this subtle point, Cardinal Lugo fell back into his native Spanish
20  *Diario di Ugo Calefini*, ed. G. Pardi, Ferrara, 1938, vol. 1, pp. 178–9. Here the chronicler lists the gifts the Jews offered to the marquis in January 1477; pheasants, cheeses, cakes, sweetmeats, dozens of chickens, etc.
21  A. Panella, 'Una sentenza di Niccolò Porcinari podestà di Firenze', *Rivista Abruzzese di scienze, lettere ed arti*, 24, 1905, pp. 337–67
22  'La Madonna della Vittoria', now in the Louvre, was commissioned from Mantegna in the following circumstances: In 1493 the banker Daniel Norsa bought a house at Mantua with a façade decorated with a painting of the Virgin. With the authorisation of the local bishop, he had it erased. The people were incensed, and incidents took place in front of the house during Holy Week in 1494 and 1495. In May 1495 Norsa wrote to Luigi Gonzaga, marquis d'Este, to ask for his protection. The marquis, having won the pseudo-victory of Fornovo di Taro in July 1495, decided to express his gratitude to the Virgin by razing Norsa's house to the ground and building a church on the site. In addition he commissioned a 'Virgin' from Mantegna which the Jew had to pay for (the price was 110 ducats). Thus the masterpiece was born: 'A "virgin" painted in memory of a victory which was not achieved, in expiation of a sacrilege which was not committed, and at the expense of someone who did not believe in her' (Sizeranne). At the same time, one of Mantegna's pupils perpetuated the features of the Norsa family on the predella of another 'Virgin', at present in the Sant'Andrea basilica at Mantua: Paolo Norsa, 'Una famiglia di banchieri: i Norsa (1350–1950)', *Bollettino dell'Archivio storico del Banco di Napoli*, Naples, pt 6, 1953; pt 13, 1959
23  The whole document has been published by A. Medin and G. Tolomei, 'Per la storia anedottica dell'Università di Padova', *Atti e memorie della R. Accademia di scienze, lettere ed arti in Padova*, 26 (2), 1911, pp. 103–22

(appendix I); but only the first eleven transactions (pp. 104–5) state the amount of interest charged; in the subsequent entries it is no longer indicated

24 'I prestiti comunali a gli Ebrei a Matelica nel secolo XIII', *Le Marche*, 7, 1907, p. 255

25 *I banchieri ebrei in Urbino nell'età ducale*, Padua, 1902, p. 11

26 Piccolomini and Mengozzi, op. cit., pp. 97, 151, 155, 237–8, 271

27 Balletti, op cit., pp. 34–8

28 Oreste Dito, *La storia calabrese e la dimora degli Ebrei in Calabria dal secolo V alla seconda metà del secolo XVI*, Rocca S. Casciano, 1916, p. 284

29 When it was published with an English translation, as *Banking and Finance among Jews in Renaissance Italy*, a critical edition of *The Eternal Life*, by Gilbert S. Rosenthal, New York, 1962, Yehiel Nissim da Pisa's treatise brought a rich store of evidence to enrich an already old debate. The scholarly rabbi-banker wrote (ch. XV, p. 122): 'We could have dispensed with the discussion of bills of exchange which are called in Italian *cambii*, since they are not currently used by the Jewish people and since at the time of the codifiers and sages they were not utilized.' But it is perhaps useful to recall that such evidence does not concern the marranos of the Iberian peninsula

30 See the discussion between J. G. van Dillen and E. F. Hekscher (in van Dillen (ed.), *History of the Principal Public Banks*, The Hague, 1934, pp. 79–123) about the profits which the Bank of Amsterdam made in the seventeenth century from its transactions with the Huys van Leening (therefore pawnbroking). The authors refer only to the size of the profits and do not consider why the bank tried to hide them. In passing (p. 100), van Dillen mentioned 'the absolute secrecy exercised by the management of the Bank'. Contemporaries attributed 'fabulous' profits to the transactions in question (p. 163)

31 See Felice Fossati, 'Gli Ebrei a Vigevano nel secolo XV', *Archivio storico Lombardo*, 20, 1913, pp. 199–215

32 The letter from Cosimo I to Jacob Abravanel has been published by Cassuto, op. cit., pp. 384–5, doc. XXVI

33 Castelli, op. cit., pp. 89–99, 116–17

*Chapter VII   The* Banchieri

1 G. S. Rosenthal, *Banking and Finance among Jews in Renaissance Italy*, New York, 1962, pp. 40–1 (English text)

2 Ibid., Rosenthal's introduction, quoting Colon's Responsum no. 132

3 In modern times this situation was sanctioned by legislation: see for example the eighteenth-century Prussian laws which introduced the privileged category of *Generalpriviligierte Juden*, or nineteenth- and twentieth-century Tsarist legislation which exempted Jews who were 'merchants of the first guild' from most legal discriminations

4 Andrea Balletti, *Gli Ebrei e gli Estensi*, Reggio di Emilia, 1930, p. 53 n. 1 (quoting the 'Descrizione delle bocche e biade delle città' of 1473)

5 Domenico Gnoli, '*Descriptio urbis* o censimento della popolazione di Roma avanti il sacco borbonica', *Archivio della Società Romana di storia patria*, 17, 1894

6 Attilio Milano, 'I *Capitoli* di Daniel da Pisa e la comunità di Roma', *Rassegna mensile di Israel*, 10, 1935, pp. 334–5, doc. 2

7 Giuseppe Velletri owed 1,000 *scudi*, the amount of his daughter's dowry, to his son-in-law, Aron Castelnuovo. In July 1682, three months before the closing of the Jewish banks in Rome, he gave up all the income from his bank for the next five years to the Castelnuovo family for 4,278 *scudi*. From the balance of this sum, 2,400 *scudi* were to be used to pay the Tedesco family for his sister Regina's dowry. As a result, Aron Castelnuovo and Santono Tedesco started a lawsuit against Giuseppe Velletri in spring 1683, the outcome of which is not known; Archivio di Stato di Roma, series Ufficio notariale per gli Ebrei di Roma, vol. 34, c. 672

8 For Karl Marx's family tree, see B. Wachstein, 'Die Abstammung von Karl Marx', in *Festskrift David Simonsen*, Copenhagen, 1923, p. 284

9 When the Jews of Regensburg were accused in 1476 of ritual murder, Colon ordered all the Jewish communities in Germany to contribute to a collection of funds for them. The opinions of this Italian rabbi carried authority throughout Europe. See the text of this decision, which is interesting from more than one point of view, in *The History of Anti-Semitism*, vol. 1, London, 1974, pp. 157–8 n. 19

10 'Documenti sui banchieri ebrei a Modena nel secolo XVI', *Rassegna mensile di Israel*, 11, 1937, pp. 450–5

11 *Les Rothschild*, Club français du Livre, Paris, 1960, p. 246

12 *The Jewish Community*, Philadelphia, 1942, vol. 2, p. 10

13 Personal communication to the author

14 *Legge ebraica e leggi locali*, Milan, 1945, p. 319

15 Compare the list in sermon 43 by St Bernardino, which is also much longer than that of Yehiel Nissim: the borrower, the notary, the witnesses, the lawyers and judges if there is a lawsuit, etc.

16 Jewish law forbids the consumption of animals killed other than by a ritual slaughterer. In addition, hunting is *par excellence* the amusement of the warrior, and consequently an abomination to the orthodox Jew of the Diaspora—could this indicate a fear of identifying or a refusal to identify with the persecutors? From the psycho-social point of view, the Jewish attitude to hunting has not been studied, as far as I know; it could be an interesting question in the sociology of Judaism

17 Reubeni's diary is published in *Das Reisebericht von David Reubeni*, ed. E. Biberfeld, Berlin, 1892; but compare what the chronicler Joseph Ha-Cohen had to say on the subject: 'This man . . . announced that on the orders of the Christian kings he was going to lead the Jews from their states in order to bring them to their country and to their home; he spoke of this design to the pope himself, and the Jews were terrified of it. But, they said to him, what will happen to our wives if we go off to war, and to the children they have brought into the world'; *La Vallée des pleurs*, ed. Julien Sée, Paris, 1881, pp. 115–16

18 The official seventeenth-century marriage contracts from Rome that I

have studied mention dowries of 1,000 to 2,000 *scudi* in the case of the richest families; see also the table 'Doti dei banchieri ebrei dal 1625 al 1674', drawn up by Attilio Milano, *Rassegna mensile di Israel*, 6, 1931, p. 59; out of sixty dowries, only four were for more than 2,000 *scudi*, the average being 1,080 *scudi*. For an earlier period, Umberto Cassuto, *Gli Ebrei a Firenze*, Florence, 1918, p. 222, speaks of average dowries of 500 florins [the florin was worth about twice as much as the papal *scudo*]

*Chapter VIII   The Jew in the Italian City*

1   See Pio Pecchiai, *Roma nel Cinquecento*, Bologna, 1948, pp. 371 ff. ('I provvedimenti contro le donne di mala vita e contro gli ebrei'); also on prostitutes, Jean Delumeau, *La Vie économique et sociale de Rome dans la seconde moitié du XVIe siècle*, Paris, 1957, vol. 1, pp. 416–32. 'The same jurisdiction, same punishments, same burial place, same prohibition on concealing what they are', wrote Emmanuel Rodocanachi some time ago; *Le Saint-Siège et les Juifs*, Paris, 1891, p. 165 n. 3

2   See Bernardino Ghetti, 'Gli Ebrei e il Monte di Pietà in Recanati nei secoli XV et XVI', *Atti e memorie della Deputazione di storia patria per le Marche*, n.s. 4, 1907, p. 15; the Recanati council noted that Jews were better dressed than Christians, with the result that in the absence of a distinctive sign, a Christian attired with some elegance was taken for a Jew!

3   'several among us, willingly sharing with them the food of the body [that is to say by participating at their meals], have also allowed themselves to be seduced by their spiritual nourishment . . . Many women live as domestics or as paid workers of the Jews, who lure some from their faith . . . matters have reached the point where the ignorant Christians claim that the Jews preach better than our own priests.' See *The History of Anti-Semitism*, vol. 1, London, 1974, p. 30

4   See Andrea Balletti, *Gli Ebrei e gli Estensi*, Reggio di Emilia, 1930, who quotes a court record preserved at the Archivio di Stato di Reggio

5   'Qualche note sul tipo dell'Ebreo nel teatro popolare italiano', *Giornale storico della letteratura italiana*, 60 (2), 1912, pp. 383–96; see also Cesare Levi, 'Il tipo dell'Ebreo nel teatro', *Rivista teatrale italiana*, 10, 1906, pp. 362–5

6   *Histoire des Juifs en Espagne chrétienne*, Tel-Aviv, 1959, pp. 472–4 (Hebrew)

7   *La Spagna nella vita italiana*, Bari, 1922, pp. 214 ff. Even more informative on the relationship between anti-Hispanicism and anti-Judaism is the study by A. Farinelli, *Marrano, storia di un vituperio*, Geneva, 1925

8   *The Mediterranean and the Mediterranean World in the Age of Philip II*, London, 1972, pp. 415–16

9   To confine ourselves to the Jews of Italy, the number of defections by conversion, in the town of Rome alone between 1634 and 1790, is put at 2,432 and as a whole, according to Roberto Bachi, 'La demografia dell'Ebraismo italiano prima dell'emancipazione', in *Scritti in onore di Dante Lattes*, Rome, 1938, pp. 256–320 (p. 319), exercised a 'by no means

negligible' influence on the demography of Italian Jewry. Is it possible to suppose: (a) that on average, conversions corresponded to a minimum psychological resistance potential; (b) that the consequently superior resistance potential of the residual group might have the significance of a process of hereditary natural selection? It must be admitted that human biologists, at present, have reservations while they are still uncertain about the hereditary transmission of mental characteristics. On the other hand, one is on more positive scientific ground in assuming that a process of natural selection, by the elimination of biologically less resistant lines, operated within the ghetto as a result of the extremely unsalubrious living conditions which prevailed there. I warmly thank Dr B. Minz, head of research at the CNRS, who has been kind enough to draw my attention to the numerous areas of ignorance which still beset these questions

10 See the research by L. C. and S. P. Dunn on the Jews of Rome, challenging the classical views which deny any ethno-racial specificity to Jewish populations: 'The Roman Jewish community', *Scientific American*, March 1957, pp. 118–28; S. P. Dunn, 'The Roman Jewish community: a study in historical causation', *Jewish Journal of Sociology*, 2, 1959, pp. 185–201; 'Are Jews a race?', *Issues*, 15 (1), 1961, pp. 34–45

*Chapter IX   Franciscan Propaganda and the First Monti di Pietà*

1 Peter Browe, *Die Judenmission im Mittelalter und die Päpste*, Rome, 1942. It is significant enough in itself that the best documented account of Jewish persecutions by missionary orders should in fact be a book devoted to the mission to the Jews. 'Forced conversions . . . can with slight exaggeration be called *the* method of this period' (p. 215)

2 Although the interesting aspects of the question have not passed unnoticed by a few researchers (for example Bernhard Blumenkranz, who assumes a 'connection between the Judeo–Christian conflict and the conflict of the Orthodox Church with heretics', particularly the gnostic movements; and J. Isaac, 'Jésus et Israël', *Revue des études juives*, 109, p. 124) nothing slightly more precise is available on this subject except for a few references for the period beginning with the first Crusade. It is then possible, against a background most often, it is true, of economic crises and social unrest, to point out links between eschatological aspirations and millennarian movements or heresies, and the triad: conversion of Jews; persecutions; massacres. Take for example, the case of Emicho von Leiningen, 'who regarded himself as chosen by revelation to lead the Christian army after the conversion of the Jews . . . an eschatological intention which later degenerated into massacre'; P. Alphandéry, *La Chrétienté et l'idée de Croisade*, Paris, 1954, pp. 76–8. Analysing the *Adversus Judaeos* by Joachim of Fiore (ed. A. Frugoni, Rome, 1957), the editor notes the innovation 'of making the conversion of the Jews not a problem of truth but an eschatological problem, engraved into the vision of the history of mankind' (introduction, p. xxxvii); this does not necessarily challenge the accuracy of assumptions formulated by H. de Lubac about possible Jewish

or judaising influences on Joachim (*Exégèse médiévale*, Paris, 1961, vol. 1, p. 510).

For a much later period, the figures of Vincenzo Ferrer and Bernardino da Feltre deserve very special attention from this point of view. Both are said to have come under Joachimite influences (E. Jordan, 'Joachim de Flore', in *Dictionnaire de théologie catholique*, vol. 8, pt 2, col. 1457, and Fausta Casolini, *Bernardino da Feltre*, Milan, 1939, p. 50). I think that this is an immensely interesting question as far as the development of anti-Jewish tradition within medieval Christianity is concerned. Note the remarkable flashes of insight on this subject developed by Norman Cohn in *The Pursuit of the Millennium*, London, 1957; 2nd ed., 1970

3 *The Scholastic Analysis of Usury*, Cambridge, Mass., 1957, pp. 121-6

4 *Gênes au XVe siècle*, Paris, 1961, pp. 559-60

5 Gino Barbieri, 'L'usuraio Tomaso Grassi nel racconto bandelliano e nella documentazione storica', in *Studi in onore di Amintore Fanfani*, Milan, 1962, vol. 2, pp. 19-88

6 *Die Bettelorden und das religiöse Volksleben Ober- und Mittelitaliens im XIII. Jahrhundert*, Leipzig, 1910, p. 81

7 I refer the reader to Cohn, op. cit., as well as to *The History of Anti-Semitism*, vol. 1, London, 1974, pp. 137-50, where I have tried to bring out the associations between obsessions with the devil and with the end of the world, and anti-Jewish agitation by a few great preachers at the end of the middle ages. Questions of individual psychology are thus seen to be grafted on to the historical problems mentioned a little earlier. In this context, note that sociologists in the last quarter of a century have made every effort to define the profile of the 'authoritarian personality' which is inclined to religious and political intolerance, especially antisemitism. But it can be asked to what extent their conclusions, however reliable they appear, can be used to throw light on the men and passions of the past

8 Browe, op. cit., p. 34

9 Deposition of the vice-captain of Trieste about the pestering of Jews during Holy Week; quoted by Antonio Ive, 'Banques juives et Monts-de-Piété en Istrie', *Revue des études juives*, 2, 1881, p. 183

10 An anonymous chronicle published by M. A. Shulvass in his collection *Be-tzeveth Ha-doroth* (*In the Grip of the Times*), Jerusalem, 1960

11 The information relating to the hypothetical Monti di Pietà in Bavaria, Franche-Comté or London was primarily propagated by A. Blaize who mentioned them in *Des Monts-de-Piété et des banques de prêt*, Paris, 1856, vol. 1, pp. 63-4; it recurs in a number of later authors. Father T. K. Holzapfel (*Die Anfänge der Montes Pietatis*, Munich, 1903) was the first to cast doubt on these legends

12 'Note sul Monte di Pietà di Perugia dalle origini alla seconda metà del XVI secolo', in *Archivi storici delle aziende di credito*, Rome, 1956, vol. 1, pp. 343-80

13 Note that the child had already been found at the time that the *grida* was published, as clearly emerges from the text; Paolo Norsa, 'Una famiglia

di banchieri: i Norsa', *Bollettino dell' Archivio storico del Banco di Napoli*, pt 13, Naples, 1959 ('Secolo XVI'), pp. 59–60, 130

14 The incident at Trento is said to have been preceded by a similar case in the Tyrol in 1462 (at Rinn, near Innsbruck), which also led to a cult; its most recent historian, Kurt Hruby ('Der Ritualmord von Rinn', in *Der Juden-Christ*, Vienna, 1960–1), attributes its origins to the Trento affair antedated and correspondingly modified

15 Ch. XV of the statutes of the Aquila Monte di Pietà published by Giovanni Pansa, 'Gli Ebrei in Aquila nel secolo XV', *Bollettino della Società di storia patria A. L. Antinori negli Abruzzi*, 16, 1904, p. 218. The charging of interest was made compulsory by the General Chapter of the Franciscan order which met in Florence in 1493

16 Mira, op. cit.; Zdekauer, 'La fondazione del Monte Pio di Macerata e i primordi della sua gestione', *Rivista italiana per le scienze giuridiche*, 27–9, 1899–1900

17 Op. cit.; certain quotations and descriptions here can usefully be compared with *The Book of the Lender and the Borrower*, to which I have frequently referred. See also Ive, op. cit., p. 187: 'It seems obvious to me that all that was done was to take the rules and principles of administration of the banking houses and apply them to the Monti di Pietà', and the examples this author supplies for Istria. More recently, for all Monti di Pietà, see Giuseppe Garrani, *Il carattere bancario e l'evoluzione strutturale dei primogeniti Monti di Pietà*, Milan, 1957, p. 21: 'È vero che il credito organizzato dai monti di pietà imitò nelle strumentalità techniche i banchi dei privati e le casane degli Ebrei e dei Lombardi'

18 Erected in 1556, the Cherso Monte disappeared in 1576. The following year, the municipal council decided to grant a *condotta* to 'Hieremia Ricardo Ebreo'—there had never been a licensed lender in the town before; Antonio Cella, 'Il Monte di Pietà e il banco feneratizio ebreo a Cherso', *Pagine Istriane*, 12, 1914, pp. 82–112

19 Niccolò Piccolomini and Narciso Mengozzi, *Il Monte dei Paschi di Siena*, vol. 1, Siena, 1891, pp. 221–2

20 Op. cit., pp. 397, 399. The text of such a 'letter' went as follows: 'Domini ufficiales! Rogo vos mutuetis Turchicto de Macerata florenos quater, die 29 Jan. 1476, sine pignore, quia fidus est. Amicus, legum doctor.' ['Lords, officials! I request you to lend four florins to Turchicto of Macerata on 29 January 1476 without a pledge, because he is reliable. Amicus, Doctor of Laws.']

21 Op. cit., pp. 369, 378, 371

22 Ibid., pp. 371–3

23 Zdekauer, op. cit., pp. 398–9, 410 n. 2

24 *Gli Ebrei e il Monte di Pietà in Ascoli*, Ascoli Piceno, 1940, p. 52

25 Op. cit., p. 96

26 For the 'first established' Monte di Pietà (1472–1511), Mengozzi notes a misappropriation in 1488, and another in 1497, followed by an enquiry *sopra li disordini et mancamenti del Monte di Pietà*. In 1505 it was reported that over half the capital had vanished into thin air. The Monte folded up in 1511. The following facts about the 'second established' Monte

(1569) emerge: the flight of the camerlengo and the custodian of securities, who left behind a 'considerable gap in the coffers', in 1577; other 'frauds and abstractions' committed by employees in 1586; the theft of over two hundred securities by the employees Sicuri and Turamini in 1610–14; penal proceedings 'for corruption and miscalculation' against two valuers, Alberti and Baratti in 1621; the Melari affair, a scandal involving twenty-two employees and accomplices who had squandered over 40,000 *scudi* in 1623; the flight of the auctioneer Borghesi, who had embezzled 18,096 *scudi* in 1652; the death sentence for fraud on Avveduti, a valuer, in 1680; the sentence *in absentia* for the same reason on Girolamo Gori in 1703; the misappropriation of over 28,000 *scudi* by the camerlengo Rustici in 1719; proceedings against the valuers Luti and Buoninsegni in 1734; Narciso Mengozzi, *Il Monte dei Paschi e le sue aziende*, Siena, 1913 (summary of the major nine-volume work by Piccolomini and Mengozzi)

27 Here, the Monte di Pietà was put to sleep between the end of the sixteenth century and 1647, when 200,000 lire were misappropriated by the treasurer and 272,000 lent without security—'a new and more serious failure, due to bad management and malpractice'; Norsa, op. cit., pp. 28–9

28 Ernst Dichter, *Strategie im Reich der Wünsche*, Düsseldorf, 1961, p. 162

29 'non obstante illa, quae primo aspectu longe maior videtur Montis Pietatis; nedum respectu plebis, ac populi minuti, qui ubi non habet pignora aurea, argenta, aerea, vel linea, tineis et deteriorationi non subiecta, sed habet bona lanae, seu alterius materiae ita subiectae, unde maior cura et diligentia exigitur; non leuem patitur difficultatem vel incommoditatem eius indigentiis prompte subveniendi mediante Monte Pietatis, ob inferiorum ministrorum asperitates et difficultates circa hanc bonorum speciem recipiendam.' ['in spite of the fact that at first sight it seems larger than that of the Monte di Pietà; in the case of the lowest and poorest people who do not have pledges of gold, silver, brass or linen which are not subject to moth and decay but have goods of wool or other material, which do deteriorate and for which greater care and diligence is needed, they suffer considerable difficulty or inconvenience in readily relieving their poverty by means of the Monte di Pietà because of the harsh attitude and the difficulties raised by the lesser officials when receiving these kinds of goods.'] (*Theatrum veritatis et iustitiae*, Rome, 1669, p. 28)

30 Andrea Balletti, *Gli Ebrei e gli Estensi*, Reggio di Emilia, 1930, p. 18

31 *Summa angelica*, Lyons, 1519, 'Usura', II, 14 (fo. 495a)

32 Attilio Milano, *Storia degli ebrei italiani nel Levante*, Florence, 1949, pp. 40–1

33 The Jews of Spain had been authorised to take away all their movable belongings with the exception of precious metals or objects. The Jews of Sicily were allowed to take out only personal effects that they carried with them; Milano, *Storia degli Ebrei in Italia*, Turin, 1963, pp. 216–23. Protesting against the expulsion of the Jews in 1492, the municipality of Palermo declared: 'In quisto regno non ce fa mai tale exercicio che ipsi Judei facessero publicamente usura'

34 Moritz Stern, *Urkundliche Beiträge über die Stellung der Päpste zu den Juden*, Kiel, 1893, pp. 72–3, no. 67

35  *I Banchi di Napoli dalle origini alla costituzione del Banco delle due Sicilie*, Naples, 1940, p. 36

36  Carlo Invernizzi, 'Gli Ebrei a Pavia . . .', *Bollettino della Società Pavese di storia patria*, 5, 1905, pp. 284–5; S. Simonsohn, 'Francesco II Sforza e gli Ebrei di Milano', in *Scritti in onore di Sally Mayer*, Jerusalem, 1956, pp. 308–24

37  *Continuation de la Vallée des pleurs*, [Joseph Ha-Cohen], ed. Julien Sée, Paris, 1881

38  Mario Bendiscioli, *Storia di Milano*, Milan, 1957, vol. 10, p. 301. The author points out (p. 271) that part of the Milanese archives relating to these questions was destroyed in 1943, so that verification is impossible and it is necessary to go back to the works of Carlo Invernizzi, Ettore Rota and Luigi Fumi

39  E. Greppi, 'Il banco di S. Ambrogio', *Archivio storico Lombardo*, 10, 1883, p. 515

40  Bendiscioli, op. cit., p. 300 (quoting Luigi Fumi, 'L'inquisizione romana e lo Stato di Milano', *Archivio storico Lombardo*, 17, 1910, p. 326)

41  Ha-Cohen, *La Vallée des pleurs*, p. 198: 'The inhabitants of Cremona and Pavia sent to the king's court and asked for the expulsion of the Jews from the country, promising to pay as much money as was required to reimburse the Jews. In addition, it happened that the confessor to whom the king trusted his conscience joined with them in order to persuade him to drive them out of the country as soon as possible, and the king consented to this.' Likewise Bendiscioli, op. cit., p. 301: 'Dato l'onere di questi debiti e la perdita prevista di entrate, il re impose alle città del dominio, per eseguire lo sfratto degli ebrei dallo stato, un pagamento di 32,000 ducati' ['Given the weight of these debts and the anticipated loss of income, the king imposed a payment of 32,000 ducats on the cities under his rule, in order to carry out the immediate dismissal of the Jews from the state']

42  Poliakov, *The History of Anti-Semitism*, vol. 2, London, 1974, pp. 290–2. It was to defeat this plan that Francisco Gómez Quevedo wrote his pamphlet *Isla de los Monopantos*, directed against Jewish financiers, which later seems to have constituted a source of inspiration for the *Protocols of the Elders of Zion*

43  Bendiscioli, op. cit., p. 302

*Chapter X   The Jews and the Development of Financial Techniques*

1  See Guido Pampaloni, 'Cenni storici sul Monte di Pietà di Firenze', *Archivi storici delle aziende di credito*, Rome, 1956, vol. 1, pp. 530–8. On the subject of the da Camerino legacy, see Cassuto, *Gli Ebrei a Firenze*, Florence, 1918, p. 74, Again, in 1559, Yehiel Nissim da Pisa in *The Eternal Life* holds the Christian Monti di Pietà up as an example to his co-religionists: 'Their scholars and cardinals have permitted them to take a small amount of interest for the welfare of the populace' (G. S. Rosenthal, ed., *Banking and Finance among Jews in Renaissance Italy*, New York, 1962, p. 151)

2 'Instructione al Magnifico Lorenzo'—presumed date, between May and August 1513; 'Giuliano de Medici e il pontefice Leone X', *Archivio storico italiano*, appendix, vol. 1, Florence, 1841, p. 305

3 Disposizione del Senato dei Quarantotto, 10 June 1533, *Archivi storici delle aziende di credito*, vol. 2, pp. 133–4

4 See the description of the situation in Florence in summer 1529 by Soriano, the Venetian ambassador: 'Trade with Naples is hampered by the war; exports of silk and brocade to France are similarly affected . . . trade with Flanders by the prohibition on transit through Venetian territory . . . [but] the Florentines remain extraordinarily rich despite their losses and difficulties. Eight or ten families have fortunes of over 100,000 ducats . . . More than eighty families have fortunes of 50,000 to 100,000 ducats, and a vast number have fortunes below 50,000 ducats'; quoted from Richard Ehrenberg, *Le Siècle des Fugger*, Paris, 1955, pp. 140–1

5 Giulio Mandich has used a very relevant comparison in this context, by recalling the hesitations of twentieth-century Catholics about the use of contraceptives and birth control (*Le Pacte de 'ricorsa' et le marché italien des changes au XVII^e siècle*, Paris, 1963, pp. 175–6)

6 Th. Buoninsegni, *Trattato de traffichi giusti et ordinarii . . .* , Venice, 1588, pp. 154b, 145a. A former merchant, Father Buoninsegni became confessor to a member of the ducal family after he had taken his vows; Raymond de Roover, *L'Évolution de la lettre de change*, Paris, 1953, appendix

7 *Istoria del granducato di Toscana*, Florence, 1781, vol. 2, p. 282

8 Relazione di Francesco Maria Gianni, Direttore dell'Ufficio delle Revisioni e Sindacati, *Archivi storici delle aziende di credito*, vol. 2, pp. 137–8

9 The ducal government started a lawsuit against the da Pisa on 7 July 1570 on grounds of repeated infringements of the *capitoli*; the decree introducing the ghetto was promulgated on 3 October of the same year; ten days later the action was closed by an absolution; see Cassuto, op. cit., pp. 106–14

10 The title of grand duke was important to Cosimo I to establish his precedence over the duke of Ferrara. His coronation in March 1570 at Rome was followed by a struggle to get the title recognised by the European monarchs, hence the need to please the Holy See. On this incident see Galluzzi, op. cit., vol. 2, pp. 96 ff.

11 'The Jews, who do almost all the trade with the Levant . . . ' (report by the French agent Cotolendy, 29 August 1692, Archives nationales, Paris, B1, 700); 'the Jews who do three-quarters of the trade there [Leghorn]' (report by the same agent, 15 August 1692); 'Nothing remains [at Leghorn] but its trade with the Levant and Barbary, which the Jews do almost alone . . . ' (report by the French consul de Berthollet, 27 January 1744, B1, 737, fos 285–6)

12 Brother Labat described the condition of the Jews of Leghorn as follows: 'They are free there; they do not wear any sign to distinguish them from the Christians. They are not confined to their neighbourhoods. They are rich; their business is extensive. Almost all have farms from the prince and they are protected to the point where it is proverbial in Tuscany that it would be better to beat up the grand duke than a Jew. This only makes

them all the more odious to everyone else. But they laugh at this, and I do not believe that there is any place in the world where they are more arrogant and more haughty . . . they love ostentation, especially on the occasion of their weddings' (Relation de J.-B. Labat, in A. t'Serstevens, ed., *Comédie ecclésiastique*, Paris, 1927, pp. 120 ff.)

As the governor of Leghorn had insulted the French merchant Daniel, the consul, de Berthollet, wrote to his government: 'it would be very annoying for the French nation if it were less worthy of respect than that of the Jews, who in a like case did at least have the satisfaction of seeing a similar action by the governor censured by the grand duke, with the order not to repeat the offence . . .' (4 April 1733, B1, 722, fo. 309).

Two years later, an edict forbade 'the Jews to be insulted either by word or deed, under very severe penalty; the father must answer for the son, the master for his servant, and the workmen for their lads' (8 July 1735, B1, 725, fo. 110)

13  See, for example, the various dispatches from the French agent Cotolendy in 1688, which supply information on attempts by de Seignelay to use the Jews to ferret out the real intentions of the Diwan of Algiers, at that time at war with the French (B1, 699), or information received in 1733–4 through the Jews on the course and end of the war between Turkey and Persia (B1, 722, 723)

14  The diplomatic activities of Joseph Nasi ('Juan Micas') or Solomon Ashkenasi, who negotiated the peace between Venice and Turkey in 1573, are sufficiently well known. Hermann Kellenbenz has devoted an interesting chapter of his fine book *Sephardim an der unteren Elbe* (Wiesbaden, 1958) to diplomatic agents operating in Germany. See also 'Cromwell's Jewish Intelligencers', in Lucien Wolf, *Essays in Jewish History*, London, 1934. In the Paris National Archives, for example, I found the following report by Cotolendy dated 1695 (B1, 703): 'I was advised that a man by the name of Benjamin Sacutto, Jew, staying at Algiers, entirely devoted to the English, was doing everything possible to make the Diwan promise to break the peace with us, and that the same man was the cause of the last rupture which the Algerians made at the instigation of the English. He has a brother named David Sacutto, who trades on a fairly large scale . . . This D. Sacutto, having formerly been the Emperor's Resident at Constantinople in 1665, 1666 and 1687, has retained a very great attachment to the house of Austria and it is thought that he often writes to his brother Benjamin in Algiers, in consultation with the English—of whom he is said to be a pensioner—to make these barbarians promise to break with us yet again'.

See also the epic of the Tunisian Jew Coën, who in 1711–12, after highly picturesque adventures succeeded in convincing the bey of Tunis to break the alliance with France and to substitute the Dutch alliance for it. He was backed up by the great Jews of Amsterdam (B1, 710, 'Mémoire de la négociation de Coën avec les Tunisiens')

15  A. M. Hyamson, *The Sephardim of England*, London, 1951; H. J. Bloom, *The Economic Activities of the Jews of Amsterdam in the Seventeenth and Eighteenth Centuries*, Williamsport, 1937; Kellenbenz, op. cit.; Gino

Luzzatto, 'Sulla condizione economica degli Ebrei veneziani nel secolo XVIII', in *Scritti in onore di Riccardo Bachi*, Rome, 1950, pp. 161-72, and 'Armatori ebrei a Venezia negli ultimi 250 anni della Repubblica', in *Scritti in onore di Federico Luzzatto*, Rome, 1962, pp. 160-8

*Chapter XI    The Jews and the Evolution of Christian Attitudes*

1   See my *History of Anti-Semitism*, vol. 2, London, 1974, pt 3, 'The Marrano Epic'

2   *La Vallée des pleurs*, ed. Julien Sée, Paris, 1881, pp. 139, 141

3   Thus in the nineteenth century, French Jews were commonly regarded as a Germanic tribe and were consequently enveloped in anti-German resentment, while their German co-religionists on the other side of the Rhine were criticised for their pro-western or pro-French sympathies

4   All that is available on this subject is the text itself of the bull of banishment, *Hebraeorum gens* (26 February 1569), and replies by Pius V to the archbishop of Avignon and Cardinal Georges d'Armagnac who intervened on behalf of the Jews of the Comtat Venaissin (3 and 4 May 1569). Article 2 of the bull justified the exception as follows: 'Urbe Roma, et Ancona dumtaxat exceptis, ubi eos solos Hebraeos, qui nunc eas habitant, ad praedictam memoriam amplius excitandam praesequendasque cum orientalibus negotiationis, mutuosque commeatus cum eisdem permittimus tolerandos' ['with the exception of the city of Rome and of Ancona, where only those Jews who now inhabit them in order to promote further the memory of which I have spoken and to conduct business with persons of the East we permit to be tolerated'].

To Cardinal d'Armagnac, Pius V wrote that he in no way denied the usefulness of the Jewish evidence ('quod necque Nos negamus, et fidei nostrae utile esse existimamus' ['which we do not deny either, and which we think to be useful']), but that the two ghettos he was retaining seemed to him sufficient to this end ('Tolerantia igitur Judaeorum satis consultum est, quoniam duobus in locis Ecclesiae subjectis, Romae, Anconaeque tolerantur: ceteris in locis, neque necesse, neque utile est, propter eas causas, quae in Bulla expositae sunt.' ['Therefore, we have done enough in toleration of the Jews, since they are tolerated in two places subject to the Church, Rome and Ancona. In other places it is neither necessary nor useful for those reasons which have been set forth in the bull.']); *Annales ecclesiastici*, continued by Jacob de Laderchio, vol. 23, Rome, 1758, p. 265

5   Clemens Bauer, 'Die Epochen der Papstfinanz', *Historische Zeitschrift*, 137, 1928, pp. 492, 496

6   Jean Delumeau, *La Vie économique et sociale de Rome dans la seconde moitié du XVIe siècle*, Paris, 1957, vol. 2, pp. 887 ff.

7   See for example, for the conversion of the Moriscos, Fernand Braudel, *The Mediterranean and the Mediterranean World in the Age of Philip II*, London, 1972, vol. 2, pp. 780 ff.; for the conversion of Catholic nuns by Protestant pastors, Philippe Dollinger, 'La tolérance à Strasbourg au XVIe siècle', in *Éventail de l'histoire vivante*, Paris, 1953, vol. 2, p. 247

8  Giulio Morosini, *Via delle fede, mostrata a'gli Ebrei*, Rome, 1683, vol. 2, p. 1424
9  The maintenance of the Home for Converted Jews was made the responsibility of the Jewish community in 1554 by the *Pastoris aeterni vices* bull (31 August 1554), which said that it was only justice, since in any case the community had shouldered the responsibility for converts prior to baptism. Jewish petitions answered this by stating that, at every baptism, their community lost a valuable taxpayer, who was transformed into a pensioner; see Emmanuel Rodocanachi, *Le Saint-Siège et les Juifs*, Paris, 1891, pp. 228, 280; T. K. Hoffmann, *Ursprung und Anfangstätigkeit des ersten päpstlichen Missionsinstituts*, Münster, 1923
10  A grand baptism of this type took place in Rome in 1581: the neophyte, who belonged to the rich Corcos family, naturally adopted the name of his godfather, Gregory XIII Buoncompagno; see Hoffmann, op. cit., p. 161, which gives the genealogical information. See also, for a later period, Ermanno Loevinson, 'Judentaufen von Papst Klemens XI 1704 in eigener Person vollzogen', *Monatsschrift für Geschichte und Wissenschaft des Judentums*, 36, 1928, pp. 395–400. This sort of ceremony made a strong impression on foreign observers: see Francis Stewart, 'Jews in Rome', *Jewish Quarterly Review*, 19, 1907, pp. 398 ff.
11  The distinction between 'economic causes' and 'religious causes' of antisemitism is so fallacious! Even today, relationships between Jews and non-Jews are most frequently carried on at a commercial level, which generates antagonism. To the extent that social exclusion proceeds from the combined secular efforts of Church and rabbis, 'economic causes' boil down to 'religious causes'
12  *Il ghetto di Roma*, Rome, 1964, pp. 190–1
13  *Description de la ville de Rome, en faveur des étrangers*, Lyons, 1690, p. 343
14  *De morbis artificium, Essai sur les maladies des artisans*, Paris, 1777, p. 379
15  These ceremonies have often been described. In 1623 Urban VII prescribed that when representatives of the Jewish 'Università' were granted audiences, they would no longer kiss his foot but the floor beneath his foot, so transforming an act of devotion into an act of vassalage, as Milano points out. On the occasion of the annual carnival, when the Jews also paid their respects to the Roman Senate, the registrar of the Senate, it is said, ritually placed his foot on the nape of a rabbi's neck before dismissing the delegation; Attilio Milano, *Storia degli Ebrei in Italia*, Turin, 1963, 'Atti di omaggio e manifestazioni di derisione', pp. 598–603
16  Anonymous tract, *Il vero stato degli Hebrei di Roma*, Rome, 1668, p. 19
17  'Cum ex huius modi vacatione dicto ill. mo d. cardinali camerario tam ratione suae ordinariae iurisditionis quam emolumentorum per hebreos bancherios Urbis pro tempore existentes ei solvi solitorum damnus redundet'. ['Since from a vacancy of this kind, a loss occurs to the said lord cardinal camerlengo, not only on account of his ordinary jurisdiction but also because of the emoluments paid to him by the Jewish bankers of the city existing at any time'.] As a result of this, the new concessionary, Samuel Zadich, 'teutonici hebreo', promised to compensate the cardinal. The position had become vacant on the resignation of Laudadeus Rabi Benedicti da Sicilia; it seems certain that another arrangement was con-

cluded directly between the two Jews, and that all that was involved was a formal sale; *RCA*, vol. 1226, c. 185

18  At Ancona, according to data published in Loevinson, op. cit., 272 licences were issued for *banchi* for periods varying between three and ten years between 1587 and 1669. Of this number, 27 carried 'the special privilege of the bankers of Rome' and must have been licences for pawnbroking banks; the others seem to me to have corresponded to a simple commercial patent, implying at the same time permission to stay

19  See Donato Tamilia, *Il sacro Monte di Pietà di Roma*, Rome, 1900, and Mario Tosi, *Il sacro Monte di Pietà di Roma e le sue amministrazioni*, Rome, 1937. According to Tamilia, op. cit., p. 85, direct financial relations between the Monte di Pietà and the papal government began in 1640; they became closer in 1682, when Innocent XI entrusted the administration of the Monti di Pietà to the Treasurer General of the Holy See

20  Although the text of the dispensation does not specifically say so, it is certain that it was justified in the eyes of the pope by the law of Moses, which allowed polygamy to the Jews. However, in Christian Europe, the law of the Old Testament had been amended on this point by rabbinic tradition, and in most cases, Jewish communities are seen opposing projected bigamy, so that the persons concerned have to resort to Christian authorities. The pope's order that his protégé should not be subjected to annoyance, a prohibition which figures in the text of the dispensation, was very probably made with the Jews in mind; see P. L. Bruzzone, 'Documents sur les Juifs des États pontificaux', *Revue des études juives*, 19, 1879, pp. 131–40, and S. W. Baron, *The Jewish Community*, Philadelphia, 1942, vol. 2, pp. 307–10, where other similar cases are noted

21  Henri Sée, 'Dans quelle mesure Puritains et Juifs ont-ils contribué aux progrès du capitalisme moderne?', *Revue historique*, 155, 1927, pp. 55–68; Riccardo Bachi, 'Rapporti economici fra gli ebrei e i gentili nelle diaspore', in *Israele disperso e ricostruito*, Rome, 1952, pp. 29–79

22  Rodocanachi, op. cit., p. 267

23  *Essai sur les maladies des artisans*, pp. 379–81

24  *Storia degli Ebrei in Italia*, p. 507. One might ask if the Jews of Rome and the Papal State did not find a remedy for governmental suffocation in the practice of smuggling. Only one document is available on this subject, published by Vittorio Franchini (*Gli indirizzi e la realtà del settecento economico romano*, Milan, 1950, pp. 173–4), but it is very indicative. It involves a report drawn up by the governor of the customs office in Viterbo at the beginning of the eighteenth century concerning the fraudulent introduction by Jews of cloth from Tuscany and the export of papal money in return. This trade is said to have been primarily carried on from Pitigliano, a small place in Tuscany. A Jewish colony had in fact existed in this small mountain village since the sixteenth century, and it is difficult otherwise to explain its well-known prosperity.

What is known about the part Jews played in smuggling in other countries, over the frontiers of the Tsarist empire in modern times, for example, strengthens such a presumption. Unfortunately, there is usually little documentary evidence for such activities

*Chapter XII   The Strange Case of Venice*

1   *L'interdetto di Venezia del 1666 e i Gesuiti*, Rome, 1959, p. 5
2   Sanuto, *Diarii* . . . , Venice, 1879–1903, 8 February 1520, March 1520, May 1520, 9 March 1524, 10 April 1524; Vettore Sandi, *Principii di storia civile della repubblica di Venezia*, vol. 5, Venice, 1756, pp. 441–2; documents published by Alberto Errera, *Storia dell'economia politica nei secoli XVII e XVIII negli stati della repubblica veneta*, Venice, 1877, pp. 436–47
3   Bibliothèque nationale, Paris, MSS. fr., 11366–7, Mémoire d'un enquêteur dépêché par Noailles, sous la Régence, en prévision de la création d'un Mont-de-Piété en France
4   Report by Le Blond, French consul at Venice, 23 February 1686, Archives nationales, Paris, B1, 1158, fos 177–9
5   See Léon Poliakov, 'Un tentativo di Venezia per attirare gli Ebrei di Livorno', *Rassegna mensile di Israel*, 23, 1957, pp. 291–7
6   'Sulla condizione economica degli Ebrei veneziani nel secolo XVIII', in *Scritti in onore di Riccardo Bachi*, Città di Castello, 1950, pp. 161–72, and 'Armatori ebrei a Venezia negli ultimi 250 anni della Repubblica', in *Scritti in memoria di Federico Luzzatto*, Rome, 1962, pp. 160–8
7   *Naufrages, corsaires et assurances maritimes à Venise*, Paris, 1959, pp. 14 ff.
8   After describing how the sight of the wretched Jews of the ghetto had convinced one of his friends who was a freethinker, Roberti added that, to such an argument, 'the freethinkers have not yet found an answer. I would add that they will never find one; because I am of the opinion that one ghetto of Jews proves the truth of the religion of Jesus Christ better than a whole school of theologians'; *Del legger libri di metafisica e di divertimento* . . . , Rome, 1773, pp. 19–20
9   *Giornali veneziani del settecento*, ed. M. Berengo, Milan, 1962, pp. 346–7

*Chapter XIII   The End of the System of Papal Licences*

1   The text of this concordat was published by Attilio Milano, 'Ricerche sulle condizioni economiche degli ebrei a Roma (1555–1898)', *Rassegna mensile di Israel*, 5–6, January–July 1931. I have borrowed the data relating to the financial situation of the ghetto in Rome from this study
2   *Il sacro Monte di Pietà di Roma*, Rome, 1900, pp. 81–2
3   I am thinking of Benjamin Nelson's schematic outlines in which he compares the 'universal otherhood' of modern times with the 'tribal brotherhood' of antiquity
4   Turin, 1963, pp. 314–15
5   In fact, the 'Jewish districts' in Paris, London, Antwerp, etc., which go back no further than the nineteenth century, are populated by immigrant Jews; moreover, their population is constantly changing—in Paris, for example, the Poles of the rue des Rosiers gave way to 'North Africans'
6   'This area [the ghetto], with its population, forms a distinct enclave whose existence, social separateness, and special quality are recognized by its members and by many of their Christian neighbours, although denied with some vehemence (an interesting and significant point) by most

other Roman Jews'; Stephen P. Dunn, 'The Roman Jewish community: a study in historical causation', *Jewish Journal of Sociology*, 2, 1959, p. 186

7   See the study mentioned above, as well as 'The Roman Jewish community', *Scientific American*, March 1957. L. C. Dunn is a geneticist of international repute specialising in the study of blood groups; his son, S. P. Dunn, is a sociologist

8   'La demografia dell'Ebraismo italiano prima della emancipazione', in *Scritti in onore di Dante Lattes*, Rome, 1938, pp. 256 ff. (pp. 258–9)

*Conclusion*

1   Jean Stengers, *Les Juifs dans les Pays-Bas au Moyen Age*, Brussels, 1950, p. 173

2   Benjamin Nelson, *The Idea of Usury, from Tribal Brotherhood to Universal Otherhood*, Princeton, 1949

3   As is known, satisfactory definitions of 'Jewish people' and 'Jew' have not yet been found; the Israeli authorities themselves have had to abandon the search for a precise legal definition, despite all efforts recently made to this end. (Broadly speaking, they stick to the religious criterion.)
    There is nothing new about the discussion. It can even be said that the problem of adequate definition arose with every persecution, when it was important to say who was a Jew and who was not. In its current form and terminology, the debate dates from the eighteenth century. It has been actively carried on for half a century between doctrinaire Marxists and Zionists. The Marxist denied the Jews the title of people because they did not possess a land of their own; the Zionists cited the historic right to the land of Palestine. Both therefore postulated that a people is defined in relation to a land

4   In the present state of anthropological knowledge, the most reliable information on the racial origins of the different populations of the world is provided by the study of blood groups (blood group serology), and notably the comparative frequency of four well-known blood groups, A, B, AB and O, as well as certain other factors of blood differentiation. In this respect, the indices of Jews in various countries or geographic regions resemble those of the people among whom they live; in addition, the divergence between Jews of various countries is approximately the same as between the non-Jewish population of the same countries. On this subject, we refer the reader to Appendix A, 'The Origin of the Jews in the Light of Group Serology', in my book *The History of Anti-Semitism*, vol. 1, London, 1974

5   It would have been necessary to study the evolution of ritual and observances, and the concept of the exile over the centuries, in the present context. In the case of the Spanish Jews, who were deeply rooted in the Iberian peninsula, G. Scholem's research has shown that the idea of the exile became a central thread of Jewish mysticism only *after* the expulsion from Spain; it is known that in the eleventh century Judah Ha-levi, who urged his co-religionists to stay faithful to the promised land, was crying in the wilderness

6 The schematic view suggested above would obviously need to be elaborated and given greater precision. A distinction might be made, for example, between 'rootedness' or love of the maternal soil (the homeland is a *mother* in every language) and the various connotations of patriotism or nationalism which, in their form of devotion to a monarch or a charismatic leader, are probably the more local expression, by extension, of the attachment to the father. But the distinction does not seem to be of great importance to the present discussion

7 An investigation by *L'Arche*, the organ of the Jewish community of France, into 'Is Judaism also a mental illness?', shows the interest that people are beginning to take in these questions. But the answers given by the psychiatrists consulted skirted the real problem. It is remarkable that psychoanalysis, which has done so much to expose the psychological motives for anti-semitism, should so far have confined itself to superficial descriptions of Jewish character traits without questioning their historical roots. Yet such research would have led the young science to make some useful reflections on its own origins. A few general ideas in this context can be found in the symposium *Die Juden und die Kultur* (Stuttgart, 1961), which brings out the inequality of the 'Jewish' cultural contribution, according to discipline, ranging from the minority contribution to the exact sciences, to the hegemony in sociology, and particularly psychology in depth, at the time they were established.

On another count, is there any need to specify that the 'Jewish type' (taken in the characterological sense) is only a statistical phenomenon? What is involved is simply a certain type of personality structure that occurs much more frequently among Jews than non-Jews. I think it can be added that this type tends to increase in the contemporary world against the background of the destruction of traditional frameworks, general urbanisation, increased social and also geographical mobility, accelerated tempo of life and the specific tensions created by these varied phenomena

8 I think it is useless to reproduce examples from the classics of Jewish history (Heinrich Graetz, S. M. Dubnow, etc.) in which such tendencies verge on manichaeism *sui generis*. But this is how S. W. Baron, generally considered one of the most scientific contemporary Jewish historians, expresses himself in his introductory chapter in *A Social and Religious History of the Jews*, New York, 1962, vol. 1, pp. 8, 15: 'At this point it may be well to distinguish between what we have designated the religious conception of history's victory over nature and the scientific conception of man's increasing dominion over nature. While, according to the latter, man gradually masters the forces of nature and makes its laws subservient to his own equally natural needs, Isaiah's messianism preaches the final transformation of the immutable laws of nature themselves. In the meantime, the Jew's ideal should be, not mastery over nature, but independence of it, the achievement of supremacy over it by refusing to recognise its superior powers. This attitude, however, does not involve extreme asceticism . . . But whenever there is a conflict between nature and the Law, the latter is to be recognised as supreme . . . from the eighth century onward, the Jews began again to live in other lands among varied alien

majorities. This cannot be a mere accident of history. To insist that "peculiar" destinies of individuals and nations "happen" precisely to those individuals and nations with an innate disposition for them, may seem to be reaching out too perilously into the realm of metaphysics. Under the same circumstances, however, many other peoples would certainly have perished and disappeared from history. That the Jews survived is largely due to the fact that they were prepared for their subsequent destinies by their early history'

9 Some excellent recent works on the trade of the 'New Christians' or on the great Jewish bankers in the nineteenth century describe these business-men while practically disregarding their qualities as marranos and Jews

10 See R. M. Loewenstein, *Chrétiens et Juifs*, Paris, 1951, and B. Grunberger, 'Der Antisemit und der Oedipuskomplex', *Psyché*, August 1962

11 Bernard Gille, *La Banque et le crédit en France de 1815 à 1848*, Paris, 1959, pp. 271–92

# Index